CLERICAL ERROR

ROBERT BLAIR KAISER

CLERICAL ERROR

A True Story

Continuum

NEW YORK

2002

The Continuum International Publishing Group Inc
370 Lexington Avenue, New York, NY 10017

Printed in the United States of America

Library of Congress Cataloging-in-Publication Data

Kaiser, Robert Blair.
   Clerical error : a true story / Robert Blair Kaiser.
     p. cm.
   ISBN 0-8264-1384-6
   1. Kaiser, Robert Blair. 2. Catholics – United States – Biography.
3. Journalists – Vatican City – Biography. 4. Journalists – United
States – Biography. 5. Vatican Council (2nd : 1962-1965) I. Title.
BX4705.K219 A3 2002
282'.092 – dc21

                             2002000375

This is a growing-up tale, like the classic English novel, *Tom Jones* — what the Germans call a Bildungsroman. But this is not a romance, it is a true story. (I have changed a few names, to protect the innocent.) People have been reading and enjoying these coming-of-age stories for eons. I think they do so because they are fascinated with their own growing up, looking for clues on how they can grow up, too. To them, to the looking-for-clues folk, I dedicate this book.

Strange thing about my coming-of-age story: I began my journey at seventeen by renouncing the world, the flesh, and the devil to become a postulant in the California Province of the Society of Jesus. I know now that this was an unconscious move on my part *not* to grow up. With the help of the Jesuits (and despite them) I managed to grow up anyway, quite belatedly and against the backdrop of the dramatic coming-of-age of the Catholic Church itself, at Vatican II.

CLERICAL ERROR

1

On the winding drive up the hill from Los Gatos, I couldn't see the Novitiate. Then, one more bend of the road, and there it was, looming up at me so suddenly I felt it was going to fall on me. Still in the car, I goggled at a painted statue that was too big for the courtyard, an effeminate figure — with a beard — holding his heart in his hand. My greeter spoke to me as I climbed out of the car, but I didn't hear him. I couldn't wait to flee the perpendency of that façade, and the scary statue. And I wondered what folly I'd embarked upon — minor me, a very young seventeen, hardly shaving yet, daring to enter the mighty Jesuit Order.

The greeter was one of the legendary Callanan brothers from my own alma mater, Loyola High in Los Angeles, Jack Callanan. I was grateful when he led me off to a redwood-shaded walk and helped me calm down, ambling along with both hands stuck in the cincture of his cassock, arms casually akimbo. "That's the Juniors' side of the house," he said, nodding behind him. And then, waving at the nearer building, "This is where the Novices live."

"A lot of trees over here," I said.

"Olive trees," he said. "Weeping willow, elm, oak, maple, eucalyptus. This whole hillside below us — " He waved his arm to the north. "It's in prunes and plums. Countryside's all pink in the spring."

I was soothed by the leafy greenness there, a cool contrast to the hot stare I had seen on the face of that building. I nodded with pleasure at the rows of rose bushes that stretched on both sides of the walkway in front of me, framing the open gateway to the Novices' garden, where a small printed sign said CLOISTER. And I brightened when I saw Bob Jay, my teammate on the baseball team at Loyola High, who had preceded me here by a year. Well, I thought, maybe I'll just stay for dinner, then leave.

Bob Jay was barely friendly, even seemed bemused at my presence here. Well, we were even. At this point, I was wondering, too. Did I really belong here? He told me to call him "Brother," and then he handed me over to my "guardian angel," a dark Irishman named McDonough, with a crewcut full of unruly cowlicks and a wide forehead. I was disappointed that Bob Jay wasn't going to be my guardian angel. I couldn't help feeling that I'd been given this, uh, Brother McDonough so he could whip me into shape, more effectively, perhaps, than my high school chums who had come to the Novitiate a year ahead of me.

Brother McDonough took me inside to pick out a simple black cotton jacket, which I was to wear over my T-shirt at all times. Then he led me into the Novices' chapel. I didn't pray, too curious about the statues on either side of the altar, which were realistic, life-sized impressions of, I guessed, two Jesuit saints. One of them clutched a lily in one hand and a book in the other. The other figure was holding a cross in both hands and staring at it. Over the altar, I noted a large, illuminated oil portrait of another young man in a black cassock. A very young man, with girlish features, who was holding a lily to his breast with one hand and gazing upward, to the heavens. What was this with the lilies?

When we left the chapel, I said, "Who's the guy in the painting over the altar?"

"Guy?"

"Yeah," I said, ignoring the implied reprimand. "The guy in the painting right over the middle of the altar?"

Too deliberately, Brother McDonough said, "St. Stanislaus Kostka — was — no — guy."

I later learned that Stanislaus Kostka, the patron saint of Jesuit Novices, was a nobleman's son who had died of pneumonia in 1568 while still a Novice. Back in his father's palace in Poland, he had had a habit of fainting whenever he heard someone utter a profanity. When, against his father's wishes, he entered the Jesuit Novitiate in Rome, his mother had sent a valet along with him. My angel was right: St. Stanislaus was not "a guy."

Next day, August 15, vow day, young men who had completed two years of training in the Novitiate were to take their simple vows of poverty, chastity, and obedience in the Society of Jesus, and they did so in the main chapel of the Novitiate of the Sacred Heart, while a strong tenor voice from the choir loft sang with excruciating sweetness the words of a prayer written four hundred years before by the founder of the Jesuits, St. Ignatius Loyola himself.

Suscipe, Domine,
Suscipe, Domine,
Universam libertatem meam.
Accipe memoriam, intellectum,
atque voluntatem omnem.

The Latin words in the little black book they'd given me, the *Liber Devotionum*, were printed in English on a facing page.

Receive, Lord,
Receive, Lord,
All my liberty.
Take my memory, my understanding,
and my entire will.

All right, I said to myself, this is what I chose. I'd come because I'd admired the Jesuits, the priests and the scholastics at Loyola High. They'd taken an interest in me, instructed me in an ancient faith, given me a superb secondary education, and, once they'd told me that I would make a good Jesuit, I began to endow the men in the Order with all the qualities of King Arthur's knights, Mountbatten's commandos, and Hoover's F.B.I. Did they really think I could be one of them? Well, okay, I would join. I hadn't really thought too much about the cost of joining up — and making this kind of sacrifice. "All of my liberty, my memory, my understanding, my entire will." All that, plus poverty, chastity, and obedience. This was going to be some gift. All of me? Is this what God wanted?

The rest of the day was a celebration for all. The vow boys strolled around the grounds in twos and threes, wearing new cassocks and stiff, black three-cornered hats called birettas and then, in the afternoon, we had a baseball game, First Year versus Second Year. I was not a great natural athlete, but I'd played a lot of ball in school, and managed to letter on two league championship teams at Loyola. I was a better bunter than a hitter, I knew how to run the bases, and I had a wicked tongue, which I used to rattle opposing pitchers.

I led off the game by drawing a walk, stole second, and scored from there on a groundout to deep short with a diving, dusty slide that avoided the catcher's tag after a throw that had me beat. That was all that was needed to make a newcomer bolder than he should have been. I started right in razzing the pitcher, a tall righthander named Richard Overstreet. When Bob Jay told me that Brother Overstreet was the golden-voiced tenor who had sung the beautiful "Suscipe" that morning, I had the special opening I needed to make him lose some concentration.

"Hey, choirboy," I shouted. Instead of ignoring me, he whirled and pointed and said he'd soon take care of me. His reaction only encouraged me to continue references to his pretty voice and his pretty face. In the fifth inning, with a man on third and one out, I squared away to squeeze in the tying run against Brother Overstreet. He threw a high, hard one and came charging in, his blue eyes wide and eager. I missed the bunt and the runner was out. My fault. All of a sudden, the game was over. We didn't play nine-inning games. We played for two hours, then marched down the hill in twos or threes, and said the rosary together, out loud.

At 5:30, the entire community, almost two hundred strong, gathered for a feast to celebrate the simple vows that had been taken that day. In the refectory, after the grace before meals, one of the novices read from a pulpit high above our heads in solemn tones. It was one of the daily chapters of an ongoing history of the Jesuits.

> *Fasti Breviores* for August the fifteenth. In fifteen hundred and thirty four, in the little Church of Our Lady of Montmartre, Paris, St. Ignatius and his first nine companions . . . took their first, or simple, vows at the Mass celebrated by Blessed Peter Faber, the only priest among them. . . . In fifteen hundred and forty nine, the landing at Cangoxima, Japan, of St. Francis Xavier, Father Cosmos de Torres and John Fernandez, after a stormy voyage. . . . In fifteen hundred and sixty eight, at Rome, the happy death of the angelic St. Stanislaus on Our Lady's feast. He twice received Holy Communion from the hands of an angel, and on one occasion Our Lady placed the Holy Child Jesus in his arms. . . . In seventeen hundred and ninety, at Lulworth Castle, England, Father John Carroll, of Maryland, was consecrated the first bishop of Baltimore. . . .

After that reading, the rector said *Satis,* "Enough," and gave the signal that we could talk. Then the waiters, wearing white aprons over their black cassocks, started to serve. It was the kind of dinner I had read about in books. It went on for almost three hours and the menu included shrimp cocktail, quail with wild rice, lime sherbet (to purge the taste of the quail), strip sirloin steaks and a glorious ice cream parfait. The waiters poured five successive wines from the Novitiate's own vast cellar of sherry, sauternes, burgundy, black muscat, and port, and then came around at the very end of the meal to pour shots of brandy or crème de menthe.

Afterward, we were allowed to mingle with those who had taken their vows that day. Some of them plied us, incredibly enough after that feast, with boxes and boxes of chocolates. I took the occasion to talk to Brother Overstreet. I walked over to him with an outstretched hand and a smile. "No hard feelings?" I said.

"Why should there be?" he said, blandly. "We won, you lost. In fact, you could have tied the game with a good bunt. And you didn't." He raised his eyebrows, and made a slight explosive sound with his lips that seemed to emphasize his point with a finality that no one could argue with. I certainly couldn't. He moved off to joke with one of the others.

I turned to my guardian angel hovering nearby and said, "Say, Brother McDonough, just who is this, uh (I wanted to say snotty) Brother — Overstreet — anyway?"

He laughed and said, "Oh, don't mind him."

"Yeah," I said, "but who is he? Where does he come from?"

He told me that Brother Overstreet had served four years in the U.S. Navy before he joined the California Province. "I think he's from Washington, D.C. His uncle is the president of Georgetown."

"I'm not impressed by that," I lied, "but if he can make it here, so can I." Now I didn't want to turn around and go home at all.

2

I soon began to wonder whether I really wanted to go ahead with this life. It was torture. For one thing, a succession of sexy young women started invading my inner space, which came as a surprise because I'd never dated more than two or three times in high school. In fact, during my teens, I stayed away from girls, particularly girls at dances, after one disastrous freshman dance at St. Mary's High in Phoenix. Dancing with a young woman who was almost exactly my height, her nipples boring right into mine, I sprung an enormous erection. I couldn't hide it, couldn't melt it. When the dance ended, I hobbled over to the edge of the dance floor, red-faced and then angry with my grubby classmates, who were chortling over my misfortune.

Needless to say, I was scared by my own feelings, and would continue to be puzzled by them for some time. Going off to a boys' boarding school was a way of getting away from sex. So was joining the Jesuits. But coming here to the Novitiate didn't get me away. Now, in my first few days as a Postulant, my wild young imagination was playing tricks on me, slipping in sexy pictures of girls I had known, most of them in eighth grade, of Anna Mae and Geri and Katherine and Anne and Betty Marie and Patti. But why here, why in this holy place?

❧

THE NOVITIATE of the Sacred Heart. Novices' wing. Second floor. Cubicle D-2. I begin my afternoon meditation. A warm sweet breeze enters the window and kisses my left ear. And then the sudden buzzing of a swarm of cicadas deflects the caress. I shift my weight from one knee to the other on my low wooden kneeler, a piece of wood hardly bigger than a shoebox. I am supposed to be meditating on the Hidden Life of Jesus, as outlined a half-hour before by Father Master. I look at my notes and try to focus on the encounter of Jesus with the Elders in the Temple, and on Mary and Joseph, who think he is lost. The method, Father Master has said, can be something like replaying a favorite movie, or scripting one.

I see Jesus talking to the Elders. Then I cut to Mary and Joseph, roaming the dusty streets, looking for the kid. They're frowning. Now I cut back to Jesus. He's about ten years old, smooth cheeked, curly black hair, earnest, well spoken. He's just asked one of the Elders a brilliant-naive question and the elder is fumbling for the right words. Waiting, he has all the impatience of a boy, toeing along a pattern in the tile floor of the temple with his leather sandal. It is a leather sandal very much like the one Katherine used to wear when I walked her home from the pool on those warm evenings back in Phoenix.

Now the scene switches to Technicolor. I see an idealized version of the way Katherine looked on one particular night last July. She is wearing very little: a red tube top that reveals her perfect, high, young, rounded breasts, and a pair of crisp white shorts, and I cannot even imagine what is hidden inside them because I have never seen a girl down there or even the kinds of pictures that young men can examine so freely these days on the Internet. She has the longest, barest, smoothest legs I have ever walked beside and they taper down nicely to her delicate ankles, encircled by the leather strap on her sandals —

The sandals remind me: I am supposed to be thinking of Christ's sandals, not Katherine's. What am I doing? I grit my teeth. It has happened again. It always seems to happen during meditation. One moment, I am exploring the Holy Places and the next I am having visions of these young women, images that overwhelm and obliterate those of Jesus and Mary and Joseph and the Elders in the temple. Anna Mae's warm lap, Geri's sexy lisp, Katherine's long lashes, Anne's tiny waist, Betty Marie's boobs, Patti's moist lips. . . . I am lost in the contemplation of laps and lisps and lashes. I shake my head. I know: it doesn't make any sense here, during a holy meditation. Try to explain that to a fantasy on the rampage.

A bell rings. Not a ding-dong, medieval-sounding church bell with a tongue and clapper but the quick burst of an electric bell, a buzzing order to change positions. Kneel fifteen minutes. Then stand for fifteen. Then sit for fifteen. Then kneel. Now I stand, pull at the annoying wetness in my shorts and scream silently to myself. "Stop these sexy thoughts. Stop.

Stop. Stop. You're here in religion, you've left the world — and the flesh. In a few days, if you make it through your postulancy, you'll be signing your name with an 'N.S.J.' Novice, Society of Jesus." That has a nice ring to it. Novice, Society of Jesus. I am proud that I have gotten this far.

For years, when I was growing up on Detroit's West Side, I had read everything I could find on West Point, glorying in the toughness of the U.S. Army officer's training, aspiring with all my heart to become one of the cadets, one of the best. Then, my parents (who had no religion at all) were divorced and I moved to Phoenix with my mother and her sister's family, the O'Briens, who enrolled me in a Catholic school called St. Francis Xavier. That school gave me a kind of moral anchor in the confusing seas that threatened to swamp my little rowboat.

Both my mother and my father (whom I visited in the summers) were making other, romantic friends and I hated that. My mother was in her early thirties, and she had every right to try to make a new life for herself, and so did my father. I couldn't see it then. I made it clear to both of them that I wouldn't tolerate any fooling around, which meant that I'd find a way to leave them both. Now, I started looking to the Church as both mother and father. I thought the Church could give me a refuge from all this, this messy marriage-and-divorce business.

It just so happened that the priests at St. Francis Xavier were Jesuits. One of them was Father Richard O'Rourke; he became the coach of our eighth-grade basketball team and he took a special interest in me and told me more about his Order, which was something like an army. I hardly dared suggest the possibility at first, but I thought, if I could join their army, I'd be a member of an elite corps (just like at West Point) — and I'd never have to marry, either, would I? I went to my eighth-grade nun and asked if the Jesuits would take someone like me. She smiled and told me I'd have to become a Catholic first, and then, maybe then I could be a Jesuit, after my high school years — if I passed the Jesuits' rigid, almost service academy standards.

And so, I became a Catholic, to the cheers of my classmates, who believed they had a hand in my conversion. I am sure they did, for they were kids who knew how to be good without being goody goody, which I found darned attractive. And then, after my freshman year at St. Mary's, Father O'Rourke arranged a scholarship for me, to the Jesuits' Loyola High in Los Angeles. I was only fourteen. The Jesuits had helped me run away from home. By my senior year, it seemed like a natural thing to pass right on into the Order itself.

Now, however, at this point in my Novitiate, ten days through a twelve-day orientation period called postulancy, I wondered whether I was really cut out for this army, this Company of Jesus. These secret fantasies made me feel like a sex-crazed impostor who had somehow been able to conceal his depravity and slip through the fine mesh screens of at least three official Jesuit interviewers.

And then came the insects. I couldn't see them, but I could feel them, all over me, night and day, on the attack. They came when I was kneeling at prayer, or, worse, when I was lying on my narrow bed, quietly smashing them into submission — quietly, because I didn't want the others in the room to hear me.

There were seven other young men in my room, a long narrow affair broken into cubicles by thin half-walls, gray-painted pine partitions that screened off sight, but not sound. During meditation, I could hear the clatter of a holy card dropping accidentally on the floor three cubicles down the line. I imagined the others could do the same, and since I never heard anyone else slapping at their bugs, and never saw a single bug, dead or alive, I soon figured out that the insects were crawling around in my imagination, nowhere else, and I was not anxious for anyone to know about my unreal creatures, not the bugs of my present, nor the beauties of my past.

A part of me said to get out before I went buggy. Another part of me took the reasoned stand that this was simply a case of nerves, understandable enough, under the circumstances. Others were getting through this — I thought of Overstreet — and so could I. I told myself I had come out of a roomy freedom into the most rigidly structured regime ever devised by man. Here, bells rang all day long, from five in the morning until nine at night, sometimes at ten- or fifteen-minute intervals, and when a bell rang everyone obeyed instantly, because the buzz of the bell was the voice of God. When God spoke, good Jesuits responded, as the Rule said, "even to the letter unended." That meant that if a bell rang when I was writing down the lights of my morning meditation (for example) and I was on the upswing of an "e," I dropped my pen immediately and raced to the next exercise, in silence.

The whole day was spent in silence, except for certain short, stated moments, during a two-hour work or play period in the afternoon, twenty minutes after lunch every day, and a half-hour after supper. If it was absolutely necessary to speak during a time of silence, we spoke in Latin, a rule calculated to help us keep things brief and to the point. There were drinking fountains in the hall, but if we wanted to use one, we had to ask the room beadle for permission: *Licetne bibere?* "May I get a drink?"

Everyone spoke Latin at table, too. Communicating with waiters was easiest in sign language. A wave and the passing of an empty egg platter brought more eggs. We didn't specify how we wanted them. If scrambled was on the menu for breakfast, we ate scrambled.

At the midday and evening meals, there wasn't much need (or temptation) to talk anyway. We had readings. From a high lectern in the middle of the refectory, a reader intoned a daily bit from the *Fasti Breviores* — items culled from the stormy history of the Order, its men hiding in priest holes during the reign of Henry VIII, being burned at the stake in Japan, imprisoned in Portugal by a villainous prime minister named Pombal. Then the reader would take up where he had left off the day before in the reading of a tract selected by Father Silva, the Juniors' hammy professor of rhetoric and Shakespeare, who would correct the readers' mispronounced words with a merry good humor. His sallies were always funnier to the Juniors than they were to us Novices.

Silence at table was just a part of the continual self-denial here at the Novitiate. At recreation on my second or third night at Los Gatos, I found out we couldn't even cross our legs.

"It's a kind of self-imposed penance," my angel explained. "We call crossed legs 'an Arsenius' because of the ancient monk, Arsenius. As part of his own self-imposed penance, he never crossed his legs."

"Gee. Yeah," I said, impressed with a guy who spent a whole lifetime not crossing his legs. I wondered what he *did* do. Or was it possible, I asked myself, that in the life of Christian perfection that I was learning, one reached the Hall of Fame by simply *not* doing something? I put both my feet flat on the ground in front of the bench we were sitting on. I wondered if it was O.K. to rest my hands on my knees. Sometimes, it was comfortable to put your hands on your knees. I looked sideways at my angel as he put his hands on his knees. I sighed in relief and pondered why I had drawn this guy as my angel, this Brother Robert McDonough, who had been some kind of Marine hero at Okinawa.

Brother McDonough said, "You'll find Arsenius in *Rodriguez.*"

"Who's Rodriguez?" I said.

"That's the book you were reading this morning at 9:30."

"Oh?" I frowned, trying to remember what Brother McDonough was talking about. "The big book with the black cotton dust jacket?" I asked. *"The Practice of Christian Perfection?"*

· 12 ·

"Right," he said. "By Alphonsus Rodriguez. We just call the book *Rodriguez*." He paused and smiled at me. "Some just call it 'Rod.'"

I smiled back, appreciating the allowed informality — that we could call this distinguished writer Rod.

Alphonsus Rodriguez, he told me, was a Portuguese Jesuit who had gone to the trouble, two or three centuries ago, to compile a three-volume treatise on all the Christian virtues. There were chapters on poverty and chastity and obedience and faith and hope and charity, exciting stuff like that. I liked to read and I had inhaled a couple tons of books as a youngster but I had always read because I found something I wanted to read, not something I had to. Reading Rodriguez was torture.

On this very day, I had whizzed through a chapter of anecdotes in Rodriguez about the way the saints practiced the virtue of Holy Purity. When St. Patrick was afflicted by a sexy thought, I learned, he flung himself into a freezing lake. On another page of Rod, I learned that St. Columcill, no doubt practicing angelic virtue in a more moderate part of Ireland, used to throw himself into a thorny thicket.

For a moment, standing there in my cubicle and trying to meditate, I considered the fact that there was a line of rose bushes just outside my window, one story down, but I rejected the idea of plunging into them if Katherine slipped off her tube top during this afternoon's meditation. I really didn't want to make a scene. I could just imagine myself lying there in the rose bushes with all the Novices on my side of the house breaking their recollection by craning their necks out the window to see what had happened to me. And then, maybe I'd shout up at them (in Latin, of course), "Mind your own business."

But my brothers wouldn't look out the window at me lying in the rose bushes, would they? They would keep modesty of the eyes, tending to their own thing. Father Master had told us, "You keep your rule, and I'll keep mine." It was a cryptic message at first, but I soon learned what the Master meant: "Don't worry about anyone but yourself. If the other guy seems to be breaking the rule, it's none of your business. You don't judge. Let God judge."

In this boot camp, I even had a drill sergeant, Father Dan Kelleher, the second in command, who seemed duty-bound to test me in devious ways. He didn't know about my private trials, the beauties, the bugs, of my imagination — and neither did anyone else. But he knew that I knew that he was a baseball nut who lived and died for the annual Junior-Novice game every spring, and that he was already counting on me to help his Novices win. So what did he do? He had me playing handball, not baseball. The idea, I guessed, was that I wasn't supposed to have too much fun.

I knew I'd have to expect these trials. I'd read all about the hazings of West Point; why should I expect anything less here in the Jesuits? On my first trip to the shower stalls on the main floor, I shivered under a freezing stream of water while I muttered quiet prayers of resignation. "Oh, God," I said, "cold showers for two years?" The water didn't turn warm. If anything, it got a little colder. "Okay, okay," I said, "I can take it." Then, as I toweled my shivering, skinny frame, I saw steam rising from the other stalls and I reached back into the shower, tested both faucets and found that the hot and cold water faucets had been reversed in my shower. I had had hot water available all the time. I felt foolish about that at first. On second thought, I felt very virtuous indeed, for I had accepted two years of cold showers — and had gotten extra merit with the Lord for accepting them — at a very small outlay of suffering.

This was something else I learned in the Novitiate, to take a cost accountant's approach to the spiritual life. We received indulgences, for example, for pious little acts. An indulgence was supposed to lessen our sentences in Purgatory. For example, we got a thirty days indulgence for saying a particular prayer, like "Jesus, Mary, and Joseph, pray for us." That was called "an ejaculation," and no one ever tittered at the double entendre. In the Novitiate, the word had only one holy, sober, indulgenced meaning.

Another bell rang to signal a third change of position during this meditation. Fifteen minutes kneeling. Fifteen minutes standing. Fifteen minutes, sitting. Now I sat down and told myself that this meditation wasn't much of a meditation. What it was was woolgathering. I tried to pray — that is, I tried to talk to Jesus. "You had a hidden life, Jesus," I said. "And now I am having a hidden life. I don't think you exactly enjoyed it. Neither do I. But if I must live it, I will."

Not five minutes later, another bell rang, kneelers rattled and everyone started tramping out of their cubicles and down the hall to the refectory. I had no watch to consult. Only the beadle had a watch. It was obviously dinnertime. I'd lost fifteen minutes somehow. I must have daydreamed right through one bell. "Oh, well," I said sarcastically to myself, "Time flies when you're havin' fun."

3

When I arrived at the Novitiate, I had been amazed to find we had no radio, or movies, no newspapers or magazines (although my Jesuit teachers had had them at Loyola High) — and that we couldn't even read novels. "You'll get a chance to read novels in the Juniorate," Brother McDonough told me. "If you like stories, you've got a lot of saints to read about. There are a couple hundred Jesuit saints. The Jesuits have more saints than any other order. And you'll have time to read the whole Bible. And Thomas à Kempis. And some different lives of Christ. And Rodriguez."

I laughed. Rodriguez! Hah! Brother McDonough was a real joker. Or was he? He was only one of a large contingent here who had been in the armed forces during World War II, and I had the feeling as I talked to him that he had seen everything and done everything before he entered the Soc (pronounced Sock) and chose it anyway and was a truly happy man. I knew I had seen very little, first hand, and experienced even less and I wondered what it was that I wanted here. Oh, sure, I was now telling myself that I wanted to serve God and I had a notion that I could do that best as a Jesuit. But wasn't I also trying to escape the real world? Was that a worthy motive for being here? I doubted it was.

Maybe I'd find inspiration in the lives of the saints. I picked up a book that Brother McDonough had recommended, *A Saint in the Slave Trade* by Sir Arnold Lunn, an English convert. It was about Peter Claver, a Jesuit, who ministered to the slaves in South America, circa 1800. Well written. It read like a novel. I could almost hear the creaking of the mast and the luff of the rigging as Father Claver's ship pulled into the harbor at Cartagena. And when Lunn recounted some of Claver's more vivid ministries — he specialized, for instance, in sucking the pus out of the ulcerated sores of the African slaves — I almost threw up at my desk.

At their best, these stories about the holy heroes were good, because they put Christianity in concrete, particular terms. They showed how the faith was actually lived by real people at different epochs in history. If you were lucky enough to be a queen, you could look up to Margaret of Cortona, who had been a queen before she was widowed and joined a religious order. If, on the other hand, you were a bum, you could develop a devotion to Benedict Joseph Labret, who was a holy vagabond. Both Margaret and Benedict, according to the Church, had practiced "heroic virtues" on earth and were now "in heaven." Therefore, they could intercede for us before the throne of the Almighty. Throne. All these spiritual writers, it seemed, used kingly metaphors when they talked about God.

This teaching tended to make God sound like a man and I was not sure I could go along with all this anthropomorphizing, but then, how else could men talk about God, except in human terms? And as the Master told us more than once, any way to God was a good way. If it helped someone to think of God as a king, who was I to challenge?

As I read, I couldn't help hearing whispered voices coming over the partitions. It was Brother Costaregni, a postulant, in earnest conversation with my angel, Brother McDonough, down in Brother McDonough's cubicle. "But I can't *stand* this!" said Brother Costaregni, raising his voice for a moment in anger and frustration. If anyone spoke at this time, it should have been in Latin. Since Brother Costaregni could not, by his own admission, "stand it," I assumed that my angel had a special duty to help a brother get through a crisis, even if he had to whisper in English. I could not hear much of what they were saying. But it was a comfort for me to know that another was having trouble with the life. It was nice not to be alone.

Dan Costaregni was a husky young man, with dark curly hair and a noble Roman nose. He had played varsity football at Loyola University in Los Angeles with Al Pollard and Don Klosterman and an all-star cast of janizaries who were going to put Loyola in the big time. He had come all the way from Connecticut, in fact, for no other reason than to play football. After two years at Loyola, he was transfixed by the Jesuits. He wanted to become a Jesuit, too, and serve God like they did. The only trouble was, as far as I could tell from the story Brother Costaregni was telling, he had also been living the sweet life, Los Angeles-style, for two years. And he could not help thinking about that life now. His uncle was a Hollywood agent and he had made things nice for Dan.

"You know where I'd be right now if I wasn't here?" he demanded. "I'd be in Uncle Porkie's yellow Buick convertible driving along Wilshire Boulevard with the top down and the wind blowing in my hair and a beautiful blonde sitting close to me in the front seat." He groaned with pleasure at the memory of it. "That's where I'd be."

Because Brother Costaregni raised his voice, Brother McDonough followed suit. He told Brother Costaregni that no one ever said this would be easy. "But now is the time you can show that you are a real man, now is the time that you reach in and grab a handful of guts and show your-self — not me, not Father Master, not any of these guys here — you show yourself you've got — what — it — takes."

Brother McDonough's voice came across the partition like a low growl. He was right, I said to myself. This was good advice for me, too, I said, as one of my imaginary bugs crawled up my right arm and up into the hair on the back of my neck. It was a warm night, but I shivered with a kind of masochistic anticipation. Whatever Brother Costaregni did, I would show myself that I had what it takes. I would make it.

✑

TWO NIGHTS LATER, after a large dinner occasioned by the final vows of a priest-professor living at the Novitiate, one that lasted more than two hours and featured four wines, I dreamed of Patti. I was dancing with her in a palmy paradise I had never seen before, dancing very close, and her nipples were brushing mine and she put her tongue in my left ear and whispered my name, "Bob, Bob, Bob." My wet dream woke me up, then and there. Oh, I sighed to myself, this is wrong. What am I doing here? But as I lay there on my back, not moving or rolling over on to my own dampness, I found it was very easy to go back to sleep.

In the morning, the bell rang and the cubicle beadle cried, *Benedicamus Domino*. "Let us bless the Lord." I joined the chorus of replies with a shout of *Deo gratias*, "Thanks be to God," and whipped off my pajamas, now hardened in front, donned a tattered robe and slippers and trotted down to the shower room to wash off the mess. The hot water made me feel better. But I knew now I must tell Father Master and let him decide: should I stay or leave?

"Bless me, Father, for I have sinned," I told the Master. I was kneeling on his *prie dieu*, he was sitting next to it. "It has been a week since my last confession. Since then, I accuse myself of many impure thoughts. Last night, I, I had a wet dream. I do not think I can stay here. I am not doing well. I can't meditate."

The Master had his face buried in his hand. He looked like he was asleep. He grunted at me and opened one eye to look at me. "A wet dream is not a sin. Impure thoughts are not necessarily sinful." I nodded. "Did you take pleasure in them?"

"No," I said, lying quickly. I really did "take pleasure" in my visions and if I didn't I would have been something of a freak and the Creator Someone Who Had Made A Big Mistake because it was He who had made me the way I was, pleasurable visions, wet dreams and all. I made up for the lie by adding just as quickly that I hated myself for having these dreams.

"No, Brother," said the Master. "Don't hate yourself. You're only living the natural life of a man. A young man. It takes time to change that, to learn to live the supernatural life of grace. Purity is a virtue, but it's not the only virtue. You have faith, you have hope, you have charity." I nodded again. I did not know what to say, but I wanted the Master to know that I was listening. "Don't be so hard on yourself. Pray a little more. Now make a good Act of Contrition for whatever sins you may have committed and for your penance say one Hail Mary."

One Hail Mary. Not a very stiff penance, I told myself as I rattled off the Act of Contrition in English while the Master said the magic words of the absolution in Latin. Maybe I had not been so sinful after all. I rose, then I turned back to the Master. "But Father, should I stay?"

"And why not?" He half turned toward me and the look on his face was fierce.

Haltingly, I said, "I, I feel that everyone else is way up here." I measured a height with my hand, about seven feet. "And I am way down here." Three feet.

"Hummph."

"What?"

"You don't know about the others," he said. "Don't worry about them. Worry about yourself. Now git."

I hesitated. I thought I saw a slight smile on the Master's face. I wondered what there was to smile about.

Later that day, I found that my name was on a list of those postulants who were supposed to receive cassocks that afternoon. Apparently, I had passed my postulancy, along with thirty-nine of the forty-three others who had entered with me. Four of my class had already left, and two of them had never smiled once while they plodded through the regimen. I told myself that I should smile more. If only the beauties and the bugs would go away. . . .

Strangely enough, they did go away, in a wondrous way, the very next morning. After I rose and went through my morning ablutions, I put on my first cassock and hurried on down to the novice's chapel. I was only dimly aware of the others coming and going for what we called "first visit" to the Blessed Sacrament. As I knelt there in the pew, I felt that the very weight of the cassock seemed to calm me down — as, in the novel by Lloyd Douglas, Christ's seamless robe had quieted the anxiety of the Roman centurion who had been afflicted with a nameless psychosis since the day he had presided over the Crucifixion.

And then, back up in my own cubicle, I started my meditation and found no insects crawling up my arms or lisping beauties invading my thoughts. I discovered I could concentrate for a good portion of my meditation, and I found myself talking to Jesus like a brother, earnestly, fondly. When I received Communion that morning at Mass, I did not walk back to my place in the pew, I floated.

☙

I TOOK Father Master's advice. I stopped trying to compare myself to my fellow novices and concentrated on doing what I was doing. And I began to do better. I had my fantasy life under control, for the most part. The nerve bugs had gone away, and I was getting used to "Common Order" — the same schedule every day, bells ringing with regularity, the daily reading periods, the talks by the Master, one at 11:00 in the morning and another at 4:30 in the afternoon, and another at 8:30 in the evening, good food, a two hour work period every afternoon.

On Tuesdays, we'd trek out to our villa in the redwoods, and on Sundays, instead of an afternoon work period, we usually had game time, and I found that now I was almost always assigned to play baseball. I still dreaded the 2:00 P.M. lineup on the third floor corridor when the beadle read out the names of who was going to do what. I always hoped that it would be hardball for me and not handball, or, worse, walking with a couple of novices who had become incapacitated with bad cases of poison oak. I knew, I knew: I was supposed to be "indifferent." But I couldn't help how I felt, could I? Anyway, I rationalized, I wasn't being all that selfish. I was one of the better ballplayers in the Novitiate, wasn't

I? And wouldn't my presence on the field make for a better game — for the others?

I'd begun to feel a sense of comradeship with the others who were good ballplayers. I now felt somewhat friendlier to Brother Overstreet and a lot closer to Brothers Weber, Jay, Welch, Boyle, and Carroll (Los Angelenos who had preceded me by a year), and to the ballplayers in my own class, Brothers Schall, Schlossman, Conn, Costaregni, Tierney, and Maher.

Generally, we only played a few innings before it was time to quit. Then, the game beadle would shout, *Oremus* and we would immediately kneel wherever we had been standing, say a Hail Mary, and then, in silence, change from our spikes to our walking shoes and team up in threes to say the rosary together in Latin while hustling down the hill. Some recited the beads slowly and carefully. Some of us preferred going fast. Personally, I didn't get that much out of repeating fifty-three Hail Marys and six Our Fathers and it was hopeless to try and think about the Five Joyful Mysteries (in the life of Jesus and Mary) while I was trotting down the hill after a tight ball game. Better to find one or two of the Brothers of the Speedy Rosary — Brothers Schall and Maher were the fastest — get it over with and on to something else.

"Something else" in the early fall was the new swimming pool. Each day, we had a choice of going in for a shower after our work/play time or swimming in the Novitiate's new pool. Most of the ballplayers preferred the pool. It was a beautifully tiled affair, surrounded by walls of the native sandstone, and it overlooked not only the Novitiate grounds but much of the Santa Clara Valley as well.

Brother Phil Callaghan, a jovial second year man who was also one of the better house gossips, said the Rector had had a hard time getting Rome's approval for something as frivolous to Roman eyes as this tiled luxury. "So then," Brother Callaghan explained, "the Rector told Rome he needed a large water storage tank for fire protection — and to reduce the insurance premiums on the winery. That was a different story," he said, rolling his eyes.

Brother Maher listened to that tale and shrugged. What did Rome know anyway? Brother Maher was in a particularly good position to know that papal infallibility didn't extend on down to the Jesuit general, sometimes called the Black Pope. He had an uncle who worked on the general's staff, and he knew that his uncle (and the general) were just as human as anyone else, just as subject to the same human prejudices.

This gave Brother Maher a kind of self-assurance that I admired. He could take a more cavalier attitude, for instance, toward some of the rules that made no sense to him. One of them: a local directive, a long-standing protocol, that the Novices and Juniors had to wear T-shirts in the pool. Brother Marc Calegari had looked in an old custom book and had found the T-shirt rule dated back to at least 1938, when they had built a small pool at our villa up in the redwoods.

One day, Brother Maher challenged the T-shirt rule in one of the Master's open question and answer sessions. The Master said he didn't want to talk about it. It was just the rule, period. "Jeez," whispered Brother Maher, red in the face. He did not argue. Later that afternoon, however, he formed a conspiracy at the pool with two of our better divers. "If the Master shows up at the pool today," he said, "we go to the tower, right?"

The Master did show up and Brother Maher sauntered over to the tower, followed by two others. A little murmur of voices rose around the pool. Somehow, Brother Callaghan had gotten wind of what was up and he couldn't help telling others. Everyone stopped swimming and playing volleyball in the shallow end to watch the scene unfold. I didn't know whom to watch, Brother Maher and his co-conspirators or the fascinated onlookers. The onlookers were something of a sight themselves. You could tell the second year men from the rookies instantly: the rookies had fairly normal knees, but the veterans all had gigantic knobs growing on theirs. They were calluses, huge pads that nature had given them as a protection against all those hours kneeling in prayer.

Brother Maher dived first. He was tall and lean and a superb athlete. He did a forward one and a half somersault in a tuck position — a little more than a one and a half, actually: the first thing that hit the water was Brother Maher's back and shoulders, flexed to make the T-shirt stretch to the limit as it smacked the water. Result: one torn T-shirt. Brother Jay followed. It looked like a game of follow the leader. Same one and three-quarter somersault, same entry, same kind of torn T-shirt. By the time Brother Costaregni was in the air, everyone in the pool area knew what was going to happen. The Master had a grim look on his face. Or was it grim? Looking at him out of the corner of my eye, I thought I detected the Master's mouth working, almost as if he were suppressing a smile. Splat. Brother Costaregni hit the water. When he climbed up the ladder as nonchalantly as the others, his T-shirt was in ribbons.

Before supper that evening, Brothers Maher, Jay, and Costaregni knelt in the main aisle of the refectory. After grace was said and the thundering of more than two hundred chairs had subsided, the three of them, performing a ritual called a *culpa,* accused themselves, in turn, of "failing in poverty" — that is, deliberately destroying three perfectly good T-shirts. That night, a short note on the bulletin board, in Latin, announced the abrogation of the T-shirt rule at the pool, *paupertatis causa,* for reasons of poverty. Young men who were really poor couldn't go around destroying T-shirts.

Brother Maher had made his point, and obviously the Master had agreed with him: no sense ruining good clothing for the sake of an outmoded rule. The rule was outmoded, of course, because, as youngsters "out in the world" (one of our favorite Novitiate phrases), we hadn't been tempted to impure thoughts by the sight of male nipples. We'd taken them for granted — until this rule told us there was something about them that needed covering up (yeah!) with wet T-shirts.

The fact that there was any danger of Novices being sexually attracted to one another was a possibility I hadn't imagined, and I still find it hard to think that there was any fooling around of that kind in my Novitiate, where the Rule of Touch was kept with absolute scrupulosity. (I still remember Rule 32: "No one shall touch another, not even in jest, except when going or coming from a long journey.")

Still, our Master must have worried about this in at least a minimal way. I recall that at some point early in my Novitiate, he took up the subject of particular friendships. "In religion," he said, "you have no special friends." Jesuits were to be *omnia omnibus,* "all things to all men." In the Novitiate, there were would be no cliques. That was why recreation partners were assigned each week by the beadle. That was why the beadle kept changing the work and play crews all the time. Particular friendships violated the virtue of charity because presumably, if you were more of a friend to A, then you were less of a friend to B. And, I now realize, if you had no particular friend, then you certainly wouldn't fall into unspeakable practices or unnatural acts.

The Master never mentioned the word "homosexuality." But I guessed that was his reason for warning us about particular friendships. I had read of homosexuals and I knew one classmate at Loyola High who used to go to MacArthur Park in Los Angeles with a gang from his neighborhood to beat up on them. I never made the logical leap: that if homosexuality happened "out in the world," it could happen here. Nevertheless, blindly, I took the Master's words seriously, too seriously. No particular friendships?

Well, then, there'd be no friendships at all: whenever I had an option, I shunned the Novices I liked best. After the next ball game for example, I deliberately avoided Brothers Maher and Schall, and attached myself to two others I didn't have a special affinity with, and fretted my way through a long, slow, tiresome session with the beads.

4

On a Monday night in the third week of September or so, I came out to the Novices' courtyard after supper and got the news: the grapes were ready for picking. "The beadles are up distributing the grape knives," said Brother Blake. Phil Blake was a comedian and a storyteller. "They're wicked-looking hooks" — with a crooked index finger, he showed how wicked looking — "with wooden handles and leather straps, and a glove to protect your other hand." He said there would be a special rec at seven thirty and the Master would give us the whole scoop.

The Master did. He told us to be sure we got proper footgear from the sub-beadle, if we didn't already have a pair of heavy boots. And one good pair of denims and a denim jacket. "You're going to get your Levis dirty the first day, but not much dirtier on the days after that," he said. "So you'll just wear these Levis for the entire grape season." The season, he said, would last four, five, maybe six weeks. "It all depends," he said, "on how good you are at getting in the harvest."

We had an excellent winery at the Novitiate, first built by the Jesuit Fathers from Turin, Italy, who missionized California during the days of the Gold Rush. A full-time team of "temporal coadjutors" — that is, lay brothers with the three vows who would never be priests — ran the presses and the machinery and the rooms full of vats just east of the Juniors' wing, producing sacramental wines and table wines marketed nationally under the label "Novitiate of Los Gatos." When the grapes that grew all around us were ready, they needed all hands to help get in the harvest.

The Master pointed out that we'd been leading the hardest kind of life, the every-day-the-same kind of life called "Common Order." He noted that the Long Retreat, which started at the beginning of November, was even more rigorous. "That's why grape season's good for you. You'll get in good shape, working in the grape fields. The grapes will get you ready for the Long Retreat, physically, mentally.

"Some of you are used to hard work," he continued. "Some of you aren't." He paused and looked out at the faces in front of him. I imagined he was looking at me. The Master smiled one of his rare smiles. "I advise you to take your siestas. Just find a big grapevine and curl up under it. It's primitive, but you'll find, if you've been working all morning, you can use the rest. Then you'll go back and pick until four o'clock. No afternoon meditation. Say three rosaries instead, on the way home. Pool time till five thirty. Dinner at six. During grape season, the Juniors will wait table. You'll do scullery afterwards, as usual.

"This is something you'll never forget," said the Master. "A time when you'll be close to God's earth, close to God's grapes, and I hope, close to God, too."

As usual, the Master was right. I wasn't very proficient at prayer, but I could work, and I threw myself into the grape season, one hundred and fifty percent. Our first day, we gathered in back of the Novitiate and climbed into a flatbed truck. There must have been sixty or seventy of us, crammed in together like so many cattle. Brother Roger Falge, the sub-beadle, announced that we should all keep a mental count of the number of boxes we picked each day and turn in the number on an unsigned slip of paper in the evening. He'd announce the day's top number each evening, "just so you know how you're doing." The all-time record: sixty-three boxes in one day.

Someone asked him who'd set that record. The sub-beadle said he wasn't supposed to talk about that. "We wouldn't want anyone to get vain-glory." That didn't stop me from vowing to break the record. That day, I honed my grape knife to a razor-sharp edge, but reality soon set in: I only picked nine boxes. That night at recreation, however, I was encouraged to learn that the day's nameless leader had picked only fourteen. "We were working on young vines today," Brother Jay told me. "Wait'll you see some of the fields. Wait'll Guadalupe. You'll get a whole boxful off one vine." I dreamt that night about Guadalupe and its heavy vines.

Grape season was good for me. I found myself getting stronger, more confident about myself and my future in the Order. When I hit my first vine in the morning, I'd cut loose the biggest bunch I could find and cram it into my mouth, letting only the cool sweet juice run down my throat, then toss the mangled clump into my box. When I filled a box, I'd carry it out to the end of the row and start filling another. I picked furiously, but never came very close to the daily winner's tally. Others weren't as gung ho (or as compulsive) as I. Some of the brothers fooled around a bit, yammered and chattered their way along until silence was imposed at eleven, and then tried to make up for lost time by picking fast until lunchtime.

The lunches were huge, more like full-course dinners, served steaming hot from an Army-surplus truck on big steel Army trays, eaten cross-legged on the ground, while someone read aloud in the noonday sun. Sometimes I took a siesta. Sometimes, I'd join a little conversation group around the Master, who drove out to the fields at noon in a brown Dodge, following the food truck. If the Master got good questions, he could be a fascinating storyteller. He had been the provincial superior of the Jesuits in California, he'd studied in Rome, he knew the late Jesuit general Vladimir Ledochowski, and he could quote extensively from the wit and wisdom of this great Pole who led the Society through the trials of two world wars.

Then a group of Novices whom I privately dubbed The Brethren of the Strict Pious Observance (there wasn't a ballplayer among them) started taking over the sessions, asking the Master to tell them about the visions at Fatima and Lourdes. Once, Brother Edward Malatesta actually came right out and asked the Master to tell us about the stigmata of St. Teresa of Avila. I was startled by this showy piety. Could Brother Malatesta really be interested in St. Teresa's bloody hands? Could anyone? Even if the story of her stigmata were true, which I doubted, who really gave a darn? But no. I was judging Brother Malatesta. I shouldn't do that. I shouldn't judge motives. This would give me some material for my nighttime examen. If someone wanted to kiss it up with the Master, that was his business, wasn't it? I wouldn't judge.

After lunch the next day, a bright, sunny one at Guadalupe (and in my mind's eye now, so many years later, all the days there were bright and sunny), I rounded up Brothers Schlossman, Maher, and Malatesta and asked the Master if we could start picking grapes right away, during siesta. We admitted we were all pushing to break our own records and we didn't want to snooze away our opportunities. The Master gave us a mock-serious frown, then softened and said it would be O.K. — just this once.

With hoots, the four of us hurried off to a pile of grape boxes, and ran down a dusty lane to the south. It wasn't quite two o'clock, and I had already picked forty-seven boxes for the day. I wasn't sure what any of the others had tallied. They didn't say and I didn't ask. That would have been vainglory. But it wasn't vainglorious for me to tell myself. With purity of intention, the Master had said, anything was possible and you didn't forego outstanding work just to avoid vainglory.

Then I slipped on my pride. "Hey," I cried out to one of the others, as I lugged two full boxes to the road, "wait'll those suckers in the Juniorate hear that four of us broke their record today." I hurried back down the row with two empty boxes and tore into the huge bunches of grapes, so huge that ten of them would fill a box.

Silentium, cried the beadle from some distance away. It was three o'clock. One more hour to pick. O.K., I thought. In that time I was sure I could fill fifteen boxes. When the beadle approached with some empty boxes, I looked up and cried, "Right here. Boxes here!" — slashing my left wrist in the process. I had sharpened my hook knife at lunchtime. It stopped just short of the bone and entered the artery.

"Damn," I cried. My wrist started spurting. I put my hand high above my head and tried to find a pressure point so I could stop the flow. "Bro," I said to Brother Schall, "I'm cut."

He ran over, took one look at me, grabbed his own grapeknife and twisted the leather strap around my arm.

"C'mon, we've got to get you to a doc."

Fortunately, the Master was still there. I climbed into his brown Dodge and he drove me right to town. I felt like some kind of freak, trotting into the doctor's office in my grapey Levis, stiff with juice and earth, and smelling like a winery.

There wasn't much pain, and the arterial blood had stopped pumping. I submitted to my stitches with stoic calm, offering up the hurt for my mother and father and brother. That was the positive side of suffering, the Master had said. Your own pain, offered up to God, built credits for others. So this injury was good. Except for one thing: now I probably wouldn't — .

"No record today, huh, Brother?" said the Master, who was standing by as the doctor sewed me up. I looked up at him and grinned. How did he know what I was thinking? Well, he was a wise man, and I was growing to like him. He was definitely taking the place of a man I didn't know very well, my father. I needed a father, someone who would understand me, and help me grow in wisdom and age and grace.

THAT NIGHT, when we all returned to our cubicles after evening recreation, we found knotted whips of heavy cord lying on our desks and two wide, intricately interlocking chains made of piano wire. I couldn't figure out what the chains were for, but I guessed what the whip was. I'd read in Rod about monks who took "the discipline" and Arnold Lunn had told me Peter Claver had beaten himself with a leather whip till he bled, as an expiation for the sins of the slavers. I thought the discipline was a relic of the past. I certainly didn't expect to ever see one, much less use one. But the Master made an invitation that night during his evening talk.

The Master told us that "the discipline" (as it was called) was an ancient ascetic practice, just one of a group of corporal penances used by monks from time immemorial that helped them control their "baser instincts" — the idea being that "if you don't beat the devil inside you, he'll beat you." The Master may have seen some of us frowning. "You may not exactly understand how this happens," he said. "You'll only find out when you try it. If you try it." No one had to use the discipline. In fact, you had to ask the Master's permission to do so.

As for the chains we found on our desks, the Master explained that one fit tightly around the bicep and the other around the thigh. "They either fit tightly," he explained, "or they just don't stay on at all. You put them on when you dress in the morning and take them off before morning Mass." In my cubicle, I had already tested the sharp points of the chains with my finger. They looked mean. Now that I understood what I was to do with them, I wondered if I could stand them. "And, by the way," said the Master, "you wear the chains with the points turned in, next to the skin, not out, so as to jab your brother." He smiled, indicating that he was joking — to make a point.

He explained himself. "Some penitential souls make others suffer more than themselves. Well, let me tell you this: if you make life less pleasant for others because you're wearing a hair shirt, then you're on the wrong track. You're putting the hair shirt on them. Better, then, not to wear a hair shirt at all."

I knew the Master was speaking figuratively. I'd seen no hair shirt along with the whips and the chains. The monks of the desert had woven shirts of horse hair, and wore them under their robes as a penance, but as far as I knew making hair shirts was a lost art, and wearing them completely passé.

The next afternoon, after grapes, just before dinner, I wasn't so sure. When I came into my cubicle, I saw Brother Costaregni standing there with a sad, disgusted look on his face. He stopped me to show me his hair shirt. Brother Blake was standing there with him, fingering its roughness along with him and telling him that yes, it was just like his, rather more of a burlap vest, but no mistaking its use. "*Est* prickly," he said, making an effort to keep the rule of speaking only Latin, but unable to call up the Latin adjective for itchy. He drew open the front of his cassock and showed us both an expanse of burlap. Brother Costaregni's eyes bulged and he shook his head in disbelief. "You gonna wear yours?" he said to me. I shrugged.

Brother Blake said, *Pater Magister dixit.* "Father Master said we should."

Hodie? said Brother Costaregni. "We gotta wear 'em today?"

Brother Blake said that the Master had told us the night before. Brother Costaregni said he didn't remember the Master's saying anything about a hair shirt. Brother Blake looked at me, gave me a furious wink that asked me to confirm. Aha, I thought, what a great practical joke! I was nodding solemnly when Brother Overstreet waltzed into the cubicle, pulled open his cassock to show us his hair shirt and asked whether we had tried ours yet. So Brother Overstreet was in on it, too.

With a groan, Brother Costaregni grabbed his vest, moved into his bedroom area and pulled the curtain closed. We waited, trying to control our laughter and almost exploding when we heard Brother Costaregni fuming and growling. We did explode when he emerged with his cassock on and his arms stuck straight out, like a vulture about to take off. "It doesn't fit," he said, leaving aside any attempt at all to speak Latin. He writhed in agony.

"Right," said Brother Overstreet, wiping a tear from his eye. "You're right."

In mock anger, Brother Blake said this was just horrible and that if he were Brother Costaregni, he'd go tell the beadle immediately. How dare they give him a hair shirt that didn't fit?

Brother Costaregni agreed. He would go tell the beadle. "I'll show him," he said, stomping out of the room.

After a minute or so, the three of us, Brothers Blake, Overstreet, and I, trailed out of the room and headed toward the beadle's office on the second floor. Brother Koch, who worked in the tailor shop and had stitched together the ersatz hair shirt that morning, stopped us. Brother Costaregni, he said, had bypassed the beadle's office and gone straight to the Master.

"He's with the Master now," reported Brother Koch.

Brother Blake clapped his hands and roared and doubled over and then said, "C'mon, let's be in on the payoff." He started up to the third floor. Brother Overstreet and I followed. We stood in a line across from the Master's door, exchanging looks and smiling. Brother Costaregni was taking a good, long time in there. What was happening? We would later learn that he and the Master were laughing together over the practical joke we had played, good medicine for a young man who was probably having a harder time in the Novitiate than any of us.

Eventually, he emerged, looking sheepish and wiping his eyes. When he saw us standing outside, he raised his arms and gave a laughing, silent shout. We grinned back in silence and tried to beat a hasty retreat to our cubics. The Master's voice called us back. "Uhhh, Brothers," he said softly. "Could you come in here please? No, not you, Brother Costaregni. The three of you."

"Dummy up," said Brother Overstreet, "I'll handle this." Richard Overstreet was a bright, caustic fellow, one of our own wise men from the East. I was willing to trust him. We filed in and lined up in front of the Master's desk, just as a bell rang calling us to supper. Saved by the bell, I thought.

No, the Master was going to give us a trial. "Well," he said, fingering the burlap vest that Brother Costaregni had left in his office. He looked unnecessarily severe.

"Yes, Father?" said Brother Overstreet, his voice all innocence.

"Well, what do you have to say for yourselves?" Generally, he kept us off balance. Now, somehow, the situation was reversed.

"About what, Father?" said Brother Overstreet. My heart was racing.

"Well, come on now," the Master said. "You pulled this trick on Brother Costaregni, didn't you? All three of you?"

Strictly speaking, I didn't have the same role in "pulling this" as the other two. So Brother Overstreet could say no—and he did.

"You didn't make this, this hair shirt, and encourage Brother Costaregni to wear it?"

"No, Father," said Brother Overstreet. Of course, we knew Brother Koch had made it.

The Master looked at Brother Blake.

"No, Father," he said.

He looked at me. I said, "No, Father."

The Master looked surprised, shook his head, threw up his hands. It looked like he was going to dismiss us. Then he changed his mind. "I think, Brothers, that you will say a *culpa* in front of the whole community."

He reached into a desk drawer and drew out three mimeographed slips. "Tonight. Before supper. You kneel in the center aisle of the refectory. You stay kneeling during grace. Then you recite these, in turn." He handed us the slips. We took the slips and read silently to ourselves.

> Reverend Fathers and dear Brothers in Christ, I say unto you my *culpa* for all my faults and negligences in the observance of our Holy Rule, and, in particular for _____ .

"Any questions?" said the Master, his jaw working nervously. I had one: were we going to be convicted and sentenced without a trial? I didn't ask it.

Brother Overstreet asked the obvious one. "Uh, yes, Father. What do we put in the blank?"

Trying to gain the upper hand, the Master said, "What do you think?"

Brother Overstreet gave him a mischievous grin. "For breaking silence?"

The Master, massaging his cheeks with his right hand, said, "All right. That'll be all right." He turned his back on us and looked out the window. "Go on now," he said. "or you'll be late." The *Angelus* bell started to ring.

During evening recreation that night, the Novices' courtyard (now so chilly that we needed to wear sweaters over our cassocks) rang with laughter over replays of the hair shirt story. Brother Costaregni glowed with good-natured embarrassment as he told the story on himself. "I couldn't even lower my arms," he said, holding them out stiffly from his side to demonstrate.

I found Brother Overstreet at the edge of the smiling crowd. I asked him why he had decided to brazen things out with the Master. "Just for fun," he said. "And anyway, what were we going to tell him, that we, in our infinite wisdom, had decided that Brother Costaregni needed a little loosening up? Oh, no. The less a man on trial says, the better."

I nodded. I guessed he was right. But the next morning, when we were gathering by the big grape truck for yet another assault on the vines, the Master himself appeared among us and took me and Brother Overstreet and Brother Blake aside. "Brother Overstreet," he said, "why did you lie to me yesterday evening?"

"It wasn't a lie, Father," he said blandly.

"It wasn't?"

"No," said Brother Overstreet. "After all, what is a lie? A lie is nothing more or less than a deception." The Master nodded and allowed a sardonic grin to appear on his face. "Well," continued Brother Overstreet, "you weren't deceived, Father. And these good brothers" — he pointed his grape knife at me and Brother Blake — "they weren't deceived. And I certainly wasn't deceived. So where was the lie?" He pursed his lips and made a popping sound with them, for emphasis, and batted his cool blue eyes.

The Master stood there for a moment, amazed. Then he threw back his head and laughed. So did Brother Blake and I. A pretty good joke, I thought. Heh, heh. And I admired the Master. Even though the joke was at the Master's expense, he could enjoy it.

Up to a point. The Master also had to have the last laugh. "Brother Overstreet," he said, "you'll have to say another *culpa* tonight." He waved Brother Blake and me back to the truck, where the others were now climbing aboard, and took Brother Overstreet aside and whispered in his ear.

That night, before supper, Brother Overstreet was kneeling in the middle of the refectory's center aisle when everyone marched in. After grace, Brother Overstreet announced in a quiet voice that could only be heard by those within twenty feet or so, "Reverend Fathers and dear Brothers in Christ, I say unto you my *culpa* for all my faults and neg-ligences in the observance of our Holy Rule, and in particular for — being a smart ass."

Those of us close enough to hear, including the Master, whooped over that one. And, as he made his way to the back of the refectory to find a seat at the table, even the great Brother Overstreet was blushing.

5

Anyone might guess that by now, more than fifty years later, I would have forgotten my Long Retreat during the month of November 1948. I cannot forget it, because in these thirty days of silence, I acquired a new way of looking at the world and my place in it. The world I saw had been redeemed by God-become-flesh, and charged with God's grandeur. It was a world in which I could see God in all things and all things in God, a world that I could love and enjoy and help make a better place — if I cared to carry on the work of Christ's redemption in my own time and space.

Anyone picking up the thin volume called *The Spiritual Exercises of St. Ignatius* today, as I did on the eve of my first thirty-day retreat, might read through it in a half hour and wonder how I found such a message in the terse set of meditations, instructions, and considerations that St. Ignatius compiled. The answer is that St. Ignatius didn't write a book to be read, but a series of things to do — he called them Exercises — that could help a young idealist make himself a principal actor in the Christian drama. The basic stuff of that drama, of course, were the stories from the Gospels of Matthew, Mark, Luke, and John. Upon these, St. Ignatius had imposed a kind of poetry that appealed to the romantic in me. His pervading metaphor was a military one, which figured, given his background.

St. Ignatius — his given name was Iñigo de Recalde — was born into a noble Basque family in a place called Loyola, lived as a military man, and almost died as a military man when he was struck by a cannonball in the battle of Pamplona in 1521. Because the iron hit him in the knee rather than in the neck, he was spared a hero's death, and forced into premature retirement while he recuperated for months in a fortress-like monastery at Montserrat. The silent monks who staffed the place must have been as entertaining as a convention of undertakers, so Iñigo whiled away the months reading the only two books in the house, a life of Christ and a volume on the lives of the saints.

On one night, he had a vision of the Blessed Virgin Mary, who told him she wanted him to found a new army, recruit others, and fight for the greater glory, not of any earthly prince, but of God. Iñigo accepted the challenge, took himself to the world's foremost center of learning at the time, the University of Paris, and persuaded some other students, mostly Spaniards, to join him in a new Order, which would not bear his name (as the Benedictines, the Franciscans, and the Dominicans bore the names of their founders) but that of Jesus himself, and it wouldn't be called an Order either, but "the Company." The term in Spanish, *la compañía,* was a military one, and Iñigo would always think of his men as troops, fighting a new kind of war, "for the Kingdom."

Iñigo's *Spiritual Exercises* would illumine the high meaning in this new kind of war, and test my toughness, too. Thirty days silence, thirty days meditation, thirty days prayer, thirty days penance. It would be a grim beginning, like Beast Barracks at West Point, maybe, but something I looked forward to with anticipation. I had no thought that I couldn't stand the gaff.

Imagine my disappointment, then, when I found that we would not just plunge into this retreat without making what seemed an elaborate institutional bow to human weakness: The night before the Long Retreat began, we had a big feast.

Did we really need squab and filet mignon and four wines? At the time, it seemed an unnecessary extravagance. Now I can see that this feast was no concession to our weakness but a celebration of our humanity. We were like so many soldiers who knew that a battle lay ahead: this would be our last laughing meal before our mission that began in the morning. My young tongue had not yet learned to like wine, but I soon became drunk mainly with joy, soaking in what would soon be denied, the loquacious company, the sense of being together, of sharing — thoughts, ideas, feelings, laughter.

Such, I mused during grace after that meal, was the heightening emotional effect of this thing called self-denial. Later that night, I observed how my own emotions were chilled when I saw two signs in big black letters on the bulletin board: *FLAGELLATIO* and *CATENULAE.* For the first time, we would be allowed to whip ourselves — that very night — and clamp the sharp wire chains on our thighs the next morning.

Back in my cubicle after evening litanies, I drew my curtain, slipped off my cassock and my T-shirt, opened my narrow closet, grabbed my little cat o' nine tails — and waited. When the bell rang, I would begin. I stood there in the dark and wondered. Would it hurt? How much would it hurt? Could I even do it? Why didn't they ring the darn bell? There, there it was. I started flailing away, but I heard no others doing it. I stopped. Then another short bell. Ah, that was it. I had started a little too soon. The first bell was a warning to get ready. The whipping was to start on the second bell — as my ears plainly told me, for now the room was filled with the sounds of seven other whips cracking on seven other backs. I started in on myself again. God, it hurt. When would the third bell ring? I kept going, and now tears started filling my eyes. Could I keep it up? I did, until the merciful third bell rang. I threw my whip on the bed and fell to the floor on my knees. "God," I said, "God, I don't like this."

But if I didn't like it (in some perverse way), I wouldn't have stayed on. And I did. During the Long Retreat, some would leave. In fact, under the strains of this regime, two of my classmates cracked. About halfway through the Long Retreat, they found one young Novice walking down the hall stark naked. They carted him off to a local hospital for electroshock therapy, and we never saw him again. Another came down with such excruciating headaches that he simply had to get out. I didn't crack. I was fascinated and challenged by the high call (accompanied, perforce, by high sacrifice) that Christ was apparently making to me.

I say "apparently" because I was a firm believer then in something we called Providence — in the idea that nothing happens, not even human tragedy, that doesn't somehow fit in God's plan. I think I still hold to a slight variation of that today. By some mysterious chain of circumstances, my family's breakup, a move to Phoenix, Arizona, a chance meeting with Father O'Rourke in Phoenix, the loving attention of another Jesuit in Los Angeles named Karl Von der Ahe, I found myself here in the Novitiate. Why? Had I come primarily to escape from my own sexuality? It didn't matter now. The only important thing: I was here. Obviously, God had used those feelings of mine as a way of bringing me here in this special place so that I could hear a special call and make a special response to it.

Those who wanted to distinguish themselves in Christ's service? St. Ignatius suggested that they would go beyond a mere offering of themselves but would also act against their sensuality and carnal and worldly love by making a total commitment to Christ, to seek to imitate Him "in bearing all wrongs and all abuse and all poverty, both actual and spiritual."

I shivered at that. I didn't much cotton to the thought of bearing wrongs and abuse. But since Ignatius believed that helping to bear Christ's cross was the only gateway to glory, I prayed for such a cross, if that was God's will. It would take many more meditations at the feet of many more crucifixes before I started to accept the idea that I would seek to imitate Christ in bearing all wrongs and all abuse, and I doubt that I ever accepted it completely, as a rational life strategy — although, when wrongs and abuse come along, even today, I still try to accept them as part of the cross I asked for long ago. Some of my psychologist friends can only frown at this expression of what they consider an obvious pathology. (Still, they have their crosses, too. I wonder: do they have any better way of bearing them?)

On the following day, there was another key Ignatian meditation — on the Incarnation — in which I was bidden to imagine (much as if I were writing my own movie script) the Three Divine Persons looking "down upon the whole expanse or circuit of all the earth, filled with human beings, some white, some black, some at peace and some at war, some weeping, some laughing, some well, some sick, some coming into the world, some dying ... all nations in great blindness, going down to death and descending into hell."

It was in this context that St. Ignatius imagined (and bid me imagine, too) the Three Divine Persons determining to work the redemption of the human race and then making their dramatic move, sending an angel to tell a young Jewish girl that she would be the mother of the Messiah. After observing all the details of this drama in my mind's eye, I was bidden by St. Ignatius to reflect upon all of it, and close the meditation conversing with any or all of the actors: the Three Divine Persons, the eternal Word incarnate, or his Mother, our Lady and then, "according to the light received, beg for grace to follow and imitate more closely our Lord, who has just become man for me."

The charm of this approach, for me, lay in the fact that my call made me something of a major historical figure, at least in my own grandiose imagination. Kneeling there in my little cubicle, I let my fertile fancy go. I panned over the whole face of the earth, zeroed in on the intimate little scene "in the city of Nazareth in the province of Galilee" — and then put myself in the middle of the redemption scenario itself. God wanted me to be a follower and an imitator of Christ, like Jesus, *Jesu-ita?* That was an offer I couldn't refuse.

The retreat went on for three more weeks. I was aware of my fellow Novices, but only remotely. My more real world was peopled by me and the men and women of the Gospel — for I was writing myself into the Jesus scenario. I trekked with Him and the other disciples along the Sea of Galilee, helped them gather up twelve full baskets of leftovers after He fed the multitude on a few loaves and fishes, ate the Pascal Lamb with them in an upper room and watched Judas leave the gathering to go out and sell my Lord. I helped Jesus carry His cross to Golgotha, listened to His seven last words, and, aroused by Mary Magdalene and the other Mary, ran to the tomb on the first Easter morning alongside John while Peter came puffing up behind and found it empty. Afterward, on the road to a place called Emmaus, I stumbled along with two disciples whose hopes had been dashed — until a stranger fell in step with us, showed us how it was fitting that Jesus should suffer, die, and rise again. The stranger shared a meal with us and made us know when He broke bread with us that he was the Christ. "Were not our hearts burning within us when he spoke?" the disciple said after the man had disappeared. Uh huh, I said. My heart was burning, too.

On the thirtieth and final day of the Retreat, I dedicated myself to this Arsonist of the heart with words suggested by St. Ignatius in his *Contemplatio ad Amorem:*

> Take, Lord, and receive all my liberty,
> my memory, my understanding, and my entire will,
> all that I have and possess.
> You have given it to me.
> To You, Lord, I return it.
> All is Yours.
> Dispose of it wholly according to Your will.
> Give me Your love and Your grace.
> This is enough for me.

In my Novitiate prayer life, I would use the words often. They were the words of the *Suscipe,* that indescribably sweet song sung by Brother Overstreet when I'd first entered Los Gatos, a song that he would sing again when I would take my first simple vows of poverty, chastity, and obedience:

Suscipe, Domine,
Suscipe, Domine,
Universam libertatem meam.
Accipe memoriam, intellectum,
atque voluntatem omnem.

6

As I look back now on that life in the Novitiate, I see it as a kind of boot camp, the kind you find in the U.S. Marine Corps. The discipline was supposed to make us into the kind of men who could take orders, so that, later on, we'd be the kind of shock troops our superiors (or even, in special cases, the pope himself) could send anywhere in the world, on any mission. It was also a life that seemed designed to keep us psychologically immature. But of course, this is one reason I joined the Jesuits in the first place: to keep from growing up, like some latter day Peter Pan.

We sustained our immaturity in a number of ways, even in our games and amusements. Most of the games we played were the games of men-who-are-still-boys. Some of them were pathological, like those described by the psychologist Eric Berne in a classic called *Games People Play.* Others were innocent strategies to make our highly institutionalized lives a little more human, a little more livable.

Almost everything, however, was programmed. Tuesdays, we would walk to our villa, several miles up into the redwoods of the Santa Cruz Mountains, play softball, tennis, and basketball, have huge lunches, pray a bit, play some more, and then walk home again, no more than three miles. There were some villa days when we could sign up for longer treks of ten or twenty or even forty miles, round trip, to any of a number of peaks in our mountain range. We were in marvelous physical shape, could run for hours, and some of us frequently did. I remember running the last five miles home one afternoon, after a visit to a peak called Loma Prieta, because we were late and I didn't want to show up at table without a shower.

We played no football at villa, not even the version of touchless touch football played by the Juniors, with no blocking, and no running. That game was a strictly pass-catch affair. You scored a touchdown only by receiving the ball in the end zone. Touchless touch football was due, of course, to our Rule 32 — "No one shall touch another, not even in jest" — which we observed to the letter during our first four years. We'd heard on the grapevine that up at Mount St. Michael's in Spokane, where we would spend our fifth, sixth, and seventh years in the Society, they played a real solid game of touch football and even got to listen to Notre Dame games on the radio. As Novices, however, we were like the monks of the desert, dedicated to a life of prayer and penance — with no football, which was probably too much of a man's game to help us remain the little boys we were meant to be in the Novitiate.

We put an immense amount of effort into Christmas, the holiday most beloved by little boys. After the Long Retreat had ended on December 8, we started getting ready for Christmas. We enhanced the ultimate enjoyment of it all by first denying ourselves, descending into a period of special prayer and self-denial, in keeping with the penitential season observed through the entire Church, called Advent. We fasted and beat ourselves with whips three times a week and meditated on sin and death and the last judgment.

We also began transforming the house into a piney-scented forest of garlands and wreaths. In both the refectory and in several chapels, we built crèches, rustic models of the stable at Bethlehem, complete with figurines of Mary and Joseph and donkeys and oxen. We transformed our rec room into an auditorium. Some of the brothers built a stage at one end and others of us were encouraged to produce plays like T. S. Eliot's "Murder in the Cathedral." We copied scripts, recruited and rehearsed actors, built sets, made costumes, planned the lighting. Some of us even wrote plays of our own. Since we were to present a play every night for each of the Twelve Nights of Christmas, there was more than enough work for everyone.

Christmas Eve was special, with the brethren scurrying about placing a great profusion of poinsettias on the altars, polishing the chalices and ciboria, running the waxers and buffers up and down all the corridors, washing the last of the windows, stuffing the turkeys, baking the racks of Danish pastries for our snack after midnight Mass. Finally, after a meager supper, we retired early and slept for a couple of hours — until just before midnight when the voices of the Juniors' choir filled our halls with a literal call to come and adore. *Adeste fideles, laeti triumphantes*, sang the choir. "O come all ye faithful, joyful and triumphant.... O come let us adore Him.... O come ye, O come ye to Bethlehem."

By the time we had whipped on our cassocks and made our way to the chapel, the Juniors' choir was "in Christmas concert" in the loft of the chapel. Their carols put me into a state very close to a swoon. Today, friends still call me one of "the last of the great romantics" and I am sure that the romanticism in me had come to full bloom during that Christmastide of 1948, in the flush of my first fervor as a Jesuit Novice. Oh, God was good, I thought, as the sounds of the choir came floating down and filled my every pore. Oh, all His creatures were good. One carol, *Gesu Bambino,* seemed to epitomize all the sweetness of the night:

> When blossoms flowered 'mid the snows
> Upon a winter's night,
> Was born the Child, the Christmas rose,
> The king of Love and Light.

The organ and the backup voices of the choir rose and fell in a manner that made me feel as if I were gliding along a rolling, snow-covered meadow in a sleigh. As the choir's voices swelled, I thought my heart would burst.

> The angels sang, the shepherds sang,
> The grateful earth rejoiced.
> And at his blessed birth the stars,
> Their exultation voiced.*

The Christmas liturgy was as perfect as Jesuits ever bothered make it. Three priests in new white vestments celebrated a solemn High Mass, and then the rector said a second, Low Mass, a quick quiet affair. During it, I had an earnest, one-way conversation with the Baby Jesus, whose chubby, glowing likeness I could see in the crèche on the Novices' side of the chapel. Ah, the wonder of the Christmas story, that God, God! would make Himself into a little child and be laid in a feed box for animals!

After the second Mass, we trooped downstairs to the candlelit refectory for the once-a-year treat, midnight cocoa, along with Danish pastries

---

*Lyrics by Frederick H. Martens, from Pietro A. Yon's "Gesu Bambino," copyright 1917, renewed 1945, by J. Fischer & Bro., Melville, NY 11746.

and Christmas cookies, which we ate and drank in a thankful silence, meditating on the Bethlehem scene that was set up in the center of the refectory.

When the Twelve Days of Christmas had ended, we settled into something called "Common Order," a dull routine of meditation, meals, lectures by the Master (called exhortations), and a variety of spiritual reading: Scripture, Rodriguez, the lives of the saints, à Kempis. (In retrospect, I don't know why we made so much of Thomas à Kempis, a medieval monk whose philosophy could hardly help us become the worldly guys envisioned by the Order's founder. À Kempis believed that every time he went out among men, he returned to his cell "less a man." St. Ignatius was a "more" man.)

In the Master's exhortations, he tried to give us the benefit of everything he knew and thought he knew. I now think his barrel full of certainties was too full — of beliefs about the nature of God, the Trinity, the angels and the saints and the creation of the world, and the necessity of always having Mass in Latin. But my Master had some solid wisdom which made sense then and still makes sense today, about true and false spirituality, about true and false religion, about the men and women in it who were only human.

Perhaps because the Master believed that "the human (or sinful) element in the Church of God" was and would be a danger to us in our future work if we did not get a good grip on ourselves, he made sure that we lived a pretty grim life, according to the principle, "If it gives pleasure, reject it; if it gives pain, embrace it." I suspect that this wasn't the Master's idea: as the Master, he had to pass on this particular perversion. It was our received tradition.

But even in the midst of this doctrine, we got a more solid theoretical teaching from the Master about what it meant to be a follower of the Christ who had said, "I am come that you may have life and have it more abundantly."

"Life is to enjoy," said the Master. "God made the peach taste good so you'd enjoy eating it." And living that life didn't mean going around in sackcloth and ashes all the time, spreading gloom, much less "embracing pain." This wasn't just his opinion, said the Master. It was the opinion of the official Church, which, for centuries, had taught (against reformers like Savanarola who were "always holier than the Church") that Christians never had to opt for the harder way just because it was harder. The Church had condemned those moral theologians, he said, who had taught a doctrine called "Probabiliorism" — that anyone, faced with a moral dilemma, always had to choose the more probably moral course. According to the more solid teaching, whenever there was a real doubt, a man or woman was free to opt even for the less probable moral course. The principle was formulated in the Latin *Lex dubia non obligat*, "a doubtful law does not oblige." Otherwise, life would be too gloomy, too Calvinistic, and a far cry from the freedom of the sons and daughters of God that Christ had come to proclaim.

That was the theory. In practice, at least in the Novitiate, we put bounds on our own freedom. We went to absurd lengths to deny ourselves, even the taste of a peach or a draft of cold milk, the smell of a garden rose, or the nighttime view of the twinkling valley below. At the sound of bells every fifteen minutes or so, we jumped through all the myriad exercises of each day, instantly, "even to the letter unended." Obedience, the Master kept reiterating, was the preeminent virtue of a good Jesuit, as poverty was for a Franciscan or recollection for a Trappist.

Of course, there were other virtues, too. Each of us tried to select one to work on each month, even kept count on a pocket abacus of the number of times we "practiced" that virtue, or slipped into a repetition of its opposite. I was born and bred into an impatient and irascible family. (My grandfather, Charlie Blair, used to heave decks of cards across the room during heated poker games.) And so, for the entire two years of my Novitiate, I worked on patience. Though I never learned patience, I learned, at least, to suppress many of its outward manifestations, which made life a bit easier on those around me.

I discussed this besetting fault with my Master of Novices several times. He insisted that virtues are "acquired by a repetition of their acts." The way to be patient, therefore, was to exercise patience at those times and places where my patience would be tried. By the end of my first year Novitiate, he had the perfect job for me, one that would try my patience a thousand times a day. He put me in charge of running the kitchen and refectory for our community of almost three hundred — Novices, Juniors, priest-professors, lay brothers.

Though this community surpassed the size of a squadron, we did not eat like infantrymen, on metal trays, cafeteria style, but were served family-style, at tables of eight, on huge platters, by waiters in cassocks and white aprons. There was an immense amount of clearing to do after meal: pots, pans, dishes, glasses, and silverware to wash in a kitchen area that was hopelessly outdated, tables to be reset for the next meal, ad infinitum, three times a day. As scullery boss, I presided over all this activity, the only one in the place wearing a white apron over my cassock. (The others wore aprons of denim.) I commanded all the crews — waiters, dishwashers, potscrubbers, floor sweepers, table setters, trying the obedience of all (and my own patience) by assigning every job before, during, and after every meal. I gave several thousand orders daily, in Latin, and more than several thousand if, as frequently happened, the dishwashing machines broke down in a steamy room we called *machina* or the giant tubs and drains started overflowing in a dank dungeon called *ollis* where we did the pots.

I loved it. What I liked about being scullery boss was making everything come together. I made the whole operation into a scullery Olympics, where each day I tried to see how we could cut minutes, or even seconds, off the previous day's record. The payoff was not only mine, seeing the job done faster than anyone had ever done it before, but the community's as well, because the sooner we finished, the sooner we commenced those periods after dinner and supper called "recreation."

We started getting out to recreation so early, in fact, that the Master soon realized he could start drawing men away from scullery duty to put them on special jobs, thereby accomplishing two things simultaneously. He could make things harder for me (in keeping with his role as the chief giver-of-trials in the Novitiate) and also get some of his own pet projects realized more quickly. Soon, I began to see more and more men diverted from scullery to our Novitiate workshop, which we called *Taberna,* where a number of the Master's favorites manufactured heavy cast-iron, anodized crucifixes which would be presented to each Novice on his vow day.

I didn't complain. I reacted to the challenge of doing the scullery just as fast with fewer men by working out a number of strategies. Instead of assigning men to the dishwashing detail according to some random process, for example, I started putting my speediest washers of dishes and scrubbers of pots in the crews that labored during the meal. These whiz kids could usually finish 98 percent of the work by the time the community was saying grace. After the meal, therefore, I didn't have to send four or five men to "help in *machina*" or "help in *ollis.*" I could use the men elsewhere, setting tables, or sweeping the floors.

The Master noted what I was doing, of course, and kept assigning more and more men to other projects — canning plums, or making new cassocks, or cataloging books in the library — until, gradually, almost every one was on some special job or another. I used to have thirty men line up after supper for assignments; now I was lucky to see a half-dozen. I couldn't think of any new efficiencies. The few of us who ended up doing the former work of thirty began arriving at recreation later and later. Soon we weren't arriving at all, because recreation had already ended by the time we'd finished setting the tables. The hell with that, I said hotly to myself. I started sending my half dozen men out to recreation when the job was only half done and started sweeping floors and setting tables myself — on into the night — until the Master called me in and demanded to know what I was doing.

He tried to look surprised when I told him, but I could see the twinkle in his eyes, and he laughed right out loud when I said, "You know how many Novices lined up after supper tonight? One. Brother Gourdeau." Brother Gourdeau moved — and worked — as efficiently as a stringed marionette. "I asked Brother Gourdeau, as sarcastically as I could in Latin, 'Don't you have a special opus?' I shouldn't have tried to be cute. He blinked and said that, yes, by golly, he'd forgotten that he did. He hung up his apron and beat it — while I stood there with my mouth open."

The Master couldn't hold back his mirth. After we'd both finished laughing, he asked me what I thought we ought to do. "Eliminate some of the special projects," I said. I didn't mention his pet, *Taberna,* preferring to let his own conscience be his guide, but I pointed out that the Novitiate had its own elite, men who never touched a pot or washed a dish or set knives on a table, the beadle, the sub-beadle, and the sub-sub-beadle. "If I could only assign them and some of the other privileged characters around here to wait on table . . . "

He smiled and said, "Why not have them scrubbing pots?"

I raised my palms and shrugged. Here I was proposing to drag my classmates away from their goldbricking and put them back in the long black line. That was injury enough. Why add insult, too?

"O.K.," he said. "Assign them to wait tables if you wish. What they have to do they can do at other times."

I nodded and, without advising the beadle, sub-beadle, or any of the other favored characters what I was doing, I posted the new assignments on my pegboard the following day. I was actually surprised, when I got to recreation that night (just as it was ending), to find that Brother Glen Smith, beadle, and Brother Jim Schall, sub-beadle, were lying in wait, angrily demanding to know what I was trying to do. In Latin, I told them that Father Master had given me authority to put them to work. Why?

How? They were all over me. I stood my ground and tried to spell things out. If they didn't like it, they could take it up with the Master.

I walked away and left the two of them muttering to each another, but I knew they probably admired the way I'd been able to turn things around. They were the kind of men who knew me and liked me anyway. I wasn't so sure that I could describe some of my other classmates in the same way.

Some of them were pretty weird. But then, I must have seemed pretty weird to them, too. I had a quick tongue, a volatile temper, a competitive nature: I liked to win, to have my own way, to bring others to my opinions. Under a regime where I examined my conscience twice each day, I came to know more and more of these things about myself. And where I failed to see for myself, my brothers told me.

They told me so on a dull gray afternoon in March of my second year in something called an *Exercitium Caritatis,* or "Exercise of Charity." These were truth sessions — something like those the Communists imposed on every village and hamlet in China soon after the party takeover in China during the late forties and early fifties. With them, the Red Chinese could gain group control over individuals who were different (and therefore subversive). I assume now that our "Exercises of Charity" had the same inner purpose, control, though they were ostensibly "for our own good."

The *Exercitium Caritatis* worked like this: All the Novices sat in hard-backed chairs arranged in a large circle. Each week, the Master would call out a Novice to go to the center of the circle, make the sign of the cross, kiss the floor, kneel, fold his hands and listen as each man stood and told the Master what defects they had noticed in Brother So and So. Generally, the circle could do two men during each session, giving each of them a half-hour's rundown on their defects.

"Father," I would say, "it seems to me that Brother Hombach is supercilious. He doesn't listen to the opinions of others. And sometimes he goes on reading *America* at the bulletin board after the bell has rung calling us to something else." Then I would sit down and the man next to me would stand and deliver his analysis. And so on, until everyone had had his say. Then the Master would invite the next victim to go to the middle.

When my day came, most of my brothers had a lot to say — so much, in fact, that they needed the whole hour to detail their observations. I took a perverse enjoyment in this: I am probably an Enneagram 4; I liked being noticed, and I rather liked the discovery that my brothers couldn't put me in some neat pigeonholes, couldn't even agree which of my ways were defects and which were virtues.

Brother Wolf said I was too naive and Brother Blake said I was too knowing. Brother Wagner said I was too familiar and Brother Smith said I was standoffish. Brother Ryan said, "Father, it seems to me that Brother is too loose. Why, one day after we had put the refectory back together after a big feast, he just lay right down in the middle of the floor."

"Father," said Brother Brill, "it seems to me that Brother is too tense. As scullery boss, he's such a driving force...." Many others had scullery stories to tell. It was obvious that in my role as field marshal of the scullery, I had nettled many of my mates. One of them, Brother Maher, picked up on that and, to my surprise, tried to defend me. He pointed out that I had to give a thousand orders a day. "And it isn't always easy to take some of the orders he has to give. It's hard to go into that scullery line after a big feast, when you know there's a ton of dirty pots down stairs, and hear him say, *Muta vestimenta et adjuva in ollis.*"

Everyone in the circle knew what that meant: Go down to the change room, doff your cassock and don rubber boots, a Levi jacket and a big black rubber apron, because you're going to scrub pots. They roared, because they not only knew that Brother Maher was right, they also knew how much he hated working in that steamy dungeon called *ollis.* He sat down soberly, and out of the corner of my eye I could see that he seemed pleased that he had made his point so well; he burst right out laughing.

Though my mind was telling me that I was enjoying all of this, too, and that I would earnestly try to reform my ways according to the manifest wishes of my brethren, I found, to my surprise, that my body was giving me a different message. During the closing prayer, after I had risen from my knees and returned to my place in the circle, I found that all the valves in my stomach were opening and closing in peculiar, uncomfortable ways. Hiccuping after this exercise, I went to the Master's office and told him I was sick. He said, "Yes, I can see. Your stomach is backing up. I can smell your breath way over here." He clapped a hand over his mouth, pulled on his bulbous nose, squeezed his cheeks and then said, finally, "Go lie down. Skip dinner. Or, if you feel like it, go down later and eat at second table with the waiters."

Lying on the narrow bed in my cubicle, I went around the circle, reviewing my brothers' remarks again and again. I found some consolation in the fact that their observations were all so contradictory. They couldn't all be right, I said. Therefore, I reasoned fallaciously, none of them were right.

I had grateful thoughts about Brother Maher's intervention on my behalf. In the ethos of the Novitiate, however, I couldn't show my gratitude. I even had to demonstrate the opposite. The very next day, we had a big feast and I had completely forgotten that I needed an extra man scrubbing pots that night — until Brother Maher appeared before me in line. The sight of him reminded me. And, once I was reminded, I couldn't play favorites by skipping him and condemning the next man in line to the dungeon of the greasy cauldrons.

Muta vestimenta, I said stiffly, *et adjuva in ollis.*

"Jeez!" he cried, and crumpled like a man who'd just been socked in the stomach. He recovered and hurried off toward the change room, muttering — not in Latin, for he was talking to himself — "Try to stick up for a guy and what do you get for it? Jeez! Try to stick up for a guy!"

7

I made my first profession in the Society on August 15, 1950, along with thirty-eight others in my class. The ceremony was a solemn one, with each of us vowing in turn *paupertatem, castitatem, et obedientiam perpetuam in Societe Jesu,* "poverty, chastity and perpetual obedience in the Society of Jesus." I wandered around in something of a rosy cloud, hardly able to believe that I had made it through the Novitiate, unwilling to take off my new tailored cassock or my new linen collar or that stiff medieval hat called a biretta, even for a moment.

I still have a picture of myself taken that day. It shows a tanned young man with a far off gaze in his eye and a serious set to his jaw, his biretta at an important tilt. The entire look said this young man knew what he was about — and that it was all business, God's business.

The serious business ahead was called "Juniorate," an entirely new phase of training. If the Novitiate was a boot camp, then Juniorate was no less than an Officers Candidate School. The Novitiate had helped me establish my pieties, my dedication to "the Kingdom." But I had learned that a Jesuit had to have more than piety and dedication, he had to acquire an expertise that would make him an outstanding officer in Christ's army, which was formed not to conquer, but to serve.

Jesuits weren't Trappists who would serve the world simply by praying for it and making a better liqueur. They were men who followed in the footsteps of those learned missionaries who did not go off to Brazil and India and China and Japan to tell people how they could resign themselves to the miseries of this world in order to win some bliss in the next, but tried, instead, to help them use their wit to make this world (redeemed by Christ) a gentler, happier place, a place that people could live, and love, in.

The Jesuit tradition was rather a worldly one. Jesuits weren't monks and they weren't friars. Unlike all the other religious orders up to the time of Ignatius Loyola, Jesuits didn't bother about singing the daily office at stated times of the day, they spoke it privately, whenever they could find time. They weren't attached to a particular monastery for life, they went out into the world and became "all things to all men, so they could win all men to Christ." They didn't just "do good." They did "the *greater* good" — hence the Order's motto, *ad majorem Dei gloriam*, for the *greater* glory of God. In the early history of the Order, this free-swinging, non-formalistic approach (Iñigo de Loyola had prescribed no uniform and urged his men to dress like the people they were working with) took the Jesuits into a newly emerging world of science, into the courts and governments and universities of Europe, into the vanguard of exploration into Asia and the New World, into the front lines of the Church's battle against "the Protestant revolt."

That tradition hadn't been an unbroken one. The Jesuits did such a good job being relevant to the world of eighteenth-century Europe that they created powerful political enemies who brought pressure on Pope Clement XIV to suppress the Order (which he did in 1773).

(It's a common human phenomenon: those who rise to the top in any profession quickly find they are targets to everyone below them. Even today, Jesuits try to avoid becoming too visible; too much visibility can anger even the pope.)

Another pope, Pius VII, restored the Order in 1814, but the men who led that restored Order were weak and fearful. They believed that the Society could only survive in the nineteenth century by sticking more to "the sacred sciences" and establishing a non-Ignatian spirituality that emphasized withdrawal from a world that was essentially evil. By 1948, of course, the effect of that withdrawal was all too apparent. The world had taken shape under the influences of forces that were decidedly not Christian, and the result was two world wars and the Holocaust.

Some leaders in the Church, including two Jesuit generals, had begun to see that the Church should try to do more. In letters to the whole Society, read in our refectory over and over again, both Vladimir Ledochowski, the general of the Jesuits during World War I and World War II, and Jean Baptist Janssens, his successor since 1946, had outlined a new Jesuit approach to the entirely worldly work of advancing "the Kingdom." Ours would be an "intellectual apostolate." Men with ideas were the ones shaping the world; Jesuits would have to be among them.

The notion may sound banal today. But it was hardly self-evident in 1950, a year when Pope Pius XII was condemning the work of some of the Church's best scholars, including that of Pierre Teilhard de Chardin, the French paleontologist and philosopher, a Jesuit whose mysticism won a respectful hearing everywhere (except perhaps in the Roman Curia and among a few fearful members of his own Order) precisely because he was also a man of science.

We didn't read Teilhard in the Juniorate. We did read another French visionary of the time, or rather, we had his pastoral letter, "Growth or Decline," read to us in the refectory. He was Emmanuel Suhard, the cardinal-archbishop of Paris, a quiet, do-nothing prelate during the war, who had had a profound conversion when he stepped into the ruin of postwar France and discovered that his country, nominally Catholic, was not even Christian any longer. What to do? I can still remember the core of Suhard's message. Roll up your sleeves and get out in the real world. His actual words were stirring.

> Being an apostle means taking on everything and penetrating everything belonging to man and the world he has made . . . to extend the benefits of the Redemption to the whole created world. The Christian has not only the right but the duty to complete creation and then make of that an offering to the Creator. To convert the world, it is not enough to be a saint and to preach the gospel; or rather, it is not possible to be a saint and invoke the gospel we preach without doing all we can to assure for all men conditions of work, housing, food, rest and human culture without which life ceases to be human.

"Completing creation." Such a task, said Cardinal Suhard, would not be easy, nor could it be done in a generation or two. It would have to be done by men of learning and scholarship.

So I had my global vision: I would try to develop the critical tools necessary to help remake society, to help the world's movers and shakers make life more human. It was a vision that would gradually lead me out of the Society, when I would finally come to the conclusion that I could "complete creation" more effectively out of the Order than I could in it. The irony was that my Jesuit education itself was the thing that would give me the critical tools to make this independent judgment.

The critical tools would come first from my classical schooling. The Fathers at Los Gatos didn't teach us clumsy Church Latin and New Testament Greek, but the elegances of the historian Livy, of the orator Cicero, of the poets Virgil and Horace, the Homeric Greek of the *Iliad* and the *Odyssey,* and the Attic Greek of the dramatists Sophocles and Aeschylus. They told us we weren't studying the classics as mere tools that would help us get through philosophy and theology, but in order to develop the "perfect eloquence" of the Renaissance man, which, they hoped, would be just as valid in the twentieth century as it was in the seventeenth when the Jesuit *Ratio Studiorum* (or plan of studies) was written.

As part of that plan, I read Dante and Shakespeare and Molière and Tolstoy. I listened to Bach and Brahms and Beethoven. I tried to appreciate the genius of Michelangelo and Da Vinci, El Greco and Reubens. I analyzed the poetry of Pope and Dryden, Wordsworth and Byron, and tried to emulate the prose style of Dickens and Thackeray and Robert Louis Stevenson. I wrote speeches by imitating Edmund Burke and Winston Churchill and Franklin D. Roosevelt.

In the Juniorate, there was a rule which said we weren't supposed to read "novels or other mere worldly works which, even thought not prohibited, could be a danger to morals or the religious spirit." One day, reading Shakespeare's "Measure for Measure" brought on a symphony of sexy thoughts, so I went to John F. X. Connolly, my rector, and asked him whether I should go on reading that play. He said that only I could be the judge of what I could read and couldn't read. "You have to grow up," he said, "and learn to make your own judgments."

I nodded, but I didn't really understand. Understanding what it means to grow up doesn't come until men and women actually start to take responsibility for their own decisions. Afraid of doing that, I wouldn't begin taking responsibility for some time, choosing not to pay attention to that part of me that was sexual and learning in the process how to disown my own feelings. In the meantime, I contented myself with following the rules and reading safer stuff. My first Christmas vacation in the Juniorate, I read *David Copperfield* by Charles Dickens, and I spent most of my first summer vacation at our villa in the redwoods reading Tolstoy's *War and Peace.* But even those novels were "dangerous." For light reading, I ended up with *Luke Delmage* and *The Triumph of Failure,* the moralistic novels of Canon Patrick Augustine Sheehan, priest of County Limerick.

Still and all, I got a good schooling, one that probably had no equal in the English-speaking world of 1950 (if for no other reason than this, that I worked at it about twelve hours a day, with hardly any distractions, certainly not the distractions of dating and drinking that characterized collegiate life in the 1950s). I did well. I learned to read. I learned to write. I learned to think (if not feel). And superiors told me that if I kept on doing well, I could also look forward to getting my doctorate in some other field — in sociology, or history, or economics, or political science — and at one of the best universities in the world to boot. Father Connolly wondered if I wanted to go to Harvard? To Berkeley or Cal Tech? To Oxford or the Sorbonne?

I didn't know, yet. "It's okay," he told me. I would have three or six or ten years to decide, no hurry. He said I could proceed on my course, just like most of my other classmates: three years Philosophy at Mount St. Michael's in Spokane; three years Regency in one of our Province's high schools; then four years Theology, probably at Alma College in the Santa Cruz Mountains. After this I could begin Special Studies.

I should have appreciated the leisurely pace of it all, an academic free ride enjoyed by only the richest, most privileged young Americans in the 1950s, but I believe the trip gave me guilt pangs. It was ironic. I was vowed to poverty, but lived as if I were rich; I dined on filet mignon, I was learning to drink cabernet, I read Horatian odes, I listened to Bach. There was little scullery, little manual labor. I never had to wash a sock, shop for food, or wonder if I could afford a haircut. I was a gentleman.

∿

MY CURRICULUM at the Mount in Spokane was elitist, too — for few young men (even then) could afford the luxury of an M.A. in philosophy, which, in the long run, was and still is among the most useful of academic degrees. I studied Aristotle and St. Thomas Aquinas — their philosophy of being, of knowledge, of the mind, of the world, of God, and their ethics — took some surveys on ancient and modern philosophy and some special courses in Hegel and Marx.

But philosophy was abstract and boring and hard to keep bearing down on with the intensity and drive that I had learned in the Novitiate and Juniorate. I was desperate to find my own specialty, something more concrete, something more immediately relevant to those who peopled St. Ignatius's key meditation on the Incarnation, "some white, some black, some at peace, some at war, some weeping, some laughing, some well, some sick, some coming into the world, some dying...."

I found that, though the Society wanted me to get a grounding in philosophy, it wouldn't insist on making me a professional philosopher if my interests lay elsewhere — which they did. I found more juice and more joy in politics and economics and history, and discovered that none of the faculty seemed to mind that I spent more time on these than I did on Aquinas. My first week at the Mount, I came upon a copy of a current bestseller, *Witness*, by Whittaker Chambers, and stayed away from classes for several days while I raced through that narrative, fascinated by the tale of a man who had given his life for a faith that failed. I was grateful to Chambers; he brought me up to date on some of the current American history that I had missed while I was reading Rodriguez.

And so, though I earned an M.A. in philosophy, as my California superiors expected, I also won approval to do my thesis on "Journalism and Prudence" — an application of the ideas of Aristotle and Aquinas to the problems of interpretive reporting in a democratic society. This project seemed more interesting to me than some of the head-busting theses my classmates had chosen — for example, "The Real Distinction between Essence and Existence" and "The Categorical Imperative of Immanuel Kant."

My thesis was a first step in my own master plan, to develop my expertise in a new academic field called "the mass media." If the Jesuits were going to have a moral influence on the world, I could not imagine any better place than the fields of news and entertainment. I wasn't exactly sure how I could get involved in either of these areas, as a Jesuit, but I wanted to prepare myself, then make some new things happen. As far as I knew, no California Jesuit had ever attempted to do something creative in the film world.

(Years later, Ellwood (Bud) Kieser, a Paulist priest, would make a huge impact on Hollywood by producing a long-running television series called *Insight*. They were half-hour stories that avoided organized religion; they simply dealt with men and women engaged in a struggle for "love, freedom and being human." Kieser, a six-foot-seven blond giant, persuaded some of Hollywood's best screenwriters to do the scripts, and he conned some of its best actors, actresses and directors to bring them to life. Kieser became known as "The Hollywood Priest" and went on to produce two notable feature films in the 1990s, one on Archbishop Romero, the Central American martyr, and another on Dorothy Day, the American founder of the Catholic Worker movement, before he died in September 2000.)

JP

OUR JESUIT PROFESSORS at the Mount were a heady bunch, and at least one of them, Father Alex Tourigny, was an iconoclast who believed he had a duty to purge some of our Novitiate pieties. I don't think there was a single maxim we had been taught to hold sacred in the Novitiate that he did not deny, or flout as heretical or insane or morbid. He was a corpulent man, who sometimes ate chocolate bonbons while he taught his specialty, rational psychology, and I can remember my shock when, one day, apropos of a discussion on the desires of the unconscious mind, he focused on the nocturnal habits of the Order's founder. "Now take Pater Ignati, for instance," he said, popping a chocolate into his mouth and continuing to talk as syrup dribbled down his chin. "Have you ever wondered why he spent his nights in Rome, sometimes until dawn, engaged in conversations with ladies of the evening?"

The class tittered. I could hardly believe it. St. Ignatius? The founder of the Jesuits spent his Roman nights talking to prostitutes? I wondered about that. Since our founder was an official saint, I assumed that he could do this out of the purest and most zealous motives. I looked up one of the newer biographies on Iñigo and found that Father Tourigny was right. St. Ignatius was a nightwalker, and believed that this apostolate of the streets was worthwhile if he could keep just one woman from committing one mortal sin (and, of course, stopping one, or many, men from doing likewise).

This Renaissance man had probably never even considered what unconscious and subconscious dynamics were at work here. Surely, there were a good many other sinners he could have paid attention to. He could have carved out an apostolate among the moneylenders of Rome (for charging interest on money was then a sin) but Iñigo didn't spend his time in Rome's Jewish ghetto, he spent it with hookers. I was sure that a Freudian analyst could have written an interesting paper indeed about Iñigo's special fascination.

I also began to like the Mount because I found some encouragement there to be more human, more spontaneous. At least half the men in the house, mostly the men from the Oregon Province, were a rough-and-ready bunch, down to earth, even earthy. They didn't observe some rules, like the rule of silence, and they insisted, along with the spiritual father at the Mount, who had been their superior at their Novitiate, that they were praising and serving God even when they were "just having fun." This, to me, was a more real approach, more akin to the Jesuit life I had seen lived when I boarded with the Jesuits at Loyola High in Los Angeles, and I went along with it.

I studied hard, at least nine hours a day, after classes, but I played hard, too. I played touch football every afternoon, even when the rains came and then the snows, this time real touch football. I played hockey, too, something I hadn't done since I left Detroit at the age of twelve. And I found that one of the Jesuits on the faculty, Father Bill Gaffney, was a fervent fisherman who didn't mind taking me and a couple of my classmates on his expeditions to Twin Lakes, Idaho, a couple hours' drive away. I found good trout fishing there, in stream and lake, and bass waters that were fabulous, probably because they were underfished by locals who spurned the largemouth as an inferior species.

For almost a month in the summer, the whole community pitched tents on the southern shore of Lake Pend Oreille in Idaho. Those of us who wished could fish all day, those who preferred playing bridge in the lodge that housed our kitchen and chapel and recreation rooms could do that. More often than not, Jim Schall and Dick Rolfs and I would spend our days rowing all over the lake (which was several miles wide and thirty-five miles long), trolling for rainbows and cutthroat and silver salmon, usually with little luck, until, one day, we had a revelation from an angel.

About ten o'clock one sunny morning, we got our lines crossed as we turned too tightly at the end of Bottle Bay. Since there was a nice beach right there in front of us, we rowed over and climbed out on the sand to untangle our lines and lures. "Been doing any good?" asked a shoeless young blonde wearing a pair of white shorts and a yellow tube top. I blinked at this apparition and so did my companions. A real live human attractive female person!

Trying to sound like it was the most normal thing in my life to chat with a beautiful woman, I said, cleverly, that we hadn't had a strike.

"Uh huh," she said, looking at her watch. I admired her. She happened to be a woman who knew how to look at a watch.

"It figures," she said. "It isn't time yet."

Jim and Dick and I looked at one another. "Time?" said Dick. "What do you mean, time?"

"The fish bite on a timetable," she said. "The solunar table. They're supposed to start biting today at 10:45. Come on, I'll show you." She motioned for us to follow her to a cottage at the edge of the beach. We hesitated, then smiled when a man who turned out to be her husband came out on the porch and waved us in.

They introduced themselves as Tom and Jane Stockton. We introduced ourselves. We were skeptical about the solunar table, and traded suspicious looks when the young couple told us how it worked and what success they had had fishing when the fish were hungry. But you couldn't argue with their freezer, which was filled with silver salmon — caught, they said, on a lure called a Super Duper, which looked like a silver tie clip with a treble hook on the end of it. We had some Super Dupers among our collection of spinners, but weren't using them because we were sure trout wouldn't be fooled by tie clips.

And then, as we chatted, Jane said, "Look! There's the first of the squirrels. It's just about 10:45 and the squirrels are starting to feed. They feed according to the solunar table, too." She smiled. "I think they even mate on the same timetable."

We hustled back to our boat, clipped on Super Dupers and started catching silvers as fast as we could get our lines out. A little after noon, the young couple motored over to us. "How's it going?" Jane shouted.

We'd put ourselves in silence, to make our mid-day examen, so we didn't answer right away. We just smiled and waved. And Dick replied to her question by reaching down and pulling up our string of silvers for the Stocktons to see.

"The fish have stopped biting, haven't they?"

We laughed. "Yep."

"You might as well stop for lunch," Jane said. "Come back and join us."

Giving up on the silence for a moment, I said, "We've got our lunches aboard."

"Bring 'em along," she said with a laugh. Tom, running the outboard, reached out for our bowline, attached it to his gunwale, and towed us back to their cottage.

They served us vodka gimlets, and we had lunch. Dick asked for pencil and paper and copied down the solunar table for the next two weeks. They gave us their catch of the morning, since they had "more than enough silvers." And then we were off to take advantage of the next afternoon feeding period, at 3:15. We boated a couple dozen more silvers and docked back at our lodge shortly before six with a tremendous string. The other returning fishermen goggled at our catch, but scoffed when we told them about the solunar table. "O.K., laugh, you suckers," Jim said. "But we'll catch the fish."

We did — and with far less effort than we'd been expending. Each night, we'd consult the solunar table and plan our next day accordingly. We didn't always have to start fishing at the crack of dawn and whenever the fish stopped biting, we'd beach our boat, play three-handed pinochle, have lunch, and recoup our energies for more trolling.

We did more than fish during villa season. On our first day at Pend Oreille, everyone in the community got $10,000 in play money. We set up a casino in our refectory and played bridge, pinochle, blackjack, poker, for play money, on into the night. Some of the Brethren of the Strict Pious Observance refrained, calling the games "very secular" (that is, worldly). I found it all very exhilarating. Playing for money (even play money, which we used in an auction for candy bars and gum at vacation's end) only made it more so. Poker games were always an event when my family got together on holidays; I can remember learning the game sitting on my mother's lap at age seven, and playing penny ante with my cousins, at a fourth of a cent a white chip. (When my grandmother, Nanny Blair, died at the age of eighty-eight, we included in her casket a poker deck and some poker chips — and a second deck, in case someone in the long night demanded new cards.) It was nice to play poker again.

It was also a treat to see movies once more, after a four-year hiatus. We had first-class sound projectors at the Mount and a friend of the Rector who owned a movie theater in downtown Spokane sent current and choice flicks up to us whenever we wanted them. We wanted them mainly on big feast days; the choice was made by the Rector, in consultation with the house beadle who had access to the movie reviews.

In my opinion (I never discussed it with others), they goofed one night when they ordered up an Academy Award winner, *From Here to Eternity,* with Burt Lancaster and Deborah Kerr. Did we see the famous beach scene, when these two made love in the surf? Well, no. Better. The projectionist had orders to blank out that beach scene: too sexy for us. So he just let the damn projector run for five minutes or so, while our imaginations provided a sexier scene than MGM could have gotten by the censors in 1953.

I had a wet dream that night, and I confessed it first thing the next morning. No, technically speaking it was not matter for confession, that is, a sin. But it was considered a good ascetic practice to confess it anyway. The whole experience told me that, as far as the virtue of chastity, was concerned, a total blackout of women from my life, according to the Novitiate way, was the most effective way to go. If I didn't see women, in the flesh or on the silver screen, I didn't have images of them troubling me at night. Eventually, of course, I would be out among men (and women). I would have to learn how to deal with temptation. I told myself I'd deal with that when the time came.

And so, at the Mount, I learned how to flip by the pages of a sexy layout in *Life* magazine, and how to avert my eyes when, say, on a trip to the dentist, I spied a pretty woman coming up the street. Now I wonder: what damage did I do to myself by learning to think of women primarily as temptations? The Jesuit rule said, "What concerns the vow of chastity needs no explanation, since it is plain how perfectly it ought to be observed, endeavoring to imitate angelic purity in cleanness of both body and mind." But of course we were men, not angels. My manhood began to start telling me that — more and more strongly every day.

One villa day, Tom Williams, a classmate, and I were on our way to Gonzaga University to pick up some books from the library. On our way, Father John Lindekugel, the Minister of the house, or second in command, asked if we would mind delivering a package to an address in Hillyard. Of course not. We found the address, a little white cottage next door to a church, and Tom rang the bell. The sweetest young woman I had ever seen — dressed in the habit of the Sisters of the Holy Names, fair, freckled — came to the door and shone us a dazzling smile.

I did not exactly sink to my knees. But, for what seemed like an hour or more (it was probably just a matter of a few seconds) I was paralyzed with — what? Wonder? Longing? Passion? I cannot say. Finally, I was aware that Tom was clearing his throat, because, though I was holding the package, I was making no move to hand it over. I gulped, shook my head with a dopey grin, and gave this gorgeous creature the bundle. For a moment, our eyes met, and an instant of understanding passed between us. She blushed.

That was too much. I lowered my eyes, literally closing the windows of my soul. She turned to Tom and thanked him, perhaps not trusting herself to talk to me, because I had made my feelings so very very obvious — and more, had elicited an instinctive (and no doubt unsettling) response in kind from her. She disappeared into the house and the door swung shut as if by itself.

I stood staring at the door, then cursed my own klutziness: no one should see me like this. Tom pretended he didn't see and engaged me in a discussion about Seattle U's chances in the upcoming NCAA playoffs. I never learned who this nameless sister was, and never saw her again, except in my mind's eye, where she made unexpected and unbidden appearances for months to follow. For the first time since my earliest days in the Novitiate, I started asking myself the key question: what the hell am I doing in the Jesuits?

∞

I HAD A SOLID ANSWER to my own question: I was trying to serve God. But I was beginning to learn that serving God in this manner — vowed to poverty, chastity, and obedience in the Society of Jesus — entailed some deep sacrifices, including, possibly, a sacrifice that my own feelings were rebelling against. Was my goal worth this sacrifice? I was only twenty-three and I had eight more years of this before ordination. I put those questions aside, resolving during three days of recollection before renewal of vows in December to work hard and play hard and see if I couldn't sublimate my very real desires "for the sake of the Kingdom." If others could do it, I told myself, I could do it. (I was finding out some others couldn't do it. Dan Costaregni finally "gave up." He left during those December days of recollection.)

I also found that those who seemed happiest here had found one distraction or another from the unrelenting regimen. Richard Overstreet, for one, was still going strong, possibly because he had found innocent diversion in a game called golf, which wasn't a part of our curriculum, but which a few of the men had found a way of playing once a week at a local country club without superiors being any the wiser.

I found my diversions in daily touch football games, no matter what the weather (in Spokane, it seemed to rain and snow more often than not), in my thesis and in the bootlegged copies of *Time, Life, Newsweek,* and the *New York Times* which I needed, to make my thesis ring with some sense of reality.

I found some distraction, too, in television. It came to the Mount in my second year there, 1953, when one of the house's benefactors gave the scholastics a big TV set. The rector allowed us to have it in the auditorium, but only for use between seven and eight every evening, and at other rare times when a Saturday football game was on the tube. That wasn't quite enough. A half dozen of us started some serious TV viewing after evening prayers, some good drama, things like Studio One and Playhouse 90, Imogene Coca and Sid Caesar, and a few entertainment specials. Until we got caught.

Normally, the TV set faced out into the auditorium seats, and when it wasn't in use it was covered with a blanket. For our late evening enjoyment, we turned it around so that it faced the stage and we watched from up on the boards, peeking out into the auditorium between the parted stage curtain. If we heard anyone coming down the wooden stairs, we pulled the plug on the TV and let the stage curtain swing down in front of us. To the intruder, the auditorium appeared empty and the TV set, covered with a blanket, obviously unused.

One winter's night about 10:30, however, a visitor came thumping down the stairs. The two men holding the curtain dropped it and the man holding the extension cord pulled the plug. We waited in silence for the usual: someone who would flip on the lights, see nothing, flip the lights back off and walk out. This time, the footsteps kept on coming. "Oh, hell," hissed someone peeking out where the curtains came together. "It's the Rector. Somebody must have told him. He's coming right on up."

Everyone split. There was only one way out from backstage, through a window, and that's the way almost everyone went, somewhat too noisily. I sat right where I was and watched the Rector pursuing the others. "Aha!" cried the Rector, climbing out the window after them. "I've gotcha. Aha, I've gotcha."

He would have a chase on his hands first, I said to myself, betting that the rector was probably skidding on the snow and ice outside at this very moment. I stood up and walked calmly off the stage and out into the auditorium. I saw someone else lurking in the shadows at the back of the room. I saw Richard Overstreet. He wasn't exactly one of the Brethren of the Strict Observance, but he wasn't a member of the TV club either and I had a sudden flash, that if anyone had tipped off the Rector, it was probably the man who was lurking in the shadows. I didn't stop to investigate. I walked right on out, up the wooden steps and on to the elevator to my room on the fifth floor.

I thought I'd escaped. I was wrong. The next morning, just before Mass, Steve McMahon, one of my partners in crime, told me, "I slipped on the ice. The Rector slipped on the same patch, over near the new wing, and plowed right into me." I looked at him coolly and asked him what was going to happen to him.

"Not me," said Steve. "Us. The Rector wants to see us all at eight o'clock this morning."

"O.K.," I said, wanting to smile, but looking properly chastened instead.

"I'm sorry," said Steve. "I had to tell him. He made me give him the names of all the others."

"It's O.K.," I said. I had learned in ethics that breaking man-made rules like this wasn't immoral, but that doing so was inconvenient if you were caught (because there was usually a penalty if you were). But you had to pay the penalty.

We paid it. We got a mild dressing down by the rector, and an order to say *culpas* that evening before supper, "for breaking the Great Silence and watching television without permission."

I was a little chastened by that (and a little worried that my escapade would go in my file at the California Provincial's office). I was not chastened, only proud, of the only other *culpa* I got during my stay at the Mount, for calling down Rick Curtis, an annoying Oregonian. He was waiting on table during a dinner celebrating the feast of Pentecost and he seemed to be playing some kind of bitchy game with me and my table companions by bringing us everything late. That bothered us not a bit, but then, when he did not bring us any ice cream (a rare treat at the Mount), I began to get a little steamed, started waving my hands and looking exasperated. Finally, I got his attention. He came over to our table. "Ice cream?" he said innocently. "Why, it's all gone."

I was enraged. "You slimy bastard," I said in a voice loud enough for the whole table to hear me — and cheer my protest.

Father Lindekugel, the minister, called me in the next day and said that I would have to say a *culpa*. "Fair enough," I said. I didn't have any complaint. I should have kept my mouth shut and I was prepared to leave it at that. That wasn't enough for the minister. He wanted me to grovel a bit, too.

"Aren't you sorry?" he said.

"No," I said.

That stopped him a moment. "I mean, Mister, *shouldn't* you be? Taking the name of our Lord in vain?"

"What? I didn't take the name of our Lord in vain."

"Why," he said, "you called Mr. Curtis a goddamned son of a bitch."

Very quietly, very evenly, I said, "Who told you that?" He wouldn't say who. "Well," I said, "I did not call Mr. Curtis a goddamned son of a bitch. I called him a slimy bastard." Now it was the minister's turn to be taken aback. He stuttered a moment. I counterattacked. "Now just what kind of men are we dealing with here? Sure, I lost my temper and said something

I shouldn't have. But somebody's lying about me and I'm not going to say a *culpa* unless you make him say one, too."

He wouldn't do that, and said that I'd say the *culpa* or else. I left his office, grumbling and wondering if I'd say it or not. Unlucky for me, that was just the day that Father Gaffney chose to ask the minister if he could take me with him to the private and teeming trout ponds on his brother's nearby farm; he was going to catch some rainbows for a special supper the Fathers were giving for the Oregonians who had just been ordained that spring. Father Lindekugel said, "I'm sorry, but he's in the doghouse. He certainly can't go fishing with you.

And I didn't either. I ended up saying my *culpa*, but I didn't say it the way the minister had ordered me to, "for failing in charity." Way out of the minister's earshot, I said it "for calling Mr. Curtis a slimy bastard." Many in the community who heard me said later they were inclined to think, "What was wrong with that?"

8

My next stop was something they called Regency, a three-year teaching phase, where we were to gain some more maturity before moving on to Theology, the last phase before Ordination. In Regency, I matured right out of the Order.

I was assigned to St. Ignatius High School, on a windy hill in San Francisco, along with ten others of my class. Other scholastics reported to one or another of the Province's three other high schools and a few of the older men wound up teaching on the college level, at the University of San Francisco, Santa Clara, or Loyola in Los Angeles.

The previous year, for example, Richard Overstreet, a facile scholar, and older than many in his class, had been sent to teach at the University of San Francisco. I wasn't too pleased to be thrown in with him again (the high school and university faculty lived in the same Jesuit community) but I soon discovered that he was too busy at USF to be unfriendly. And when basketball season rolled around, he made sure I always had tickets to the USF games. In 1956, the USF Dons were national champions, then in the middle of an unprecedented unbeaten streak that lasted two full seasons, due largely to the efforts of two young men named Bill Russell and K. C. Jones, and I did not miss a home game.

Furthermore, I had a supercharged life of my own, in a Jesuit high school at last. The hurly-burly of the scholastics' life at Loyola High was one of the things that had attracted me to the Society in the first place, and one of my heroes then was Robert Leonard, a husky Jesuit scholastic who taught math and coached football and swimming. Now, I would be a scholastic, too, at a school very much like Loyola, with a student body of a thousand boys, and working under the direction of Robert Leonard, who was now a priest and the principal of St. Ignatius (which we called "Ess-eye"). Father Leonard proposed that I teach English and Latin and run a spiritual program for freshmen, monitor the yards at noon, coach baseball, and publish the school paper, too. It was a job, he joked, that I could do easily in twenty-hour workdays.

I liked the idea, because I needed to be busy, needed exhaustion at the end of every day as a sign to myself that I was giving my all "for the Kingdom." In order to make the sacrifice called for by the vows, particularly the vow of chastity, I had to feel that I was doing something special, and doing it as well, or better than anyone had ever done it before. For a time, during Regency, I knew I was doing something special for the young men I taught, giving them all I had, in the classrooms, on the playing fields. In doing so, I thought I was giving them an example of someone who was full of the more abundant life that Christ said he came to commend. I was trying to show them that their religion, fully lived, was something that could make them more human, more happy individuals, with a humanity and a happiness that would bring joy to those around them. I wanted to destroy the image of religion as something that made people less human, less joyful, less real.

In the classroom, I did this mainly by creating a sense of excitement about learning. "Nobody gets bored here," I announced right from the beginning. "If you're bored in any of my classes, you can get up and leave. If you're bored, I'm not doing my job." No one ever walked out. They wouldn't dare miss the fun and laughter that has always marked a good lit class, which deals more with life than letters. One day, I had our varsity quarterback on his feet, reading Chaucer. I stopped him. "What does that mean, Gaffney?"

"Huh? What?"

"You just read that the prioress was 'nat undergrowe.'"

"Yeah."

"What's that mean?"

"I don't know."

"Well, it must mean something. Don't you have a clue?"

"'Nat undergrowe.' Hmm." He squirmed.

I moved in on his Irish Jansenism. Eyes twinkling, I said, "Well, if you were describing one of the girls from Mercy and you said she was 'nat undergrowe,' what would it mean?"

My scholar-athlete said he didn't know.

"Well, Gaffney," I said, "wouldn't it mean that she was well-stacked?"

That was in 1955, eons ago, before the so-called sexual revolution, a year so puritanical that a harmless comedy called *The Moon Is Blue* would not win the Seal of the Hollywood Production Code. Cardinal Spellman would even condemn it because someone in the picture used the altogether shocking word "virgin." Gaffney turned beet red. The class roared, delighted that a Jesuit scholastic would dare to use one of their own off-scene expressions. "Well-stacked." Not bad. The word went around the schoolyard: some of these Misters were pretty cool.

Outside the classroom, too, I was not sad, not pious, and that, too, served to make me — and the Jesuits — something real, something of this world. I did this in a special way by encouraging my young journalists to put out a magazine that took an independent, sometimes even a critical view of SI's administration. I did it also by plunging into some serious coaching.

We had a high school that was hooked on sports, with city championship contenders almost every year in every sport except football. SI had no football tradition, and a poor varsity coach, and so I could only cheer toward the end of my first year when Father Leonard hired Pat Malley, an SI alumnus by way of the University of Santa Clara and the U.S. Army, to remake the football program. Malley had a face like a sunrise and a high enthusiasm. He wasn't there long in the spring of 1956, before he asked me to help coach, and together we started recruiting the hitherto overlooked talent in our own student body. By the next fall, we had a good turnout of terrific young athletes; with them Pat took the varsity to the city playoffs and my junior varsity team ended up with eight victories, one defeat, and one tie.

By the end of my second year of teaching, however, I was exhausted by the frenetic pace, and getting more and more disaffected with the formalism that seemed to dominate the Jesuit Order in California. The Father Minister, Norton Herrold, didn't seem to care whether and how I was doing the job I had been sent here to do, but only whether or not I was following "the Rule."

For him, this came down to getting up at five in the morning and going to bed at ten at night, and I never saw him in the hallways, or met his nervous gray eyes, without feeling that he was trying to catch me in some heinous transgression, serious things like not getting up at reveille or going to bed at taps. Sometimes, I could do neither, but I had already had one run-in with him that taught me he was not the kind who would understand if I told him that my work sometimes demanded irregular hours. He would have simply said to drop the work, because "the Rule" came first, not the work. God didn't need my work.

No, God didn't need my work. But I thought the school — and the kids — did. I had transformed the school newspaper, which had been an unsightly bore, into a newsmagazine called *Inside S.I.*, done in *Time*-style. Naturally enough, a slick magazine demanded much more time and energy than a pulpy tabloid. Sometimes, it would be two in the morning when the kids and I would be putting the finishing touches on the magazine down at SI. Then, I'd have to make my way up to the faculty residence and climb the fire escape to my room (the Minister locked the front and back doors at ten) for three hours' sleep before I had to appear for a 5:30 Mass and be ready for another long day. I couldn't keep going like that forever. To survive, I just stopped showing up for 5:30 Mass. Lazy lout, I'd sleep in until six. When the Minister caught me doing that, he told me I was "not a good Religious."

The Minister's disapproval bothered me, but I went right ahead doing what I was doing, because I got a good deal of support from the other priests and scholastics at the high school, and even from the Jesuits on the faculty of the University, who, unwittingly, helped me think hard about what I was doing here. More and more, my manhood (in the form of wet dreams) was speaking to me. Was the sacrifice of that manhood really worth it, if all I caught from my superiors was disapproval?

Many of the young university priests were brilliant, innovative teachers, but I soon found that the more these men did, the less the superiors liked it. It was almost as if the superiors rewarded mediocrity and squelched excellence. Father Eugene Schallert was one who excelled. He had an idea that was probably a hundred years ahead of his time. In order to survive in a world that was coming of age, the Church would have to start de-clericalizing itself, start training laymen and laywomen to do jobs that priests had been doing for centuries.

One of his colleagues, Father Eugene Zimmers, began the process by establishing something called the Institute of Lay Theology, which trained laymen to serve as parish professionals, most especially in what then had the unfortunate term "convert making." He was disciplined for his zeal by the university president and accused of being a troublemaker by the university's chief fund-raiser, who shouted, "What the hell are all my Jewish contributors gonna think about this, this convert making?"

Gene Zimmers would later go ahead and win plaudits all over the world for founding the Institute (and making it work). In the middle of the battle, however, the university's president seemed to agree with his fund-raiser, which caused Zimmers to invite the president to go soak his head. Not good. They delayed Zimmers' final vows and the provincial told Zimmers he would not become a Professed Father (that is, one of the Order's elite), but a simple Coadjutor (literally, a helper). In reality, no one cared very much then whether a man was a Professed Father or not, but the unfairness of the whole thing bugged all of us who knew what had happened.

I remember being part of a bull session at Father Zimmers' room, where he and a number of the younger Jesuit priests on the faculty puzzled over his "demotion." Father Bud Schallert elaborated a theory to explain it all. He maintained that what we had here was "a metaphysical problem" that seemed endemic to the Order in California, and he cast the problem in the form of a question: how could there be more horses' asses in the Province than horses? And how, moreover, could all the horses' asses be in the saddle? It was a humorous analysis, and Bud Schallert used humor in order to keep on living the life, and fighting off the horses' asses. But I didn't have his sense of humor and there didn't seem to be any way around the conclusion that those who wanted to do anything creative in the Society would run into deep trouble.

I started studying all the priests around me and decided that a majority of them were embittered old men. I didn't think I wanted to be like them, or like Gerard Manley Hopkins, a late-nineteenth-century English Jesuit who so completely accepted the Order's Eleventh Rule ("better to be accounted as nothing and a fool in order to be more like our Lord") that he didn't think he should publish his poetry. That would bring him fame, something he'd been told was decidedly "not in the spirit of the Society." He once wrote to R. W. Dixon, "it is the holier lot to be unknown than to be known." Hopkins was a product of the "deny thyself" school of Jesuit spirituality, to the everlasting sorrow of some modern Jesuits, who could have given him plenty of good unselfish reasons to go on creating some of the finest poems in the English language, like this one, "Pied Beauty," published posthumously, as was most of the Hopkins poetry that survived:

> Glory be to God for dappled things —
> For skies of couple-color as a brinded cow;
> For rose-moles all in stipple upon trout that swim;
> Fresh-firecoal chestnut-falls; finches wings;

Landscape plotted and pieced — fold, fallow and plough;
And all traces, their gear and tackle and trim.
All things counter, original, spare, strange;
Whatever is fickle, freckled (who knows how?)
With swift, slow; sweet, sour; adazzle, dim;
He fathers-forth whose beauty is past change;
     Praise him.

In 1888, a little more than a year before his death, at age forty-five, Father Hopkins wrote to the poet Robert Bridges of the desolation that resulted from his self-denial: "I can give myself no sufficient reasons for going on (writing poetry). Nothing comes. I am a eunuch — but it is for the kingdom of heaven's sake."

After two years at SI, I could see that superiors still demanded subjects be eunuchs, and I said the hell with it. Eunuchs don't "complete creation" (Cardinal Suhard's words), much less do a good job teaching high-school boys in San Francisco — if they have to fight off superiors in order to do so. And if I couldn't do a good job, then the sacrifices demanded by the three vows, especially the vow of chastity, didn't make any sense. During the summer, I got an appointment to see the provincial, Carroll O'Sullivan. I told him I wanted to leave. "Why, Mister," he said with some surprise, "you're one of the best scholastics we have."

I was surprised at that. I was never sure that he knew I existed and now he was telling me, with obvious distress, how much he liked what I had been doing. In the past, I had made my obligatory visits to him when he came for his yearly calls and no tinge of human feeling ever passed between us.

The year before, I had gone in to tell him I was troubled by the idiocies of a Father Minister in San Francisco who insisted on "blind obedience." Blind obedience, I said, was inhuman. It didn't give a man any sense of self-respect. It wasn't even "Ignatian." My authority for that was T. D. Roberts, the Jesuit Archbishop of Bombay, whose book, *Black Popes*, was the best thing written, up to then, on obedience. Carroll O'Sullivan hadn't read Roberts, didn't know what I meant by "intelligent obedience" (as opposed to a concept that had always been translated "obedience of the understanding") and suggested I try praying more.

"It isn't a question of more or less prayer," I said. "The point is, will Jesuit obedience help us get the job done better or not?" He shook his head, gave me a sour look and shrugged. He didn't want to discuss it. I wouldn't let go. I tried to talk more about Jesuit obedience and the Thomistic virtue of practical wisdom. "You remember that story St. Ignatius told in his Letter on Obedience, the one about the monk who was ordered to show his unquestioning obedience by bringing a lioness to his superior, and did so?"

The provincial indicated with a shake of his head that he didn't. He looked at his watch.

"Well," I said, with a laugh, "St. Ignatius didn't tell the whole story. You see, the lioness ate the superior."

He shrugged. Obviously, he wasn't in the mood for historical footnotes, or my commentary on the spirit of Ignatian obedience. I shrugged, too, and was shortly on my way. If he didn't need me, I didn't need him.

In retrospect, I can see that Carroll O'Sullivan was only playing the hand he'd been dealt. He was a very private person, a thin-lipped ascetic who had found his own scholarly mission in chemistry (he had gotten his doctorate from Stanford) only to discover that the general now wanted him to run the California Province — perhaps on the theory that he had already made a success in the so-called intellectual apostolate, and would, therefore, be more sympathetic to others interested in running the same track. As provincial, however, he hadn't won much love from his troops. Nor did his style of government make the men feel like they were any better than prisoners in a stockade.

Now the provincial tried to draw me out. He found that I wasn't leaving because I didn't want to serve, but because I did. I told him how disappointed I was with the General Congregation of the Order that had met in Rome that year, to update the Society. The only creative thing it did was issue an order for Jesuits to stop smoking.

The provincial smiled, surprised me by agreeing with me, and telling me that he was impressed by my obvious zeal. He said that, no matter what Norton Herrold thought, I was a good religious. I nodded. I knew that I was. The only question was, could I serve God in the Order? The Provincial was trying to tell me that I could. I said, "I'd like to think so."

He had a suggestion. "Let me go ahead and ask Rome for a dispensation from your vows. But you're not out till you sign them. If you don't want to leave, you just don't sign them."

That seemed like a good move. I went back to SI, back to my English classes, back to my football team. As a third-year Regent, I sailed with the wind at my back. I needed far less time to prepare my classes, and could take more time correcting my students' essays and short stories.

I gave up the magazine to C. M. Buckley, another scholastic. And, with one season of coaching behind me, I put together a football team that was disciplined, proud, enthusiastic — and all-winning. Everyone on the squad played in every game and, up until our last game against Lincoln, we had scored about two hundred points to our opponents' eighteen.

Austin Morris, whom we called Audie, was my assistant coach, a husky guy from Piedmont, California, who still wore a crew cut. He had been a P-51 pilot in World War II, came home to graduate from Berkeley and Boalt Hall, got his law degree and then joined the Soc. Audie coached the line, I coached the backs, I coached the offense, he the defense, and soon we were drawing big crowds from the university community on Thursday afternoons to see our kids play their swarming, stunting defenses and execute a sophisticated split-T offense, with a lot of passing. Friday nights, Audie and I would generally celebrate a successful week by borrowing the old Ford pickup they used for a garbage truck on the USF campus and rattling on downtown to see a movie, laughing at our daring, because the gas gauge usually said empty, and we only had $2 each in our pockets. We drew $2 a week for "busfare," whether we were going to take a bus or not, and that $2 a week was our effective "salary."

Our Wildcat JVs won the big game of the season against Lincoln, the only other unbeaten team in the league, 19–12, but Father Tom Reed, our new principal, took that victory away from us. The refs had tossed one of my halfbacks out of the game in the first quarter when he threw a punch at a kid who was trying to gouge his eye in a pileup. I thought nothing of putting him back in later on, but, after the game, the opposing coach protested to the league office. According to the rules, putting an ineligible player back in a game draws a fifteen-yard penalty. It doesn't call for a team to forfeit the game. But that's what happened here.

"We had a league meeting yesterday," Father Reed told me as I was heading out to practice. "I forfeited the game to Lincoln. And I cancelled your last game against Sacred Heart, too."

"Just like that, huh?" I said. "Without even talking to me or anything? Well, that makes you look good with the principals of the other schools, but how do you suppose my kids are going to feel? Why don't you go and tell them you're taking the championship away from them. I'm not going to do it."

Father Reed's eyes narrowed. "Why you goddamn son of a bitch," he said.

That did it. At SI, I had felt that, no matter what Norton Herrold thought of me, the principal and the vice principal and my colleagues at the high school who knew me were with me. Now, for the principal to call me a goddamn son of a bitch!

I said, "God love ya, Tom," and walked — no, ran — to the nearest phone and dialed the provincial's residence. "My papers still there?" I said to the provincial's secretary. "Good. I'd like to come over and sign 'em." I was leaving because Tom Reed had me helped me see that there would be a good many horses' asses (Father Schallert's horses' asses, who were all in the saddle) lying in wait for me in the years ahead.

That night, I told as many of the scholastics as were assembled in our recreation room for our Friday night pour, usually muscatel, that I was going to make my exit from the Soc. I'd teach until the Christmas vacation started. Then they wouldn't see me anymore. They were shocked. When others had left the Society, they didn't tell anyone, or even say goodbye. They just quietly disappeared. Those who knew me best and liked me anyway said they were sorry. They'd miss me, but they understood.

I went to my room, sat on my bed and read for a while, but then Richard Overstreet, looking and sounding pretty soused, knocked on my door. He'd come just to talk. He had a bottle of black muscat stashed in his cassock and brought it out — to keep his buzz going, he said. I had enough of the sweet stuff and declined when he offered to pour me some. He was telling me how a man could survive in the Society if he were clever. He told me he had politicked his way into an assignment abroad. This coming summer, he was going to Special Studies at Louvain University.

"In what?" I asked. Overstreet (not his real name) was an intelligent guy, but I would have been hard-pressed to guess what specialty he was choosing.

"In Biblical archeology," he said. And why that? "Because there isn't a man in the Province who's gotten his doctorate in this field for the past twenty years. If I get one, I can write my own ticket, go anywhere in the world anytime I want, be my own boss, take vacations on the Riviera."

I was not impressed. His reasons seemed far too selfish and I didn't see how anyone could help "complete creation" by becoming an expert on Ugaritic or Hebrew. By the time Overstreet had finished off more than half his bottle of black muscat, I suggested he'd better get going back to his own room. He didn't take the hint and kept up a line of palaver about how sad he was to see me leaving. I stood up, pulled him to his feet and tried to move him to the door.

He got behind me and dropped his bottle as he put his arms around my chest and squeezed. Even through his clothing and mine, I could feel his cock jump against me as he sighed, "Honey."

I sagged. I wasn't his honey, or anybody's. I ducked under his grip with a maneuver I'd learned in a water-safety class, turned him around and pushed him out the door with my foot. He stumbled and fell against the opposite wall. He was a bigger man than I and I was surprised at my strength. He was lucky, I thought, that I opened the door first.

The next day, I packed my steamer trunk, the one I had brought with me almost ten years before, and was soon gone, believing I could surely serve God better out of the Society than in it.

9

I had come home to Phoenix for the first time in ten years, aged twenty-seven, but looking more like seventeen. I'd been "on ice" — in some kind of suspended animation. I was hardly even shaving. I suspected I had a lot of growing up to do, and soon. I knew one thing: the Jesuits were history, and I didn't ever want to look back. I was wrong. In many important ways, I was still a Jesuit at heart, and always would be, because I'd internalized the lessons I'd learned in the Order, and I would always look at the world through the prism of the Ignatian Exercises. I would be "another Christ," continuing the Incarnation, through time.

But I didn't see that then. I just wanted to live a little, and the less said, or thought, about my past, the better.

My mother was pleased I was there. "How about that?" she said, holding me tight, "home for Christmas!" When I told her I wasn't going back, she frowned and wondered whether I had disgraced myself.

"Nope," I said, "as a matter of fact, they wanted me to stay. But I couldn't grow up there. I want to grow up." My mother smiled and said she never quite understood why I'd joined the Jesuits anyway.

What would I do now? I had all the training necessary to become a teacher, but that would put me into another ivory tower. I wanted to enter the real world, come down off my arid mountaintop and plunge into a cool blue pool. I wanted a world to float in, one that would caress me all over and lap around my ears. My goal as a Jesuit, to make a better world, was terribly abstract. First, I thought, I'd like to know more about the world-as-it-was. My best entree to that real world, I decided, was not teaching but reporting for the local newspaper.

Easier decided than done. I found Orien Fifer, the managing editor of the *Arizona Republic,* both impressed with my background and suspicious of it. At that time, in January 1958, there were only a few reporters on staff who had even finished college, and here was I, fresh out of the Jesuit Order, with an M.A. in philosophy. Fifer told me he didn't have any openings just then.

Through my family connections at Turf Paradise Race Track, I got a job instead as a call taker and chart maker for the *Daily Racing Form.* It was journalism of a sort, but something way down on the ladder, an entry-level position roughly equal to that of the guy in the circus who goes around sweeping up after the elephants, pleased because he is, after all, "in show business." My first day on the job, I met the *Form*'s man in Phoenix, Pat Caudill, a lean fellow with a huge, elliptical head that made me think immediately of J. D. Salinger's Laughing Man, captured by Chinese bandits and squeezed in a vise until his head resembled a pumpkin seed.

Pat showed me how to make the racing chart, which appeared in many newspapers in double-column, length-of-the-page agate, bought from Triangle Publications so their horseplaying readers could tell how each of the nags had done the day before. By consulting the chart, a fan could learn everything he needed to know, for example, about Bettyanbull, a two-to-one favorite who had won yesterday's feature: her age, her breeding, her owner, her trainer, her jockey, and how she had run the five-furlong eighth race in one minute, twenty-seven and two-fifths seconds, how she broke and hung back and made her late move and won by a nose at the wire over Island Fortune and Melodious, to pay $3.40 to win, $2.80 to place, and $2.20 to show.

My job: to listen carefully and take down the calls that Pat Caudill gave each horse during the race, then type up the charts, in triplicate. I nodded my understanding through this first lesson and then we left the press box and walked out on an iron catwalk. During the five-minute span before the start of the first race, Pat did what I soon learned was a kind of ritual for him: through his binoculars, he studied the action on both sides of the rail. Oh sure, he was out there to size up each horse, note the boy aboard, and the color of the silks he was wearing.

He was more interested in the crowd. "Hey, there's ol' Stevens and Tessie," he chortled. "Look at them gyps." To Pat, who said he lost most of the money he'd ever made betting on the horses, most of the owners were crooks. The trainers were gyps. Most women were whores, but he enjoyed looking — and commenting — on them. "Hey, look at that bitch, the blonde in the red sweater with the big knockers," he cried. From that distance, I needed binoculars, too, to see, but when I craned my neck and squinted in the direction of the blonde, Pat laughed and told me, "Not you, Bobby, she'd tear you apart."

He was probably right. For some months, I was as skittish as a yearling, too shy to let a woman come near me, much less to make the necessary first moves. But I wasn't too shy to sell myself to Orien Fifer. The managing editor of the *Republic* was a race fan who came up to the press box every Saturday seeking information from Pat Caudill and Bill Murphy, the track announcer, and Backstretch Charlie and all the Runyonesque characters who hung out in the press box, all bettors themselves who seemed to have a fund of knowledge to share with Fifer (more, in fact, than he could use) about which horses were ready and trying. For my part, I only had a smile for him and a question, "When're you going to give me a chance on the paper?"

As the weeks wore on, I suspect that in Fifer's mind I gradually shed the look of an academic and an ex-Jesuit and became "the kid in the press box." On May 1, he was ready to walk over and whisper in my ear, "Why don't you come on down to the paper on Monday?"

I began as a summer replacement, a $75-a-week cub on the night police beat, and when the summer was over, no one said anything about my leaving. I stayed on to cover almost every beat on the paper, which was fat and affluent and in cahoots with the mines and the utilities and the railroads and had a pervasively nay-saying influence on any kind of planning or progress in Arizona that might involve more taxes.

Well, no matter. I determined to learn all I could and then move on. After six months, I moved out of my mother's home (she had remarried by now) and, with two bachelors, lived in a large house with a swimming pool and a couple dozen orange trees in the backyard, a perfect place for pool parties, of which we gave a good many. I started dating very comely young women who pretended, according to the fashion of the day, that they were virgins. It was not the healthiest kind of entree into the world for me; at twenty-seven, I really was a virgin and I would be a klutz with women until I found someone who would make the first move.

I got lucky on Christmas Eve, 1958, a year after I'd left the Jesuits, due to nothing more romantic than a case of mistaken identity. With Bill Feeney, a golfing buddy, I'd gone to a large party in the Scottsdale home of Joan, a pretty young secretary we knew, and at some point late in the evening, I conked out, fully clothed and flat on my back in one of the bedrooms. When I awoke, about four in the morning, the party was over. My friend Feeney was asleep on a couch in the darkened living room.

I was feeling frisky. I looked for the lady of the house, found what I thought was her bedroom, and lay down next to her. She woke, put her arms around me and gave me a big wet kiss. We kissed quietly for awhile and then she asked me to take my things off and climb into bed. I wasn't exactly sure how to proceed after that; I was near the goal line, but I didn't know how to get into the end zone. No matter. She slipped out of her nightdress and climbed on top of me. The moves were all hers and they were marvelous.

"Oh, Joan!" I groaned, at just about the time she cried out, "Oh, Tom!"

Tom? I said to myself. I'm not Tom, I'm Bob. And this wasn't Joan. I said nothing. I didn't think this was the time or the place for formal introductions.

We made love for at least an hour, talking little, moaning with pleasure a whole lot. Well, it wasn't really love, but it was an uncomplicated introduction to a new sport. At one point in the action, when things were coming, as they say, to a climax, my partner wondered whether I had anything. (I knew what she meant. Those were the days before the pill.) I said, "I don't, but maybe my friend who's asleep on the couch — " I rose from the bed at just the moment that the lights from a neighbor's approaching car shone in the window.

"Wait a minute," she said, when she saw my silhouette, "who the hell are you anyway?" I paused for a moment, then told her my name. She turned on her bed lamp and looked at me. "Oh, God," she said. "I don't even know you."

"Uhhh, well," I said, "you know me better than any woman I ever met."

She looked at me with some curiosity.

"You expect me to believe that?" I nodded. She shook her head, then clapped her palm to her forehead. "Oh, shit, shit, shit!" What if I get pregnant?"

"A good question," I said. "But you'd be asking the same question if I were Tom — whoever he is. Who is he anyway?"

It was now about five thirty in the morning. No time for Twenty Questions. "Out," she said. "Get out of here."

I didn't argue. By now, suddenly detumescent, and reaching for my clothes, I felt embarrassed, and a bit guilty that I had "taken advantage" of a real honey-blonde who could have made Playmate of the Month against any competition. I'd have given a week's pay to meet her all over again under more formal conditions, but now, I was sure, I had lost my chance. I slunk away in the darkness, roused my sleeping friend on the living room couch and said, "Come on, Bill, let's get out of here."

I found out that my Christmas blonde's name was Anita, but I never made any effort to see her or talk to her again, and can't help wondering now what might have happened if I'd only tried. It never occurred to me, then, to think that for more than an hour she had enjoyed the encounter as much as I, and that she had to be a little curious about me. I didn't call her then because I wasn't interested in just another pretty face. I wanted more than that: I wanted to meet someone who could be the mother of my children, someone who was bright and lively and, above all, Catholic.

I found her some six months later. One summer night toward the end of a stint on the night police beat, I ran into a couple of friends at a local pub. "It's almost closing time here," they said. "Come on. We heard about a good party over on West Clarendon."

I followed them over in my light green '56 Thunderbird convertible (a symbol of my liberation) and when we came to a house that had about a thousand beer cans scattered on the front lawn, we knew we'd found the party. There might have been a lot more people there earlier in the evening (how else explain more than a thousand beer cans?), but even now at least fifty young men and women were still dancing and drinking inside. It looked like a happy place, and I wondered who the host was. As it turned out, the party had been thrown by Mary McArdle.

Someone pointed her out to me; she was a green-eyed brunette with a decidedly Irish face and a cute little crossbite, and she was doing the Charleston, barefoot, in the middle of a circle of shouting, clapping, happy beer drinkers. When the music segued into something slow, I introduced myself, took her in my arms, and asked her a hundred questions about herself. She said she had just graduated from a Catholic college in the Midwest, and she'd come to Arizona to visit her brother. This was his house and he was away on business. Her plans? She was headed to San Diego, where she had a job offer. "No," I said, "I mean for the next few hours."

"It's two o'clock in the morning," she said.

"I know. But in Phoenix, in the summertime, we play all night." I invited her and the rest of her friends over to my place for a swim. Mary and a half dozen others came, met my housemates, swam, drank, played records. At dawn, Mary and I were still going strong, sitting cross-legged on the floor, telling each other the stories of our lives. Up to now, I had told few of my Phoenix friends that I had spent ten years in the Jesuits. Mary was different. I wanted to tell her — and she wanted to hear.

She said that she had a thing about clerics. "In Milwaukee," she said, "my girlfriends and I used to drive around the local seminary and ogle the young seminarians. We all had our fantasies about them — so tall and so straight and so handsome. We each had our favorites. We'd talk about them. We'd see them and say, 'What a waste!'"

"Not necessarily a waste," I said. "Maybe God was saving them for something, someone special. Maybe God has been saving me — for you." I wasn't handing her a line. Right then, I knew I wanted her for my wife. She knew it too. We ended up sleeping together that morning, chastely and in our clothes, and then, the next week, I took her over to meet my mother.

Mary was a young lady with few pretenses. She loved me and made that as clear as she decently could. We saw each other every night. She immediately scrapped her plans to take the job in San Diego. If I greeted her without a passionate kiss, she'd quickly complain, which surprised me, because I thought the best way I could prove my love for her was not treating her like a sex object. We got some basic things settled. "How many children do you want?" she said one night, when we were parked on a promontory overlooking the lights of the city.

"Children?" I said, twitting her. "Who wants children?"

"Well," she said, dusting her hands of me, "I guess this is the end of a beautiful friendship."

I laughed. "How many do *you* want?"

"A dozen," she said, and then paused, waiting for my reaction. I said nothing. "Ten, at least," she said by way of amendment.

I hugged her. "Oh, Mary, Mary, I want children, too, as many as God sends."

A few weeks later, we were at a dinner dance at Mountain Shadows, a posh desert resort north of the city, when I pulled an engagement ring out of my pocket and put it on Mary's third finger, left hand. We were above the pool, all lit by candles, and the orchestra was playing a schmaltzy Glenn Miller melody and Mary melted into my arms.

"Oh, Bob. Oh, Bob," she said.

Our courtship was not all candlelight and diamonds. One morning when we were packing a picnic lunch and I was nattering at her about being so pokey, she splattered me in the face with a spoonful of mustard. The woman had a temper. She also had a streak of jealousy. "Bob," she said in hushed, hurt tones one evening. "That picture of Patti Gallagher? The one you've got on your dresser?"

"Yeah," I said. "Nice picture. Pretty lady." A high-school acquaintance, Miss Gallagher was now an actress in Hollywood, but she was also an object of my fantasies during my seminary days. When I got out of the Order, I made it a point to meet her, remind her we'd met ten years before. She'd sent me her picture. I hadn't known how to make the next move with Miss Gallagher.

Mary said, "Well, you've asked me to marry you and I've said yes. I don't think it's right to have her picture in your bedroom." She smiled her twisted little crossbit smile, but she was definitely unhappy. I went to my room, took the picture off my bureau and tossed it in a boxful of junk.

My whole family came to Milwaukee when we were married in Mary's home parish and half the town, it seemed, showed up for the nuptials and for the big sit-down dinner at a local country club. Archbishop Harold Henry, a missionary from Korea, graced the ceremonies with his presence because he had been such a good friend of Mary's mother and dad, a convivial, well-mated couple who were completely taken by me.

Now, I was on my way. Feeling more and more confident, I started looking to make the most of my opportunities. I did some special reporting in Arizona for Raymond Moley, a columnist at *Newsweek,* and then, with his help, got an interview in New York with John T. McAlister, an editor at *Newsweek,* who sized me up, looked at my thin resume, flipped through my clips, and then said, "Well, I don't think we have anything for you. We generally don't get our people from newspapers in the Far West. We recruit our people mostly from *Time.*"

I was startled. "You mean," I said, "that if I want to work for *Newsweek* I have to get a job with *Time* first?" He said yes he guessed that was about the size of it.

So I got a job with *Time.* It happened like this. Some months later, in Phoenix, I had an assignment to interview a guest in the home of Clare Booth Luce in the Biltmore Estates. Her guest was one of the world's famous Jesuits, Martin D'Arcy, an author of numerous books and a former English assistant to the Jesuit general. It wasn't hard for me to speak his language, which was, in fact, my language. We had a fine time together and when my hour was up, Clare, who'd been sitting there, said she'd been reading me in the paper and wondering who I was and where I'd come from and what I wanted to do with my life.

I told her that I'd been a Jesuit. No, not a Jesuit priest, a scholastic. Her frown told me that she'd only known Jesuit priests, like the famous John Courtney Murray, who had appeared on the cover of *Time,* and that she had never met a Jesuit scholastic. I wondered whether she had ever given a thought to where Jesuit priests came from, whether she thought the stork brought them or something, but why should I insult her? I said, "I think I'd like to work for *Time.*"

She said she thought she could be of some assistance. She arranged a luncheon for me with Henry R. Luce on the following Tuesday. But my city editor sent me out to Sky Harbor Airport to interview someone coming in that day on a noon plane. Still practicing Jesuit obedience, looking upon my editor as God's vicar for me, I went on my assignment (after phoning the Luce mansion to tell a secretary that I couldn't make the lunch). When Luce, pleading an emergency in New York, had to break the next date, I figured that I'd blown my big chance, but sent him some copies of my best stories from the *Republic* anyway.

Some weeks later, to my surprise, I got a phone call from Richard N. Clurman, chief of correspondents for *Time,* who was in Los Angeles with a copy of my resume and the clips I'd sent Luce. Could I come over, at *Time's* expense, and talk to him in Los Angeles?

I flew over on a Sunday morning in May, dressed in my best suit, and found Clurman in his bathing trunks, sitting near the pool at the Beverly Hills Hotel. He had four or five Sunday papers at his side and a pile of heavy, red Time Inc. envelopes, out of which he drew my folder. He told me he was impressed with the things I'd done in three years at the *Republic.* "It's obvious," he said, "that you have a wide range. You'd probably make a good *Time* correspondent. But I'm not going to hire you." He explained that he wanted to be known at *Time* as his own man, not as someone who took orders from Mr. Luce.

I was agape. I'd left the formalism of the Jesuits. Was I aspiring to join another group of men who cared more about "the rules" than getting the job done? What did it matter how I had come to Clurman's attention? What kind of job could I do? That's what ought to matter.

"Wait a minute, Dick," said Clurman's companion who had been sitting there all along, sunning himself. It was T. George Harris, then *Time's* bureau chief in San Francisco. "I could use some help the next couple weeks in the City." He turned to me. "Could you get a leave from the paper for two weeks? Come to San Francisco and work as a bureau stringer?" Maybe the two of them were just testing me, to see how badly I really wanted to work for *Time*.

I must have passed the test. I took the two weeks vacation that was coming to me, flew to San Francisco with Mary, who was pregnant, and was confronted by Harris with an immediate assignment. "There's a priest out at USF with a new idea," he said. "Wants to train laymen to be paraprofessionals in parishes. He's doing it in something called the Institute of Lay Theology. But he won't talk to the press about it. Name's Zimmers. A Jesuit. Be a good religion story if you could break it loose."

I smiled. Gene Zimmers was one of my best friends. If I couldn't get Father Zimmers' cooperation, no one could. I went out to USF and persuaded him that the time was right for a story in *Time*. I suggested it to *Time*'s religion section, and the editors scheduled my story for the following week. It ran for three hundred lines, which was better than *Time*'s average allotment — and the story almost broke the bank at Zimmers' office, because he was soon inundated with eleven hundred applications for admission to the ILT, and it was costing him $27 apiece to screen each man. But as far as I was concerned, I'd hit a home run my first time up in the big leagues. Dick Clurman lauded my file and I followed up that performance the next week with some solid reporting and I got far more space in the magazine than a stringer should have expected.

"I'm impressed with what you did," Clurman told me over the phone when I'd returned to Phoenix. "But I'm still not convinced. Can you go work as a stringer in L.A. for the summer?" More tests, but tests that were ants to the elephants I had conquered in the Jesuits. I promptly quit my job at the *Republic* (because my new editor, J. Edward Murray, wouldn't give me a leave "to carve out a niche in some other organization"). Mary stayed on the job in Phoenix, and I hustled over to give the L.A. bureau my all.

I did. I found that the bureau chief there was stuffy and pompous, but willing enough to let me work. The other correspondents were a marvelous bunch, bright, generous guys who knew I was trying to win a job at *Time*. They let me grab off some of the better stories in our territory so I could impress New York. There was no real formula for a good *Time* story, other than the fact that it had to have a national interest, but, since I had been helping my kids at St. Ignatius High School produce a pretty good imitation of *Time*, I had given myself a training in *Time*-style journalism: the narrative lead, the pithy quote, the colorful description (far more appreciated by *Time*'s editors in New York than it was by the copyeditors at the *Republic*), above all, the attempt to add things up for the guidance of editor and reader alike, to point out something you could never do in a newspaper: the story's significance. I'd even done my M.A. thesis on the ethics of interpretive reporting. It seemed like my Jesuit training had pointed me toward the kind of reporting demanded by the editors of *Time*.

An illustration: I'd read in the L.A. *Times* about something called Nisei Week in Los Angeles. It was an ethnic celebration and the L.A. *Times* was doing its civic duty by giving the thing a half-column notice on the metropolitan page. Not much news here. Well, who knows? I said as I drove on down Olympic Boulevard to Little Tokyo. I met the P.R. people. They introduced me to the smiling, little men in charge, and then, spying a half-dozen pretty young women, I said I'd like to meet the candidates for Miss Nisei. I interviewed each of them in turn. Each one of them, of course, had her own story.

Each of their stories began in the same way: these beauties were all born in concentration camps, eighteen, nineteen years before. Wow! I said to myself. These kids' parents were the Japanese-Americans who'd been rounded up in the post–Pearl Harbor hysteria of January 1942 and taken off to "relocation camps" in the Owens Valley or places east, simply for having the wrong ethnic origin. We were at war with Germany and Italy at the same time, but no one had rounded up German-Americans or Italian-Americans. It was a chapter of U.S. history I'd barely remembered, but why not remember it now, for the readers of *Time?*

I sold the idea to the editors in New York. It ran for three full columns in the Nation section, under the heading Historical Notes, and it drew a lot of mail. It was not only a fascinating story in itself, one that illustrated the injustices of mob psychology and the shameful ways that demagogues like Sam Yorty, then a state legislator, could use irrational fears of the simpleminded to enhance their own political power. It had some contemporary significance too, because profiled in my story were some half-dozen Japanese-Americans who had been uprooted, had had their homes and businesses taken away from them, and had spent years in the camps without becoming embittered toward America. They were, in fact, some of the best citizens in L.A. There was a moral lesson here for all those Americans who thought they've been downtrodden, but neither I nor *Time* needed to moralize.

That Nisei story convinced Clurman that I was the kind of correspondent he wanted "on staff." I was at the L.A. Sports Arena, covering a story on right-wing radicals, and their Christian Anti-Communist Crusade, when I got the big phone call from Clurman at the press table right down in front of the stage where the Australian evangelist, Fred C. Schwarz, was inveighing against some aspect or another of Communist infiltration into U.S. society. Maybe it was the Communist plot to fluoridate our nation's water supply.

"How would you like to be a correspondent for *Time?*" asked Clurman.

"Is the pope in Rome?" I said. He named a salary figure that was double my Phoenix wages. I said that would be fine. I would have said it was fine if he'd said I'd have to pay *Time* for the fun of working there.

Clurman said, "Funny you should mention the pope. I'm worried about your Jesuit background. I've already decided that's one place I'll never send you, Rome."

10

Somehow, I wasn't able to take Clurman's prophecy as a final verdict. I still aspired to cover the Second Vatican Ecumenical Council in Rome. So I began to wangle some assignments from *Time*'s Religion section, to do stories on the Catholic Church wherever I could find them. I did one notable story on a maverick monsignor in Cuernavaca, Mexico, Ivan Illich. I did another on American preparations for the Council by interviewing, among others, Jesuit Father Gustave Weigel at Woodstock, Maryland, and Bishop John J. Wright in Pittsburgh. The reports proved my special competence in matters Catholic.

We were not to remain long in Southern California. The day in November 1961 that our daughter, Betsy, was born, a day when visitors to St. John's Hospital in Santa Monica could watch the glowing progress across the mountains of one of the most spectacular fires in L.A. history, Clurman asked me if I'd consider a transfer to Boston. I didn't really want to trade Southern California for Boston. I didn't know then what a vital city Boston was. I said, instantly, that I would, recalling something I'd read once in St. Augustine, *qui libenter dat, bis dat* — he who gives willingly gives twice.

I was still a Jesuit, still ready to go anywhere in the world at a moment's notice from my superiors. Clurman was now "my superior." Sometimes, I even told myself that perhaps I was pioneering a new Jesuit lifestyle. If there were any Jesuits around in the twenty-first century, it was possible they'd be living the three vows of poverty, chastity, and obedience as I was. They'd be unattached to the things of this world, they wouldn't sleep with anyone but their own wives, they'd take their marching orders from their "legitimate superiors," whoever they were, as I took my orders from the editors at *Time*.

Mary and I loved Boston. Then, two months into our stay, Ruth Mehrtens, my bureau chief, told me she'd gotten a call from Clurman. Could I take the Eastern Airlines shuttle down to New York? No, Ruth couldn't tell me what it was all about. But there was a rueful, yet loving look in her eye that told me she felt she'd be losing me soon. To what? I guessed that Clurman might want me in Rome.

I was right. Clurman hadn't remembered his promise that I'd never get a *Time* assignment in Rome. And I didn't remind him. He had seen some of my reporting. He could see that my Jesuit background hadn't left me with any bitterness toward the Church — and that I wasn't an apologist either, just a reporter who wanted to cover a good story. I'd been telling him about the upcoming Second Vatican Ecumenical Council, how it was very much like a parliament of the Church and a rare event in history. There had been only two councils in the past four hundred years, the last of them in 1869 and 1870. "There has been a whole lot of history since 1870," I said to Clurman, "and if the Church is of a mind to deal with all the changes in the world since 1870, this could be a very interesting time."

I had a hunch that the Church was of such a mind. I think that that optimism came partly from my naivete, partly from the large store that I had then of faith and hope in God's providential ways, and partly from my early estimate of Pope John XXIII. I had never taken a formal course in Church history. I didn't know then how embattled the Vatican had been in the past century, and how bitterly Rome had dealt with those who had wanted the Church to be "relevant" to the modern world, even to the point of issuing official anathemas and excommunications against some earnest men of the Church, the so-called "Modernists," whose only sin was daring to think.

I also believed in the Holy Spirit. She would inspire the bishops to do the right thing. And then there was that rumor that Giuseppe Roncalli, Pope John XXIII, had been a covert sympathizer with the Modernists. If that were true, now, at last, he was in a position to do something about reversing the craziness that had compelled Pope Pius IX to produce his famous Syllabus of Errors, which condemned a number of almost self-evident propositions — including this one: "The pope can and must try to achieve a reconciliation and a settlement with progress, liberalism, and modern civilization."

Clurman nodded. "You'll be working under Bill McHale," he said, "but he knows the Council is your project. He'll give you all the backing you need. And so will I." He'd already made his policies clear on that score. "If you have to hire a helicopter to get the story," he'd told me once, "don't phone us and ask our permission to hire the helicopter. Just go ahead and hire the helicopter. But — get the damn story."

On the evening of March 6, 1962, Mary and I and five-month-old Betsy had our supper in the first class cabin of an Alitalia flight from Boston to Rome. We dozed under light blankets and woke up the next morning over France, and then, all of a sudden, we were landing at Leonardo da Vinci Airport near Rome. A large, jovial man who identified himself as Giulio De Angelis, from the offices of "Tee-may, Lee-fay" (Time-Life) in Rome, whisked us right through customs, no inspection necessary, and into a large dark-blue Fiat.

Giulio was one of those do-everything guys that news organizations find so necessary in foreign capitals: someone who can not only get arriving correspondents and their gear into the country, but can find them apartments, along with hookups for electricity, gas, and telephones, not *fra poco* (shortly) — which, in Rome, I would soon learn, often meant a delay of several weeks — but *immediatemente,* right now.

Giulio drove like hell all the way into Rome, using his horn, and then eased up so we could gawk at the Coliseum a bit before we got to our hotel, the Bernini. The bureau had us booked in a suite overlooking the famous Tritone fountain, sculpted, as were many of Rome's fountains, by one of the great artists of the seventeenth century — Rome's last great glory days. The bellman showed us how to let the wooden shutters down over the windows. They'd keep out the light in case we wanted to take a nap, he said, and since Betsy was sleeping, we thought a nap was a fine idea for us, too. We had agreed: Betsy was almost five months old. Now we'd better get started on the production of a little Roman brother for her. Before we lowered the shutters, Mary and I saw scores of young clerics scurrying in every direction, the skirts of their multi-colored cassocks flying behind them.

We weren't in between the cool sheets for more than ten minutes before someone was knocking on our door. Naked, I padded over and peered out of the darkness and around the door at a ruddy-faced fellow who identified himself as Bill McHale. Ah, yes, my new boss, *Time*'s bureau chief in Rome. "Dinner tonight?" he asked. "Connie's busy, so I thought afterward I could show you around...." I nodded, murmured an apology about not being able to invite McHale into the room. "It's all right," he said. "I just wanted to make sure you were comfortable...." His voice trailed off.

We had dinner at a little place around the corner and found that McHale was a delightful guy. He was a jovial enthusiast, a man who could have gotten a cushy editorial job in New York, but preferred being a correspondent in the field, where he could roam free, meet people, give parties, go on exotic journeys, tell stories. After recommending the house cannelloni, McHale said that the meat was O.K. on a Friday because no one, not even the pope, practiced Friday abstinence in Rome. Why not? Because, McHale explained, the Romans had a concept of law that differed from the one we grew up with in the U.S. In Rome, law represented an ideal to strive after, but not so strenuously as to do violence to human nature.

Mary and I nodded and smiled, too secure in our own American Catholicism to believe that this represented anything authentically Catholic, but docile enough to listen to a good reporter explain the manners and mores of the people he "covered" for *Time*.

Later in the evening, McHale took us to the Vatican. We drove right up to St. Peter's Square, got out of the car and walked toward the steps of the Basilica. "You see these two statues?" said McHale. We looked up at two towering baroque figures illumined by spotlights. "Now this one," said McHale, "this one pointing down at the cobblestone pavement? This is St. Peter. Well, according to the Romans, he's saying, '*This* is where the laws are made.' And the other one, the one with his arm outstretched? This is St. Paul. He's saying, 'And *that's* where they're obeyed.'"

It was clear that McHale had become attached to Rome. He spent a couple of hours that night driving us from fountain to fountain, all of them lit up in the way that art treasures deserve to be, and told us how glad he was that we were there. He'd been without a number two man for some time, and he didn't think he was going to get a man who knew his way around the Vatican.

I told him I knew a little bit about the Church and I had some Jesuit friends here who could help me get acquainted, and didn't know my way around the Vatican, but was willing to work at that. In addition to taking some Berlitz lessons in Boston, I'd prepared for Rome by calling back to California and discovering that at least three Jesuits whom I knew were finishing their doctoral studies at the Gregorian University in Rome: Richard Hill, Charles Dullea, and Joe Powers. Ed Malatesta, one of my classmates at Los Gatos, was getting his doctorate in Paris. Gene Bianchi, another classmate, was in Special Studies in Belgium. Both of them would probably come to Rome.

Hill, Dullea, and Powers joined us for lunch at the Bernini the next day and gave us a briefing about clerical Rome. Theirs was a breezy, irreverent account of a town that was so overrun with seminarians that the authorities had forbidden them to attend the movies and the theater. "If we went, there wouldn't be room for anyone else," said Hill. There were hundreds of seminarians here, they explained, from every nation on earth, and you could tell where they came from by the color of their cassocks. The young men from the Scots College wore lavender, the fellows from the Greek College wore blue, the men from the North American College white collars, a red sash, and blue buttons on their black cassocks.

Mary asked about the students in the bright red cassocks, whom we could see hurrying across the Piazza Tritone.

Hill said they were from the German College. "The Romans have a nickname for them: *i gamberi rossi*, the red shrimp." Mary said she didn't quite see shrimp-red so much as tomato-red, and Hill quickly nodded and sought agreement from the others, too. "That's right, isn't it?" he said. "Not so much the color of shrimp, which are a kind of salmon color, but rather more of a tomato red? That's right." Mary beamed, happy to find an endorsement from these expert observers of the scene.

I liked these men, and I appreciated having them as potential news sources. Far from being pious, they were, in fact, slightly profane, and they had scandalous stories to tell about the professionals in the Church of Rome who were politicking their way to the top, like so many Washington bureaucrats, with a sense of entitlement. Powers said, "Those who run the high Roman dicasteries, the men in the Curia, feel they are the Church; everyone else merely belongs to it. It's only natural that they resist any changes in a system that's given them position and power."

I was startled. I'm not sure what picture I had had in my mind of the Church's central administration in Rome, but it certainly wasn't this one I was hearing now. If this was right, however, I might be on to another kind of story, a story of skullduggery in the highest of high places, the Vatican itself. What more could a newsman want? I demanded to know more: did anyone want to change this system?

Powers laughed, looked at the others and said, "Pope John and Cardinal Bea would like to change things. Practically the whole Roman Curia would like to keep the status quo."

"You mean," I said, "that the pope is fighting his own Curia?"

Powers seemed affronted by my incredulity. "The other day," he said, launching into a narrative tone, "I was taking a visitor through the Vatican gardens and we ran into the pope, out for a stroll. The pope found that my friend was a member of the British parliament who spoke fluent French. And so they chatted together for a time. There was no one else around, so I just stood there and listened and smiled and then, when a gardener happened by, my friend asked the pope how many people worked in the Vatican. 'Oh,' said the pope, 'about half of them.' It was a joke, of course, but the pope may have been expressing what many of us feel, that the Curia won't help him change the Church. This is why he called the Council, to get the world's bishops to help him bring the Church up to date. He hasn't said so, in so many words, but he can't tip his hand too soon. They'd do him in."

Mary laughed and the other two Jesuits smiled. Powers smiled, too. "I know, I know, it sounds bizarre. But they've poisoned popes before, popes who tried to change things."

I didn't know whether to believe him or not, but if he was right, my assignment was looking better and better.

11

How nice it would be I thought, if Pope John XXIII were on the side of the reform. There were some indications from afar, to be sure, that he was: he had called a Council, after all, to help make the old Church relevant to a new world, a process he chose to call aggiornamento. The word meant an updating — which was curious in itself, since a half dozen of his predecessors had said repeatedly that the Church should avoid modernization at any cost. I didn't see it at first, but aggiornamento was another word that described the Church's own process of growing up; in an inchoate way, then, I saw it as something good, and something, too, by the way, that would parallel my own growing up.

The more I began to understand about Rome, the less I saw of any aggiornamento.

For starters, Pope John was presiding over all the pretensions of a Renaissance court. Soon after our arrival, Mary and I went to the Vatican for a general audience and were fairly shocked at the goings-on. The pope's entrance was like something out of an epic by Cecil B. DeMille. First there was a blast of trumpets, and then the sound of marching feet and the clank of armor, which we soon saw was produced by a corps of young men called Swiss Guards, wearing breastplates above their red and yellow silk pantaloons and halberds at their hips. Other attendants and courtiers followed, each cadre dressed in costumes that looked decidedly Shakespearean: doublet and hosen and starched ruffled collars. And then came the pope, carried by eight strong guards on a mounted throne, surrounded by a dozen men waving huge ostrich feather fans. I laughed and wondered whether Jesus of Nazareth, the humble friend of my countless meditations, could have restrained his laughter if He had wandered in upon this scene as I had. How could this simple pope of peasant stock look like such a monarch? What did this have to do with any kind of Christian witness?

In the days that immediately followed, I made appointments with anyone and everyone who I thought could give me an inside view of the pope's intentions, developing perhaps two dozen good sources, mostly from English-speaking members of religious orders stationed in Rome. From them I got a mostly disquieting picture — of a pope who wanted to lead a reform within the Church, but couldn't because of an unwillingness in his own cabinet.

I couldn't see that Pope John had done much, if anything, to make his early, overarching vision for the Council a reality either. I had some evidence that Cardinal Bea's Secretariat for Promoting Christian Unity was on its own fast track, but I also learned the Roman Curia, the pope's cabinet, was plodding along like a Percheron, going through the motions of reform, but dealing, mainly, with churchy matters: Ecclesiastical garb and tonsure. Ecclesiastical offices and benefices. Obedience to ecclesiastical teachings. The boundaries of dioceses. The precepts of the Church. Pious donations.

And that, apparently, is all the Curia would allow on the upcoming conciliar agenda. My sources said that the Curia (even some of its minor functionaries) often told the pope what he could do and what he couldn't do, what he could say and what he couldn't say, and if he said the wrong thing, they changed his words in the official records. But how could a newsman prove that? I couldn't walk into the Holy Office and inquire blithely, "Well, how are you going to thwart Pope John today?" (Or, if I could, I hardly expected anyone there to tell me.) Little by little, however, the pieces began to fall into a pattern. I learned the truth, not so much by journalistic intrepidity, but by being so ubiquitous that the truth could come right up and blow in my ear.

One day, Ettore Lolli, our bureau stringer at the Vatican, a veteran reporter from *l'Osservatore Romano* (who was on our payroll for only one reason — because he could get us and our guests good seats at papal audiences) came up to the office for his monthly check. McHale had told me not to expect much from him, but I engaged him in conversation for more than an hour nonetheless, asked admiring questions about his long service at *l'Osservatore*. My patience paid off when he reported confidentially that he was an important guy because he knew how to "fix up" the pope's quotes. He did so frequently, changing the pope's words if they sounded novel or strange to him — that is, different from the kinds of things that Pope Pius XII had been saying since Lolli first started to work at *l'Osservatore* decades before.

Sometimes, other intimations about the pope's inability to make any changes whatsoever inside the Vatican would come from innocent gossip. That spring, a priest from Boston happened to meet his own Cardinal Cushing coming out of a visit to the papal chambers. The cardinal was chuckling. "Heh, heh, heh," he said, shaking his head. "This is a good one." What? What? "You know what the pope told me? *Sono nel sacco qui.* 'I'm in a bag here.' Heh, heh. 'I'm in a bag here.' That's pretty good."

That night at Necci's, I told my new Jesuit friends from the Jesuits' Biblical Institute, Ben Meyer and Bill Moran, what the pope was supposed to have told Cardinal Cushing. They looked at each other and laughed. Mary laughed. I didn't laugh. I was furious. "Why," I said, "does the pope let these people get away with it? I mean, is he the pope or isn't he? How dare anyone 'fix up' his words? How dare anybody tell him? How dare anyone put him in a bag?"

Moran took a sip of San Pellegrino, a fizzy mineral water we had found much to our liking, and smiled. "You've got to understand," he said. "The Church is only human. Over in the United States, in the insulation of our seminaries and of our parishes, we see the Church as more divine than it is. 'God tells the pope, the pope tells the bishops, the bishops tell the priests, the priests tell the nuns and the people.' You think that's what the Church is, God's pipeline? No, that's not the real Church. The real Church is a human organization, dominated by the Rome bureaucracy. The Rome bureaucracy is not unlike bureaucracies anywhere, not unlike our federal government in Washington, where presidents come and presidents go but the bureaucrats remain forever. Basically, they don't like change."

Meyer added, " 'Change? Well, sure,' they say, 'we'll change if it suits our own purposes, and when we get damn good and ready to change.' The only way the pope can beat the bureaucracy is to get the bishops in here, in a Council. That's why he called the Council, and that's why the pope is only playing a waiting game until the bishops come. Then it will be a new kind of ball game. There'll be more than two thousand bishops here, and they may not be listening to the Curia."

"If only the bishops can get some cues from the pope," said Moran. "Things will start to happen."

In the summer my friends left Rome to pursue their research projects in cooler climates, make home visits, take vacations. The McHales went on an extended home leave to the United States. I was running the bureau, and had other reporting to do as well. Jackie Kennedy came to Ravello on a vacation with her sister Lee Radziwill and I flew down to work with a dozen *Time* and *Life* photographers and reporters who came to gawk and snap and scribble.

I also did some ongoing reportage of another big story in Rome that summer: Elizabeth Taylor and Richard Burton were making *Cleopatra* in Rome, and carrying on a mad love affair which our show biz editors in New York demanded I cover. I did so by going out to the studio called Cinecitta every Friday and having lunch with members of the cast who seemed to enjoy cataloging the ups and downs of the tempestuous romance of Burton and Taylor, their fights, their flights, visits from the respective spouses, Burton's binges, Taylor's overdoses and pseudosuicides.

❧

DURING AUGUST'S DOG DAYS, I got a lucky break on my Council coverage. It came in the form of a phone call from Paris. Ed Malatesta, one of my California Jesuit classmates, just finishing up his postordination studies in France, had heard what I was up to, and he had news — or rather some sources — for me. Could I fly to Paris?

Leaving Mary and the baby in Rome, I arrived in France on August 15, when most of Paris was off on holiday and the streets were deserted except for the presence of soldiers on almost every corner armed with submachine guns. The French were in the middle of their Algerian crisis, an attempt had already been made on the life of General DeGaulle, and the army was determined to make an obvious show of force.

During our Novitiate and beyond, Ed had been one of the Brethren of the Strict Pious Observance, but now I found him, though still intense, as impatient now with the horses' asses as I ever was. He confirmed some of my own general uneasiness with the Church, the Church that felt there was only one Church, the Church of Rome. Now he was giving me another view, one that he'd picked up in his most recent studies at Chantilly — that one could be loyal to the Church without kowtowing to Rome's officialdom, that Rome's theology was only one opinion in the Church. In fact, Rome had not only become politically embattled during the Italian Risorgimento, it had become embattled intellectually as well, and had fallen light years behind the advanced theological work that had

· 94 ·

been going on for more than half a century in Germany, France, Belgium, and the Netherlands.

Not unnaturally, Vatican types produced work in keeping with a life lived behind the Vatican walls: they were there not only to protect the Vatican, but the "sacred deposit of faith" as well. The metaphor gave a clue to their bulwark mentality: the faith was something like a bar of gold bullion, and the men in the Curia, led by Cardinal Alfredo Ottaviani, were standing over it, like guards in an ecclesiastical Fort Knox.

Such a stance inhibited the kind of growth that one would expect of any living body. For years, there was a sameness about Catholic doctrine. In their seminaries, priests learned "eternal truths" and passed them on down to the people. In the late nineteenth century, the American bishops authorized something called the Baltimore Catechism; sisters were still teaching the same questions and answers, by rote, in the twentieth. Marx, Freud, and Einstein had come up with new questions, the world had gone through two major wars, six million Jews were tortured and gassed from Buchenwald to Belsen, and one lone B-29 had leveled Hiroshima and Nagasaki with two solitary bombs. The Church's questions and answers didn't seem quite so relevant anymore. What was Christianity all about anyway?

"The Council's Central Commission," Malatesta told me, "has produced documents couched in the same legalistic, scholastic language that was already out of date in Vatican One." He said, "But don't take my word for this. Come, let's go see some of the Church's scholars." We visited Benedictine and Dominican and Jesuit theologians in Paris and its environs and spent some considerable time with some of the scholars at *Études,* the highbrow monthly edited by the French Jesuits. These men were even freer with anecdotes than my friends in Rome; everyone had stories to tell of skirmishes with the Roman Curia that had already been lost — or won.

My French sources made no effort to conceal from me news of the fight then raging (behind the scenes) between Cardinal Ottaviani and Cardinal Bea. If this was going to be a Council to promote Christian unity, Bea believed, then non-Catholic observers should be there, to see for themselves exactly what was happening. Ottaviani would have none of that. He didn't want outsiders at the Council. And so, in July of 1961, he flatly opposed the sending of any Roman Catholic observers to the World Council of Churches meeting in New Delhi. For Cardinal Bea, this was a crisis.

If the Church did not send men to New Delhi, how could it possibly ask the Christian bodies represented there to send observers to Rome?

Though it was nothing he cared to do very often, Bea went to the pope on this occasion and appealed. *Io sono solamente il Papa*, said John, "I'm only the pope." He implied that he could do nothing. But he did act, and told Ottaviani that observers would indeed go to New Delhi. Ottaviani sniffed and said that, In that event, none of those observers could participate as theologians in the Vatican Council — presumably to diminish the importance, in retrospect, of the Roman Catholic presence at New Delhi. It was a small victory for Bea. But it didn't bode well for the progress of the Council itself: if Cardinal Ottaviani, the head of the Holy Office (formerly known as the Holy Office of the Inquisition) was going to buck Bea at every turn, the Council was going to be a long, hard fight.

Jean Danielou, a wiry, nervous Jesuit, was my source on that story. Ed and I bumped into him in the hallway at *Etudes,* and he stopped to tell us in very good, very excited English, about his trip to New Delhi, for he was one of the observers who had finally gone to India. Danielou also made it clear that he would be at the Council in October, Cardinal Ottaviani's prohibition notwithstanding. No, said Danielou, he wouldn't be an "official theologian." What did "official" mean anyway? Did it mean that if Danielou didn't have Ottaviani's Good Housekeeping Seal of Approval, he couldn't speak to a Council Father, or ghostwrite a speech for a bishop? Obviously not. Danielou said he couldn't miss this chance of a lifetime.

❧

WHEN I RETURNED from Paris, I found a *Life* writer in Rome, Robert Elson, a veteran Time Incer and a loyal Catholic. He was there to do a text piece on Pope John which *Life* would publish at the beginning of the Council. Elson leaned on me and I gave him all the help I could, but he was a pain in the ass because he kept second guessing my approaches to the job. He seemed disappointed that I didn't know the dean of the foreign press corps in Rome — as if I should be gathering material, second-hand, from an old-timer — whom I never saw "out on the beat." More often than not, I would see this fellow at the bar of the Foreign Press Club — interviewing another reporter.

One morning, Elson arrived at the bureau wearing his best blue serge suit: he had arranged a private audience with the pope. But I had to laugh when he returned just before lunch in a funk. He had spent about forty-five seconds with the pope, in the same room with a couple dozen men and women who each had a chance, in turn, to kiss the pope's ring and say hello. The pope told Elson he was aware of his projects and that he would "pray God to enlighten his eyes, his ears, and his tongue," so that he could write a good article. Elson didn't need prayer so much, not even the prayers of a pope, for it wasn't inspiration he was after, it was a chance to talk with the man he would write about.

Back in New York, Harry Luce, who was, for my money, the brightest journalist in the world, understood that. He worked out a trade with Cardinal Francis Spellman, one of the few men powerful enough to arrange a real interview with the pope. In order to put together something called the Vatican Pavilion at the New York World's Fair in 1963, Cardinal Spellman wanted to borrow Time Inc.'s "Illuminations" — color transparencies of the Sistine Chapel done laboriously and sensationally by *Life*'s famed Dmitri Kessel. Luce said that would be an easy favor to grant — if Spelly could help get the pope to sit for a *Time* cover, to be painted by the Italian portrait artist Pietro Annigoni, *and* arrange a real interview with the pope for the *Time* and *Life* writers in Rome.

Cardinal Spellman said that was a fair deal. Of course, there were problems of protocol. The pope could not sit *for us*. Annigoni was being paid $25,000 by Time Inc., but protocol dictated that he would have to pretend he was working for the Vatican secretary of state. Then, if the portrait was to the Secretariat's liking, the Secretariat would "donate" it to Time Inc. And the pope, like any other crowned head in Europe, did not give official interviews. However, if Elson and I would present ourselves at the pope's summer residence at Castel Gandolfo in the Alban Hills outside Rome, we might just run into John XXIII — by accident. There would be some back and forth, a conversation, but not an official interview, nothing that would create a precedent.

♨

ON A WARM MORNING in August, Elson and I and Gabriel DeSabatino, a longtime stringer in the Rome bureau, found ourselves chatting with the pope's personal secretary, Msgr. Loris Capovilla. He told us a good deal about the pope's daily schedule. He rose every day at 4:00 A.M. and retired at 10:00, after he watched the evening news on television. Sometimes, he'd get up again in the middle of the night to read for a while, then go back to bed again. At lunch, eating a customary Lombardy diet of rice, meat or fish, a green vegetable, and a little wine, he sometimes chatted with a friend, sometimes listened to music. During Lent, he heard one or two movements every day of all nine Beethoven symphonies — and prepared for this daily concert by reading the historical background of each symphony. After lunch, he snoozed in a chair for no more than a half-hour, then turned to reading daily reports from all of his cabinet officers. I asked Capovilla if the pope would be bothered by fights between conservatives and liberals at the Council.

"Perhaps the Holy Father will intervene," said Capovilla. "Perhaps he has already intervened. There are ways in which the Holy Father, in rewriting a *schema,* could arrive at some compromise that would be acceptable to both sides. Still, Pope John has no wish to flaunt his authority."

"His health good?" I asked.

Capovilla almost snapped at me. "Just look at the schedule he keeps. Of course, he's eighty-one and we have to watch him, something he doesn't always see the need for." Capovilla said the pope kept a diary recounting his day rather completely and making observations about his guests "in a pretty good reportorial fashion."

Capovilla seemed to be enjoying himself, talking about his boss. "Everybody should have a boss like this one," he said. "When Jacqueline Kennedy came to visit this summer, the Holy Father asked me how to address her. I said, 'Mrs. Kennedy,' or just 'Madame,' since she is of French origin and has lived in France. Now, while he is waiting for her in his private library, he is rehearsing to himself. 'Mrs. Kennedy. Madame. Madame. Mrs. Kennedy.' Then the doors opened and she was there and the Holy Father stood and threw open his arms and said, 'Jacqueline!'"

We were chuckling over that one when the pope sauntered by in his white cassock, alone, on his way to lunch. All of us pretended surprise at the coincidence of the encounter, but I didn't have to pretend very much because I could still hardly believe that this was Giuseppe Roncalli, His Holiness, Pope John XXIII, standing there next to me. He was shorter than I and I noticed that he wasn't wearing shoes, but some velvet slippers, and I made a mental note that I hoped he didn't have to spend much time on his feet in those brogans. He carried about two hundred pounds on a five-six frame, but he didn't seem to be as heavy as he appeared in some newsphotos. His head was bald in front, but he had a good growth of white hair in back, and he hardly ever stopped smiling at us.

We were newsmen, so we didn't kiss his ring (for the same reason that news reporters do not applaud when they cover a speech by a politician). We each shook his hand as we were introduced by Capovilla and then the pope launched into a happy monologue — in French. Since none of us spoke French, I stopped him and urged that we speak Italian. John seemed delighted with that, and shifted right into his native tongue. His voice was not that of an old man, it was high, almost youthful, and clear.

Our conversation hardly dealt with weighty policy matters. To me, John was like a fruit merchant from Boston's North End, as comfortable as an old shoe. He asked about our families. I told him I had one *bambina*. He said I shouldn't be afraid to have lots more; his brother in the Piedmont had twelve kids. I said that Mary and I wanted a dozen, too. He beamed. I beamed.

Elson had a cosmic question. The pope responded in a less-than-cosmic fashion. My turn: I asked him if he thought that Russian Orthodox observers would attend the Council.

The pope said we were all brothers; why couldn't the whole human race start loving one another? "Not long ago," he said, "I had a visit from a group of French Protestants, from the monastery of Taizé. I asked them, 'Why can't we get together?' They said, 'We have different ideas.' I said, 'Ideas, ideas. What are ideas among friends?' "

I was shocked. The sticky point about the Church for me, and for many of my friends who were not Catholics, was its insistence on this or that doctrinal formula, as if adherence to a number of abstract propositions could create a loving community. The Church had fought wars over an enclitic (the *-que* in the Nicene Creed's *Filioque*), disputing with the Greeks whether the Holy Ghost proceeded from the Father *and* the Son or from the Father *through* the Son. And now here was the pope himself saying ideas were not important. What *was* important? The pope told us several stories about the need for everyone in the world to start pulling together, to make life on earth more livable for everyone.

We exchanged some more questions and answers. The pope asked us as many questions as we asked him. Finally, we made a move to excuse ourselves. Pope John wasn't ready for us to go. He grabbed my shoulder and held on and started telling some more stories about his brothers and sisters up north. Clearly, people were more important to Pope John than ideas "which only divide."

Up close to him at last, I could confirm to myself much of what others had had to report. Pope John exuded warmth, exuberance, and love. Lord knew the world needed that. But he wasn't simply an ecclesiastical Santa Claus. He had a prepossessing wisdom, too, about the futility of ideologies themselves and, fittingly (I now realize) he chose to say so not by logical argument but in the manner of a scholar like Elie Wiesel, who would rather tell stories than spin syllogisms. Rather than bore us with a wordy argument, he preferred to tell us one simple story about a visit from the Protestants of Taizé (who now, by the way, run an ecumenical monastery in France that emphasizes what unites Christians rather than what divides them).

Pope John's style was allusive. Msgr. Capovilla preferred to spell things out. When the pope finally bounced off to his lunch, Capovilla sat the three of us down at his desk and told us more stories about the pope's efforts to further peace and understanding between peoples, whatever their ideology. Once, he recounted, when the pope was watching television coverage of the 1960 Olympic Games in Rome, he spied a Bulgarian general in the midst of a large group of athletes. He recognized the man as an old acquaintance, a man he had known during his days as a Vatican diplomat in Sofia.

That evening, the pope sent word to the Bulgarian contingent in the Olympic Village that he would like to see the general. Though this embarrassed the man in front of his confreres, he could hardly refuse the invitation. He was surprised to find that the pope did not want to give him a sermon or lecture him about communism, he only wanted to reminisce. "He didn't ask me anything," reported the general. "He just said he loved Bulgaria very much." After the general returned home, a Catholic bishop and a dozen priests who had been clapped in jail by the Reds were surprised to find themselves quietly released.

Capovilla pulled a copy of an Italian weekly out of his desk drawer. A banner headline over a story on Pope John said, *LA CROCIATA: NON SI FA PIU.* "No more Crusades." Capovilla said the newspaper was right on the mark. He tried to explain what was new and different about his boss.

"The Church is not a dam against communism," said Capovilla. "The Church cannot, should not, be against anything. It should be positively for something. This is the characteristic note of the Holy Father's attitude. Not to condemn but to affirm. When we support only one political bloc, we alienate half of humanity. The Church is for all people, for all times. It is not bound to follow the political and economic fortunes of states. It must look ahead to eventual contact with all peoples, even if it is fifty years from now. Even now it can multiply contacts and encourage other contacts on every level — political, religious, cultural, creative. Yes, we want the Russian Orthodox observers at the Council. No, we do not want any further crusade against communism. A crusade against communism is pointless."

Capovilla, like Danielou, was a lean, nervous fellow. His head was closely cropped, almost like a convict's, and his fingers often fluttered to his face as he spoke with a high animation. It seemed that he had much to tell us and not nearly enough time. The pope, he said, was simply trying to commend Christ to all humankind. He wouldn't dream of "converting" anyone—which was bad theology to begin with, since faith is a gift which God bestows when and upon whom He wants. But the pope was clearly pleased, Capovilla said, when he received a birthday greeting on November 25, 1960, from Nikita Khrushchev, who called John "a man of peace" and wished him success.

This was the first recognition by any Soviet official of any pope and it marked the beginning of suspicions that perhaps the pope was not aligned, as his predecessor had been, with "the American imperialists." The right-wing Italian press was in a furor, of course, and many in the Vatican advised the pope against any kind of reply. John replied. He cabled back to Khrushchev, "Thank you for the thought. And I will pray for the people of Russia."

Capovilla ticked off other items in the pope's new approach. He referred to *Mater et Magistra*, a twenty-five-thousand-word document which some called "a treatise on socialism" — but which, according to Capovilla, Nikita Khrushchev read and then told his ministers, "We can't laugh at *this*." The pope also turned his attention to the throbbing nationalism of Africa and moved the Church ahead several centuries by ordering thirteen native African bishops consecrated immediately. For too long, he told some, in the hearing of Capovilla, the Church had betrayed its mission by its close identification with the colonializing powers. "If a man doesn't have his liberty," he said, "he's nothing."

Capovilla also wanted to make it clear that the pope wanted to ease tensions between Christians and Jews. He had already asked Cardinal Bea to prepare a *schema* for the Council that would revise the old Catholic story about the Jews killing Christ, and thus bringing eternal damnation on them and on their children, too. It was a myth that had nurtured anti-Semitism for centuries.

This pope, Capovilla said, didn't much care for people who were always cutting themselves off — another way of describing "sects." Pope John was no sectarian, possibly the least sectarian of all the popes of history.

Capovilla pointed out how Giuseppe Roncalli had once defined a Christian to a group of Socialists at the city hall in Venice. "In this place I am at my ease, even though there may be someone here who does not call himself a Christian but who really is so because he does good." I thought that, here, we had a wide new definition of "Christian" that would exclude few in the human race.

Capovilla reemphasized the point by telling another story, about a young Jewish lad who had made the acquaintance of Giuseppe Roncalli when he was the cardinal-archbishop of Venice. The kid had wanted to be a Catholic, but Roncalli kept putting him off. "Look," he said, "you are a Jew. Be a good Jew. Becoming a Catholic would kill your parents." The young man persisted and Roncalli finally said that he could be baptized — in secret. Several years later, after his parents had died, he presented himself at the Vatican to see his old mentor, now the pope. Now he wanted the pope to give him the Sacrament of Confirmation. "All right, all right," said Pope John XXIII, "but you've got to continue being a good Jew in your own community, go to the synagogue, support the Jewish *schul,* because, by being a Catholic, you do not become any less a Jew."

Capovilla told us of other encounters the pope had had with any number of "non-Catholic" delegations. One group of Jews from Paris approached him cautiously. Not within memory had any pope received a delegation of Jews. Pope John greeted them warmly, embraced them and said, "I am Joseph, your brother."

I was flabbergasted by much of this. I'd been doing my homework. I'd read everything written about Pope John and I hadn't seen this Pope John in print, anywhere. Arnaldo Cortesi, longtime correspondent in Rome for the *New York Times,* was predicting the Council would be a dull, churchy affair of interest to few outside Catholicism. Now I realized that the pope had broad ecumenical intentions that went beyond the confines even of Christianity, and that he intended his own leadership in the Church to serve the cause of universal peace: that his goals were as political as they were ecclesial.

Now, of course, I could see that the pope was, in fact, "up to date" — maybe even a little ahead of his time. On the drive back to Rome in one of our big office cars, Elson had some cavils about Pope John's "politics" and some questions about Capovilla's ability to speak for the pope. I didn't even care to argue with him. I was lost in my own thoughts and surmises about a Council, which, if it were led by this man, would, in fact, update the Church more than anyone knew.

Elson, DeSabatino and I spent most of the afternoon debriefing one another on our conversations with Capovilla and the pope and then, about 6:00 P.M., a messenger arrived from the Vatican Secretariat of State. He had Papal medals for each of us, and a note from Pope John to me, saying that he was much taken with me — and hoped that Mary and I would indeed have twelve *bambini*.

12

Pietro Annigoni came up with a sketch of Pope John, rather than the oil painting we had expected. Somehow, it was just right for us. Annigoni had captured Roncalli's earthiness, and the unfinished quality of the work produced an image of a man who, at the age of eighty-one, was still unfinished himself. For *Time,* that was quite a symbol: Pope John would not be "finished" until his Council was finished. We had the canvas shipped off to New York, I cabled in most of my cover file on the pope, and then I jetted off to Venice with Mary to catch the sights and sounds of the Venice Film Festival.

That was all the vacation I was to get for a long time to come. Soon as I returned to Rome, I had an assignment to fly up to Milan to do some preliminary reporting on a cover story on Enrico Mattei, the head of ENI, Italy's oil and gas monopoly. I spent a week at ENI. Then McHale came back from his three-month U.S. vacation and took over the reporting on Mattei. He planned to travel with Mattei on ENI's jet to Sicily and, perhaps, to some other oil lands in North Africa. Mattei was a wheeler-dealer who was very thick with the Arabs, had already succeeded in breaking the American-Dutch-English cartel that told the Arabs how much they could charge for their own oil. He may have been the most powerful man in Italian politics at the time, principally because he had something on everyone in the country. His enemies in the Italian government undercut him at their own risk — it was said that Mattei had a dossier on everyone — and no one knew if he had any friends.

Mattei and McHale were supposed to fly back north on a Saturday night. McHale had phoned the bureau and said that Mattei might drop him off in Rome. More likely, he'd have to fly straight up to Milan with

Mattei, and then turn around and catch a commercial flight back to Rome. Mary and I and a few priest-friends were having an after-dinner brandy at our apartment in Rome, when I got a phone call from New York. It was Dick Clurman.

"Where's your bureau chief?" he said.

"Sicily," I said, "or Milan. Or on his way back to Rome." There was a pause on the other end and for a moment all I could hear was the transatlantic crackle.

"Was he with Enrico Mattei?" asked Clurman. I said he was and Clurman's voice sounded suddenly grim. "I think we've lost him," he said. "I just got an AP report that Mattei's private jet went down tonight near Milan. Check it out, will you?"

The Associated Press in Rome confirmed. The jet had gone down in the middle of an oat field. Mattei, his pilot, and Bill McHale were dead. I phoned Clurman back in New York. He said I ought to get right over and tell Connie, and if I could take a priest with me, that would be even better. We took the three priests who were then dining with us, but, even so, Connie took it very hard.

We drove home in silence, delivering the priests each to their respective houses. "We are fragile creatures," said Jesuit Father Roberto Tucci sadly, as he climbed out of the car at the headquarters of his magazine *La Civiltà Cattolica*.

We're particularly fragile, I said to myself, if there are shadowy figures out there somewhere trying to kill us. No one ever proved sabotage in the Mattei plane crash; but no one really had any stake in doing so, not Mattei's political associates, not his survivors (for charges of sabotage might muck up the insurance payoffs), not even Connie McHale, who was sick at heart over the loss of Bill. Proof of a conspiracy couldn't bring Bill back.

ઈ

ON SEPTEMBER 11, Pope John finally unmasked his most optimistic intentions on Vatican Radio; the Council, he said, was meeting "in the midst of a new political world." He noted that each of the Council Fathers who "belong in reality to all peoples and nations" was meeting to "bring his contribution of intelligence and experience to cure and heal the wounds" of two world wars "which have changed profoundly the face of all countries." In this radio message, I thought the pope was trying to spell the end of that old Augustinian view of the world as something evil and a thing apart.

It seemed to me that the pope was saying that it is we who are bad, not the world. If we want to find evil, we need look no further than our own hearts. The pope said we have only ourselves to blame for much that befalls us; we have armed conflicts, he said, because we ignore our own duties, and our own spiritual values, and fail to possess and use the powers we have to make the world a better place.

Since my days at the Mount, I had never quite seen the value of harping on what was called "the natural and the supernatural order." They were distinctions we made in our own minds, but real men and women lived in a real world and those men and women were both body and soul; the same men and women were members of many communities at once, simultaneously members of a church and citizens of a state. There were then 580 million Catholics, worldwide. (The number now is one billion.) If the Council Fathers wanted to serve them, then they also had to figure out how this Council might have an impact on the world these Catholics lived in.

And so, contrary to reports by some of the press corps in Rome who kept insisting on the Curial line that the Council would be a churchy affair with few worldly ramifications, I tried, in my reports to my editors in New York, to focus more on the impact this Council might have on a world that then seemed embroiled in a conflict that could blow up the whole human race. Indeed, only a few days later, Msgr. Jan Willebrands, Cardinal Bea's number one man in the Secretariat for Promoting Christian Unity, would make a move that couldn't help but lessen political tensions between Moscow and the so-called free world. He boarded Czechoslovakian Airlines Flight 502 heading for Sheremetievo Airport in Moscow. His mission: to talk to the top members of the Moscow Patriarchate and persuade them that John XXIII would want them, as representatives of some forty million Orthodox, to attend his Council where, Willebrands said, they would discover that John's *politique* was not that of Pius XII. Rome would be friends with Moscow.

This wasn't an altogether new idea, the idea that antipathy to an "ism" (even communism) didn't necessarily mean hatred of those who espoused it. Giovanni Guareschi, an Italian author, had written engagingly about a man named Don Camillo, who, though a priest, was friendly with the communist mayor of his little town. But to have Pope John XXIII take that position, that was something else again. Catholics (and some newspaper editors) are like children; official opinions are often more important to them than those of others who have no official standing but who still speak truth to power, those who were called, in ancient times, prophets. When a pope became a prophet, that was news that even an editor with a lot of preconceptions had to listen to.

Henry Grunwald, *Time*'s foreign editor, had to listen when I cabled my reports about Pope John's "new opening to the left" (as some unfriendly papers in Rome would have it). Grunwald didn't like what he heard, and wired back, "You can't tell me that the Church is dropping its fight against communism." It was a strange thing for an editor in New York to tell one of his reporters in the field. Grunwald, of course, was one of the most intelligent of all the editors in *Time*'s history. He had written *Time*'s cover story on Pope Pius XII in December 1953, and he knew of the Catholic Church's antipathy to communism. His only mistake was in assuming that things do not change in the Catholic Church. There were times in the Church's recent past when that was a safe assumption. Here in Rome things were changing before everyone's eyes.

And so I didn't let Grunwald's incredulity bother me. I was in Rome. My editors were not. That put me in a better position to know what was happening here. I wasn't working directly for Grunwald anyway, but for Dick Clurman, who cabled me on the eve of *Time*'s October cover story on Pope John XXIII:

ONE OF THE BEST COVER FILES I'VE EVER READ.
FASCINATING AND REMARKABLE JOB FOR WHICH
I SEND MY HIGHEST COMPLIMENTS.

With support like that, I not only served as the acting Rome bureau chief, I ate, drank, and slept the Council: total immersion. I had interviews from breakfast to midnight and beyond. I roamed the city and talked to bishops who had come in from every continent, black, brown, yellow, some of whom had obviously suffered pain and deprivation, and white men who looked too comfortable and self-assured for their own good.

There were more than eight hundred missionary bishops here at the Council, and my guess was that most of them were poor and full of uncertainties about the Council and what was expected of them. I met Paul Etoga, a husky native bishop of M'Balmayo in the Cameroons, who had just scraped together enough money to take a boat to LeHavre, hitchhike to Paris, and squeeze into a second-class railroad car for Rome. I found that Bishop Joseph Busimba of the Congo checked into Fiumicino's customs office with three elephant tusks as a gift for the pope. And I learned that Archbishop Aston Chichester, who had labored in Rhodesia for many of his eighty-four years, wandered about a Jesuit house in Rome for days and listened to talk that only confused him: "Just who is this bloke Ottavi, uh, Ottaviani?" he demanded.

In the first week of October, the Council Fathers started pouring into the hurly-burly of the Vatican's reception center on Via della Conciliazione to pick up their documents and credentials. The Maronites from Tyre and Tripoli, Baalbek, Nisibis, Cairo, and Cyprus, led by His Holiness the Patriarch Meouchi of Antioch, proud of their seven hundred years' resistance to the Turks and Arabs. The Melkites from Aleppo, Antioch, Jerusalem, and Laodicea, led by the fiery Maximos IV Saigh, claiming to be the sole representative of the Eastern Church and ready to fight for the ancient ways of the East in a Church he felt was too Romanized. And the bearded bishops of other ancient rites: the Syro-Malabars, the Malankers, the Copts, the Byzantines, the Chaldeans, the Armenians.

The European bishops flocked in, more at home than the missionaries. The 33 bishops from Catholic Ireland and the 95 from most Catholic Spain, the Spanish feeling themselves on the brink of a new future without the now-ailing Franco, the Irish full of misty memories of their part in the fight for infallibility at the First Vatican Council; both Spanish and Irish suspicious of the alien theologies of the French and the Germans. The 42 bishops from England and Wales and the 27 from Portugal, equally insular, equally hoping for an early end to an unnecessary Council. The 68 Germans, nervously fearing themselves too far out in front with their projects, the 159 French determined not to push their programs too hard, content to sit back and play a waiting game.

Some 217 bishops from the United States flew in by jet or sailed over on Italian liners, each of them accompanied by two or three clerical buddies, whom they called "theologians," and checked into the most posh Via Veneto hostelries like the Excelsior, the Flora, the Eden, the Majestic, the Boston. With scant regard for this nudge to the local economy, one Rome newspaper cracked, "The American bishops are consecrating the Via Veneto."

It was true, however, that the American bishops brought a clerical tone to the racy Veneto and added some innocently racy stories to those told in the sidewalk cafes near my office. (One of them concerned a bishop who checked into a hotel where there were already some Anglican clergymen in residence. Late that evening, when he returned to his hotel, he found himself in a double room with his pajamas laid out neatly on one twin bed and on the other — his lace surplice.)

No one knew how the bishops of this now obviously universal Church would react to the myriad number of proposals that would be laid before them. But some journalists tried to guess. Paul Hoffman of the *New York Times* wrote, "The dominant trend is averse to radical changes in Church doctrine or policy." The *Times* copy desk headlined the piece: TRADITIONALIST TENDENCY PREVAILS AMONG DELEGATES.

I wondered about that. I could not imagine the Council Fathers, the successors to the Councils of Nicaea and Ephesus and Trent, now gathered from Borneo, Little Rock, Fukuoka and Madagascar, coming to this Council to rubber stamp the Curialist view of the Church and the world. I didn't quite see how the 374 missionary bishops from the exploding Orient, nor the 296 bishops from throbbing Africa could possibly leave the push toward reform to a handful of German, Dutch, French, and Belgian bishops. I also learned that, while there were only nine bishops from the Netherlands, there were 85 other Dutch bishops hailing from what were then called "mission countries." I guessed these bishops might tend to vote with their own Cardinal Jan Alfrink, whom I had already marked as one of the liberals.

Since I was covering a parliament of the Church, I was fully aware that I was thinking, as Bishop Fulton J. Sheen charged, "in human terms." I pleaded guilty to that; I couldn't think in any other terms — and neither could Bishop Sheen, though he implied that, since the Holy Spirit was in charge here, no journalist should try reporting this event as if it were just another "human assembly." I, too, believed the Holy Spirit was in charge, but I assumed She worked, normally, through the mediation of human beings, who acted and reacted and interacted in human ways that I could report on.

So I not only thought in human terms, but, like any American reporter covering Capitol Hill, I thought in political terms as well. What reading I had done on the history of the councils told me that the Council Fathers had always had their own political agenda, and so, for me, the Capitol Hill model worked as well as any. I would soon discover that the Council Fathers, whatever their direct revelations from the Holy Spirit, tended to vote in national blocs and according to certain theological tendencies (which some called "open" and "closed") and according to the cues given them by Pope John XXIII.

I thank God that it was Pope John XXIII giving the subtle directions, for I saw his optimistic vision of the world as one that demanded, in essence, that Catholics start giving the world — and themselves — their due. This, I thought, was something new. The cardinal-electors who chose Roncalli had called him "an interim pope," because, at the age of seventy-eight, he couldn't last long; there would be another pope right behind him. But he was "interim" in quite another sense; he was a pope who served as a bridge between more authoritarian popes of the past and new popes of the future who will try to help people start thinking for themselves, especially on personal moral questions where no one else ought to try to do their thinking for them.

Back in 1962, however, I still let others do my thinking for me: Pope John, liberal cardinals, the theologians who would turn out to be the superstars of the Council. The Church was only starting to grow up. And so was I. We all needed cues.

13

On October 12, the day the Council opened, they set bleachers on both sides of the nave, twenty-eight hundred seats, in rows that ran just a little over a hundred yards, making St. Peter's look like nothing so much as a football stadium — with a baroque altar at one end instead of goal posts. Television cameras were there; television promised a visual presentation of this Roman triumph, part of the show business that had, for centuries, been a part of papal Rome.

Pope John surprised everyone by making this more than mere showbiz. To the 2,381 Council Fathers gathered in the "stadium," and to millions watching on European television, Pope John gave some important cues about the direction this Council was going to take.

One cue was nonverbal: though plans called for the Protestant and Orthodox delegate-observers to be seated in a tribune (or balcony) somewhat removed from the action, the pope changed those plans and ordered the observers be given special seats that were the equivalent to field passes at a Super Bowl game. Other Councils had been Councils of exclusion, effectively setting aside those who would not submit to the Church's authority. This Council was obviously different, this would be a Council of inclusion — and Pope John wanted these observers close to the action. Until recently, they'd been called nothing but heretics and schismatics. But now, the pope called them "separated brethren," and did them honor, and wanted them where he could see them, where the world's press could see them, close to him.

The pope's words were more than cues, they were an unequivocal call for reformation of a Church that had become fossilized, words aimed as much at the Protestant and Orthodox delegate-observers and at the world as at the Council Fathers themselves. John outlined the Church's new optimistic orientation, one that would "look to the future without fear." He scored the "prophets of gloom who were always forecasting disaster as though the end of the world were at hand." He said that he did not want this Council to indulge in condemnations, but rather to encourage good work in the world by all men of good will, "preparing and consolidating the path toward the unity of mankind." He said he didn't know how this would happen. Sufficient for this Council to be conciliatory, reformist, creative. Time would tell what other actions must follow.

He said the whole world was expecting the Church to take "a step forward." The original Italian was *un balzo avanti*, a phrase that had a happy sound for me, perhaps because I associated the word *balzo*, literally "a precipitous leap," with the English word "waltz." This picture of the Church, led by John the Round, waltzing into the future, made me smile. Then this pope dared to utter something which few Catholic theologians of the recent past would have said out loud in mixed company: "The substance of the ancient doctrine of the deposit of faith is one thing. The way in which it is presented is another."

He was making a distinction between the liberty of faith (which is expressed in the life of Christians) and the prison of theology (which is merely someone's rational thought about that life). This declaration startled me — because John's words were a paraphrase of one of the Modernist "heresies" that Pius X condemned back in 1907. (There is little doubt about this even today: this is what Pope John's detractors in the Church most hold against him, that he was a secret Modernist all along, and then, when he became pope, an open one.)

My thoughts went back to one of the original Modernists, the Jesuit George Tyrrell, dying in 1910 at the age of forty-five, two years after his condemnation, despondent not only because he'd been kicked out of the Church and denied the sacraments, but because his ideas had been quickly dismissed as inconsequential by two of his best friends. One of his ideas: that the Church was, in fact, created for man and not man for the Church, and that bishops, councils, even popes, were "witnesses to, not creators of, the Church's faith and practice."

My colleagues in the press, who had feared that the pope's talk would be simply a speech of welcome (and a bore) were impressed with it. Most of them had never heard of George Tyrrell, but they knew that the pope was making news, because he was talking about a new kind of Church, one that would ratify the Reformation launched by Martin Luther (and rejected by Rome) four hundred years before. What else did the pope mean when he said the Church had to "reform" and "update" its doctrine? The correspondent for the French daily, *Paris Presse* spoke for many when he wrote that the pope's discourse "will go right to the heart of the Catholic world. But it is also certain to arouse agitation in some quarters."

For me, a Council that made people yawn was no Council at all. But a Council that created some "agitation" was a Council that was going to do something important. The trick for me, as a new man, was to gain enough access to the event so I would know, on a daily basis, what was creating the agitation. Getting this access would not be an easy thing.

In the first place, the Council's sessions were closed and the particulars of its agenda secret. The Council had a press officer, Msgr. Fausto Vaillanc, but he was a career man in the Roman Curia; in some preconciliar hand-outs, he had already demonstrated an inability to understand what kind of Council the pope was aiming at. I couldn't cover the Council by re-lying on his bulletins, and neither could any other newsman worth his Roman expense account. Some reporters, especially the older hands, said they had other Roman sources. Newcomers like myself had a hunch that a non-Roman view of the proceedings would provide a clearer picture of what was happening inside the conciliar aula.

I quickly found out not to look for scoops from my own American bishops; they were a careful bunch who'd gotten where they were because they'd learned to make no mistakes — and did so simply by attempting nothing new. They weren't going to change that modus operandi now.

At a reception on the eve of the Council, Bishop Thomas K. Gorman of Dallas-Ft. Worth, a former chairman of the U.S. Bishops' press committee, listened patiently when I complained to him about the official Vatican press arrangements. Then he lit a foot-long cigar and said that he couldn't help me, and laughed at my eager naivete. "You won't see many headlines coming out of this Council," he said. He said that the Curia had a lock on everything and that many American bishops were saying the same thing. They thought they'd come to approve what had been prepared for them in advance by the Curia and then go home. They'd probably wind up this Council in about three weeks.

Bishop Gorman couldn't have been more mistaken. On the very first working day of the Council, the world's bishops refused to endorse a list of men chosen by the Curia to run the Council's commissions; the elder statesmen among the non-Roman cardinals asked and were granted several days' adjournment so the bishops-at-large could come up with their own nominees. I quickly learned the names of those who had led this rebellion, and, once the "secret" sessions began in earnest, I learned just as quickly that they and their aides were only too eager to tell the world's press what was happening.

Furthermore, they didn't try to keep their machinations secret. Every noontime, I could find knots of bishops and theologians from France, Germany, Belgium, and the Netherlands gathering with reporters in or around St. Peter's Square to tell them what had gone on in the sessions just ended. At 12:30 every day, for example, just outside the official Vatican press center on the Via della Conciliazione, I could always find Father Jean Danielou, whooping excitedly in a kind of football huddle with his favorite French journalists, telling them about the best speeches of the day, and how those speeches furthered the strategy of either camp (for it was already clear that the Council was dividing into two general groupings, those who wanted the Church to change and those who wanted to see it remain pretty much as it was).

I learned to listen in on those huddles, note the names of the Council Fathers who had made things happen, then run off and try to get the complete Latin texts of those important speeches from the Council Fathers who'd given them. I found I didn't have to persuade these prelates to "break the Council secret." I found they wanted the world (and, incidentally, their fellow bishops) to understand what they had said.

The Council's first debate revolved around the liturgy, the whole of the Church's worship, and those interested in updating the Church's liturgy had already determined that the Mass and the sacraments should no longer be in Latin, but in the vernacular. The vernacular meant the language of the people and it seemed to me self-evident that if the Mass was for the people then the people ought to be able to understand it. The Council Fathers debated the questions for several weeks, with members of the Roman Curia and others with a Curial mindset taking furious exception to this proposal.

Why all the debate over the vernacular? Because it is a concept that goes beyond mere language. It can also stand for whatever is home-bred, homespun, homegrown, homemade — and this, I think, is why the Roman mind was so opposed to the vernacular. For centuries, the Church had been engaged in a centralizing and expropriating control — in every respect. Allowing the Church's worship in the vernacular would mean decentralization, of not only worship, but of power in many other areas as well. The resistance to the vernacular was a resistance to a shift of power — power to the people.

Msgr. Ivan Illich, of Cuernavaca, whom I had profiled for the world a year before in the pages of *Time,* pointed this out in a book of essays entitled *Shadow Work.* In one of those essays, "Vernacular Values," he discussed the role of a Spanish grammarian, Elio Antonio de Nebrija, who in 1492 presented to Queen Isabella a new grammar of the Castilian language, with the express purpose of providing her with a new instrument of imperial domination. Illich interpreted Nebrija as a forerunner of the modern age, in which the business of government (even, I think, Church government) is expropriation — taking away from people what they can create for themselves (in this case, ordinary speech) and forcing them to take it back in a transformed version, the standardized language taught by formal educators. The expropriation of language, said Illich, foreshadowed all later expropriations, each of which drove people further in the direction of helplessness and dependence. (There was nothing more standardized, of course, than the Church's official books of prayer and the Church's official theological handbooks, in just these exact Latin words and no other.)

If the Council encouraged people everywhere to worship in their own language, then, it might make those same people less passive, and help them seize control of their own lives. In essence, the other principle debates of the first session, on the Bible and on the nature of the Church revolved around the same questions: would Rome continue to keep Catholics clueless, or would it help them grow up? I can recall no one at the Council who saw these wider implications. At Vatican II, they were simply talking about putting the Mass in English, French, Spanish, German, Portuguese, Swahili, Urdu, Tagalog, and so on, almost ad infinitum.

It was laughable to me to see that some of the Council Fathers pushing hardest to keep everything in Latin could hardly deliver the Latin speeches that had been written for them (Cardinal McIntyre of Los Angeles was one of these) or even understand them, spoken as they were in dozens of varying accents, and with varying degrees of eloquence. After the first session, even Pericle Felici, the Council's secretary-general, admitted this when he reported that his office was besieged with episcopal requests for a complete transcript of the proceedings, because the Fathers said they had understood "only generally and in an incomplete fashion" the eight-hundred-odd speeches given that fall in Rome.

◌◌

DURING THAT FIRST SESSION, many bishops kept themselves informed on the chief debates by reading *La Croix,* a French Catholic tabloid sold in Rome, which was filled with long, actual quotes from the Council floor each day, and Paris's *Le Monde,* whose Henri Fesquet turned in three or four insightful stories a week. Many of the Fathers used *La Croix* and the monthly *Informations Catholiques Internationales* as a kind of Congressional Record to keep informed about what was being said. They used *Le Monde* to assess how well it was all coming across to the world outside. *Il Messagero* was also on top of everything. Its report on the Council's first closed session sounded as if Rome's largest daily had a team inside St. Peter's. Twelve hours before the Council Fathers knew whom they had elected to the conciliar commissions (to replace the members picked by the Curia), *Il Messagero* carried the complete list.

Many of my English-speaking colleagues at first ignored these sources; they took the conciliar secrecy literally and refused to print anything that didn't come out of the official press office. For me, truth was where I found it. As a result, for a while at least in the English-speaking world, *Time* was scooping both the secular and the Catholic press in the U.S. and Canada, England, Ireland, and Australia. The Council Fathers noticed: I heard that every Tuesday, the world's bishops were passing copies of *Time* from hand to hand up and down the conciliar bleachers — and commenting on the coverage.

One Tuesday, Bishop Francis Griffiths of New York handed a copy of *Time* to Bishop Wright. "Is this the same Council we're attending?" he asked sardonically. Bishop Wright shrugged and smiled, and later, telling me about that scene during a dinner at our home, explained that the Council was a kaleidoscope. "Everyone sees the Council from his own particular point of view," he said. "Bishop Griffiths obviously doesn't buy your interpretation." I looked a bit crestfallen. Wright quickly added, with a laugh. "But I do."

Some of my English-speaking colleagues accused me of getting inside the Council sessions. With a straight face, I told them I had been getting in, and why not? The system seemed to give unfair advantage to clerics: priest-journalists were inside, other journalists weren't. So, I told them, I had donned a cassock, put a surplice on my arm and stood outside

St. Peter's early one morning until I spied a kindly-looking bishop. I told him I was a cleric from California anxious to see a Council session from the inside. Without a moment's hesitation, the bishop escorted me in, found me a seat among the Council stenographers, and made sure I had a list of the day's speakers besides. "You can't tell the players without a scorecard," were his approximate words, in French. Well, I got a raft of good notes that day, but I felt a little guilty, especially when my benefactor came by and asked me how things had gone. "Your Excellency," I said, "I have a confession to make. I'm not a priest at all. I'm a journalist."

"Perfectly all right," he replied. "I'm not a bishop. I'm a journalist, too."

Of course, the story wasn't true. Much later in the Council, Desmond Fisher, one of the many good Irish reporters who were to make their way to Rome, made life imitate art by putting on a cassock and slipping into the aula with no trouble. At the beginning, since most of the English-speaking reporters were as rule-bound as most of the English-speaking prelates, those who were reading French, Belgian, Dutch, Spanish, and Italian newspapers were getting a better, more intimate view of the Council.

In a small way, I helped change the state of affairs in the English-speaking world. I had become a member of a consortium of journalists from many different countries, led by Roberto Tucci, the Jesuit editor of *La Civiltà Cattolica* (now Cardinal Tucci), who believed that the people of the world had a right to know what was happening here, Roman secrecy or no. Each member of the consortium was promoting a more open Council among his own country's bishops, but no one was pushing the U.S. bishops to do anything special.

Finally, I did. Under the urging of Father Tucci, I asked the American bishops to institute a daily briefing for American reporters. I did so by approaching Bishop Albert Zuroweste, head of the U.S. bishops' press committee; he consulted with his committee and within a few days something dubbed "The American Bishops' Press Panel" was holding a news conference every day at two-thirty in the basement of the U.S.O. offices on the Via della Conciliazione (originally set up as a hospitality house for American servicemen and women visiting Rome).

I had done a service for my journalistic rivals: at my suggestion, Bishop Zuroweste quickly put on the panel many of my own best private sources, including Msgr. Fred McManus, from Boston, the Paulist Tom Stransky, the Augustinian Gregory Baum, and the redoubtable Bishop Wright, all dinner regulars at our home. I had an idea that Bishop Zuroweste had met with opposition from some of his colleagues, but soon, I was told, the bishops could see that having a public panel was a good idea: English-speaking reporters, at least, weren't put in the position of having to chase down anonymous and sometimes unreliable sources, or, worse, to rewrite the often tendentious columns of the Rome daily *Il Tempo*.

Now, they could quote Fred McManus, for example, who was one of the *periti* (that is, expert theologians) on the liturgical commission, and get all the explanations they needed to make the Council's first debate, on the reform of the Church's liturgy, understandable to their readers. Under McManus' guidance, and that of others on the panel, my colleagues and I began to see that the Fathers' discussions over the advisability of simplifying the Mass and allowing it to be celebrated in the language of the people, instead of in Latin, bore on the entire mission of the Church: would the Church remain locked in its old forms, or become incarnate in all the world's cultures? It was a question that provoked a good deal of serious thought and some serious journalism.

The panelists, moreover, were able to put all this in homebred, homespun, homegrown, homemade American English. They were often funny, always entertaining, and soon other bishops, theologians, delegate-observers, even interested tourists, started filling up the basement hall to catch this great daily show. The U.S.O. soon became S.R.O.

14

The guest list made sense to me. It was a reception held to introduce the Protestant and other observers at the Council. So I was not surprised to see representatives of all the major Protestant churches on the list — Episcopalians, Lutherans, Methodists, Presbyterians, and so on. The name of Douglas Steer, a Quaker, aroused my curiosity. I sought out Steer. "I didn't think the Quakers were going to send anyone," I said.

"We heard the Council would deal with the large questions of war and peace," he said. "So we felt that we had to have someone in Rome."

But the Council didn't have war and peace on its agenda. "Where did you hear this?" I inquired.

"Why," he said, "from Archbishop Roberts."

"Roberts! From Bombay? Is he here?"

He smiled, pleased with himself. "I certainly hope so. I'm supposed to see him for lunch tomorrow."

Ah ha. The most important things going on at any convention, or congress, are often off-scene. And here was an important piece of para-conciliar activity that could lead to the kind of story that *Time* tried for all the time: some deeper significance that would draw in readers (including many of my editors in New York) who didn't give much of a damn for the Catholic Church. But now, if the Council was going to involve itself in geopolitics, then I was on to a good *Time* story, the kind of story that I was being paid to uncover.

So I wanted to see Roberts. He could tell me more, I was sure, about this "war and peace" business. And I had another, more personal reason for wanting to see him. His book, *Black Popes*, had had a special meaning for me when I was in the middle of making the first adult decision of my life, the decision to leave the Jesuits. I consulted a conciliar directory of the Council Fathers and discovered a Rome phone number, nothing more, for "Roberts, T. D." I dialed the number and an Italian nun answered. She left me holding for many minutes and then an English voice came on the line and said that yes, he was Roberts. "You're from *Time?*" he said. "You want to talk to me? Jolly good." We arranged to meet the next afternoon near the Piazza Navona, at the Foyer Unitas, a community run by some valiant women from the Netherlands.

At the appointed hour, I walked into a dim, oversized kind of library room at the Foyer, and found a slight figure with great bushy eyebrows sitting under a small lamp reading his breviary. Thomas D'Esterre Roberts was wearing a black cassock speckled with a thin layer of fine cigarette ash; it gave him a slightly raffish look, like Alec Guinness playing Gulley Jimson in the movie classic, *The Horse's Mouth.* He lowered a pair of black horn-rimmed spectacles, looked over the top of them at me with a twinkle in his eye and a wrinkle of his nose, and said, "Are you a Papist?"

I burst out laughing. I could see that this was a man with a fine sense of the absurd. The word Papist was a pejorative term in England, dating back to the time of Henry VIII; the use of it now by a Roman Catholic archbishop startled me. "Not only am I a Papist," I said, "I was a Jesuit for ten years. Sometimes, I think I am still a Jesuit." His bushy eyebrows worked a bit over that news, but I could tell that this created an instant understanding between us. I only enhanced the good feelings by telling him the best thing any writer can say to another writer — that I loved his book. In this case, I was talking about *Black Popes,* the seminal treatise on authority I'd recommended in vain to my former provincial, Carroll O'Sullivan.

He wrinkled his nose again. I would soon learn that he always wrinkled his nose, like a rabbit, whenever he was pleased, or about to deliver a zinger. His Grace — that's what I called him, at first, Your Grace, in the English mode — told me he wasn't even sure he was welcome at this Council. He said that in 1960 he had gotten some haughty letters from Archbishop Gerald O'Hara, the Apostolic Delegate in England, and Cardinal Godfrey of Westminster, who told him they'd "delated" *Black Popes* to the Holy Office for "the scandalous material" contained in it, though neither of them had ever bothered telling him how *Black Popes* was "scandalous." I frowned. Perhaps Roberts had nettled the defenders of the faith with his insistence that the Church had failed to understand its own authority, failed to incorporate the modern "discovery" of decentralized democratic structures into a system that had assumed (and never let go of) the medieval structures of a monarchy. My guess was that it wasn't just *Black Popes* that caused the trouble. After all, the book had been published more than a decade ago. My guess was that Roberts had become an aging *enfant terrible* and a general pain in the ass to all those who viewed the Church and the world in conventional ways.

Roberts was far from conventional. He was the only bishop in the world who advised Pope Pius XII in 1950 not to define as infallible the dogma of the Assumption of Our Lady. And he had marched with Bertrand Russell in a daring, ban-the-bomb campaign at a time when Catholics didn't march with Protestants (or heathens) in any kind of cause. In a mock serious tone, I asked him how he could urge the Quakers to come to a Council to look in on a debate on war and peace and The Bomb when these matters weren't even on the agenda. He wrinkled his nose and said that maybe the presence of the Quakers would help *get* the question on the agenda. I pondered that. I was astonished at the archbishop's frank admission that he was a kind of agent provocateur at this Council. He must have read my mind.

"Is there anything better I can do here," he said, "than to stop the world from blowing itself up?"

I had no good answer to that. I wondered to myself whether this raffish little Englishman, or even an entire Council, could stop the world's leaders from starting a nuclear war if they wanted to. Only time would tell about that. So I changed the subject and asked him how an archbishop, even a Jesuit archbishop, could turn out to be so, well, different. He said he'd tell me if I would drive him home. Bargain. He lived in a poor convent way up the Monte del Gallo, more than half an hour's drive, which was a good thing, because he needed all of that time, and more, to tell me something of the story of his life.

First of all, he said, his elevation to the episcopacy was a mistake. He'd just been minding his own business, serving as rector of a small college in Liverpool, when he got the news (from an inquiring newspaper reporter!) that Rome was making him the next archbishop of Bombay, India. He claimed that it wasn't until he had received the holy oils of episcopal consecration that some Vatican functionary discovered he'd tabbed the wrong English Jesuit. By then, of course, it was too late.

I thought to myself that this was a happy accident. Perhaps the Holy Spirit knew what She was doing. In teeming, turbulent, overcrowded, backward Bombay (where Catholics were less than one-half of one percent of the population), T. D. Roberts became a very pastoral, very compassionate shepherd who had a surfeit of free time on his hands to do some heavy thinking about the mission of the Church in the world. He thought the Church had unwisely tied itself to the Latin culture in which it took such solid root, that the missionaries who then branched out from that root did so not only to Christianize Asia and Africa and South America but to Europeanize those continents as well. The missionaries were colonizers for a particular culture as much as witnesses to Christ's coming for all humankind.

In India, Christianity was hardly a light to the world; it was more of a dim bulb. Mohandas Gandhi's teachings were more relevant to India's masses than those of Christ, or his representatives on earth. For one thing, the representatives of Christ were foreigners. That was a barrier to the advance of the Gospel (although the Gospel's "advance" for Roberts would probably consist in its being entirely assimilated into the Indian cultures in such a manner that it would give birth to a form of Christianity that western Europeans would hardly recognize). He himself, a stranger in a strange land, was probably more of a hindrance than a help to the spread of the Gospel in India.

Roberts' first step became clear: he would have to abdicate his office. He could see that Gandhi's movement would eventually end with the banishment of the British. For that reason, Roberts sent Pope Pius XII a series of letters telling him that the Church didn't need an Englishman in Bombay, it needed a native Indian archbishop. The pope did not agree. Ever since the Vatican and Portugal had signed a concordat in 1928, English and Portuguese Jesuit missionaries had held sway over this ecclesiastical territory in alternating terms of office. The tradition wasn't ancient, but it was firmly juridicized. The pope wouldn't change it.

Roberts knew that the pope might regret that decision. He saved the situation by a bit of cunning. In 1946, when the Atlee government in England committed itself to Indian independence, he simply got the pope to agree that he should, at least, let him have an Indian auxiliary bishop. Roberts had just the chap in mind for the job, a tall, stately young priest named Valerian Gracias. Gracias was duly consecrated and then, after a decent interval, Roberts packed a valise, walked out the door and told Gracias over his shoulder to run the show — because he was taking a two-year trip around the world via tramp steamer. Gracias was still holding on when, as Roberts had expected, India went independent. In 1950, Roberts made his way to Naples, got off his steamer, entrained to Rome, and paid a call on the pope.

"You see?" Roberts told Pius XII. "Now you have a native Indian in Bombay just when you need him." The pope fixed Roberts with a long, deep, unsmiling stare, then nodded and sighed in French, *Bien.* There was only one thing wrong with this idea: it was not the pope's own idea. But, other than that, why was it not good to have a native Indian doing a fine job in Bombay? Gracias would soon become the first native Indian cardinal. As for Roberts, he had schemed himself out of a job. The pope suggested he might return to England where he could preach at the Jesuits' famous church on Farm Street. Though Pius XII made no mention of this, the "witty, charming, and ugly" George Tyrell had once been a popular preacher at the same Farm Street.

We were parked in front of Roberts' shabby convent. The archbishop hurried to a finish. "The rest of the story," he said with a wave of his hand, "you already know. *Black Popes.* Cardinal Godfrey. The Holy Office. Bertrand Russell. The Bomb." He stared ahead through the window of my VW at the macadamed bleakness of the street, not a tree or even a bush in sight.

I felt like his confessor. "You feel isolated out here?" I asked. He nodded.

Suddenly, I suggested that he might like to come home with me to dinner — that very night. I didn't have to urge him. We drove directly back to Monteverde Vecchio and as we did so Roberts asked me about Mrs. Kaiser. "How can she stand all these — people you bring home?"

"Mary?" I said. "She's got a thing about clerics. She loves 'em."

Mary needed no prompting. She loved Archbishop Roberts. He told a lot of stories, he had a brandy or two, he bounced little Betsy on his lap, he told some more stories. Mary and I had the same idea almost simultaneously. His Grace was lonely and alone. We had a spare bedroom. Why didn't he stay with us? He pondered that invitation for a millisecond and said he'd be delighted. I moved him in the next day.

❦

WITH MY OWN Council Father in residence, so to speak, I had an edge on the other journalists at the Council. I began learning things from Roberts that I couldn't get from the official daily briefings at the Press Center. For one thing, each day, he routinely handed me all the secret documents of the Council. They were in Latin. But I read Latin rather well. Roberts gave me more than that. Through him, I began to see the

Council and its changing moods through the eyes of a Council Father, and from a Council Father who was also becoming a part of my own family. Each evening, I'd get home to find him preparing for Mass, which he celebrated conversationally, primitively, on a table at one end of our triple living room. "The biggest, most undreamed of thrill of all," Mary wrote home to her family, "is having His Grace say Mass every day in our very own living room. He says Mass facing Betsy and me, with Bob next to him, serving. What a blessing for us."

Afterward, we'd have a cocktail and some dinner, and talk about the Council's proceedings, trade rumors and gossip of the day, discuss who'd said what to whom at the two bars behind the main altar at St. Peter's, the Bar Jonah and the Bar Rabbas (where they served brandy and schnapps as well as café espresso).

"They turned Ottaviani off today," T. D. reported one evening with a chuckle. "He had gone far beyond the ten-minute item limit. After a warning by the chair, he found he was speaking into a dead microphone."

Ottaviani boycotted the Council for a number of days after that, and there was no official accounting for his absence. Then T. D. came home with a story, picked up at the Bar Jonah. "Now they say the reason why Ottaviani hasn't been coming," reported T. D. with a wrinkle of his nose, "is that his chauffeur kept him waiting so long the other morning that he called a passing taxi and told the driver, 'To the Council.' " T. D. paused, then added laconically, with perfect timing, "The cabbie drove him to Trent."*

The Council sessions lasted until midday. Then the bishops would come pouring down the steps of St. Peter's like a flowing red and purple waterfall. Sometimes, I'd pick up T. D. at 12:30 and take him home for lunch. On days when I had other appointments, T. D. seemed to make his way home all right. Sometimes, he'd get a ride from one of the other Council Fathers (Cardinal Koenig of Vienna lived a few blocks away, at the Salvator Mundi Hospital), or he'd catch a municipal bus. Sometimes, he'd nap after lunch. An increasing number of visitors started arriving around teatime, allies and potential allies in his efforts to get the question of war and peace and The Bomb put on the Council's agenda. His own afternoon guest list began to include a steady stream of ban-the-bombers, Czech and Polish and Hungarian bishops who wanted to go back to their

---

*Trent, the town where Catholic bishops and theologians met in Council from 1545 to 1563 to set a strategy for the Church's four-hundred-year battle against Protestantism, is in the Italian Alps, hundreds of miles from Rome.

governments with a pacifist statement from the Council, members of the UN's Food and Agricultural Organization, English civil libertarians, Indian converts in saffron colored saris, Quakers in severe black woolen suits, ex-priests in trouble, seminarians who wanted to know how to disobey their superiors, journalists who wanted to interview him, and artists who wanted to draw him.

On one afternoon, I came home early to find an interesting guest having tea, Dominicus Yoshimatsu Noguchi, the Japanese bishop of Hiroshima. I could not speak Japanese, nor any of his other languages. He could not speak English, or any of mine. We traded pleasantries in Latin. He tried to tell me that the Japanese bishops, for all the horrors they had suffered in August 1945, did not want to be used by the world's pacifists (including Roberts). Nevertheless, I tried to tell him that I, an American, was sorry we had dropped The Bomb on his people. He nodded, and judging from the way that his eyes lit up, I could see that I had helped destroy something of his image of Americans as a bunch of thermonuclear madmen.

With our enthusiastic go-ahead, T. D. started inviting some of his new-found friends to supper and we were delighted one night to find that he'd invited Archbishop Denis Hurley of Durban, South Africa, Archbishop Eugene D'Souza of Nagpur, India, and Bishop Gerard Van Velsen of Kroonstadt, South Africa, all three of them warm, loving pastors whom I imagined made their people feel thankful to be Christians. I was collecting my own favorites among the Council Fathers,* and it wasn't hard to persuade them to come and join my Rome regulars, many of them Jesuits from scattered parts of the world.

Our spacious apartment, with its huge picture windows and sparkling marble floors, became something of a gathering place for conciliar progressives. Mary was often the only woman in the house, and she became an unflappable hostess. Practically every other night of the week, we'd have a small dinner party for eight. One Sunday night, Frank McCool, the vice-rector of the Biblicum, brought some extra, though uninvited, guests: Thurston Davis, Donald Campion and Robert Graham, all editors of *America*, the U.S. Jesuit weekly. Our sit-down supper became a buffet.

---

*Chief among them were: John Wright of Pittsburgh, Paul Hallinan of Atlanta, Leonard Cowley of Minneapolis, Peter Bartholme of St. Cloud, Leo Dworshak of Fargo, Robert Tracy of Baton Rouge, Ernest Primeau of Manchester, Emmett Carter of London, Ontario, Joseph Blomjous of Mwanza, Tanzania, Vincent McCauley of Fort Portal, Uganda, and Guilford Young of Hobart, Tasmania.

That was such a success that we told our friends to invite their friends, every Sunday. We'd always have room for one more, we said, and the very next week the "one more" turned into several score more. A kind of institution was born at Vatican II: the Kaisers' Sunday nights.

Roberts blossomed. Far from being isolated in his resistance to the antediluvian minds of the Roman Curia, he found that his venturesome opinions were shared by many others, including some of the best prelates in Christendom. With him, they thought (and said out loud) that the Church was overloaded with excess baggage, myth, superstition and nonsense. With him, they voted on all the important reforms of Vatican II, most of which tended to make the Church less Roman — and more Catholic.

For me, having Roberts around was also a private delight. Every morning, after I had gotten Betsy up and changed her diaper and played with her for awhile, I'd drive him to the Council. He hated the regal trappings of his office, mumbled when he got tangled in his robes as we climbed into my yellow Volkswagen, and made clear his antipathy for humbug whenever he had a chance. One morning, when a pilgrim in St. Peter's Square asked him to bless her rosary, he grimaced and gave it a perfunctory wave. He wore no episcopal ring and if anyone asked him about it (thinking they might be expected to kiss it), he said with a grin and a wrinkle of his nose that he kept it in his back pocket.

But he was not a gruff one. He and Betsy devised a little game. She'd sit in his lap and pull on his bushy eyebrows and tweak his parrot-like beak until he'd cry. But his tears weren't tears of pain, they were tears of joy from a love-starved old man who should have had a family of his own.

15

I was a little miffed. Ben Meyer and Bill Moran, my friends from the Biblical Institute, were my dinner guests at least once a week, and they had known that I was putting in long hours trying to understand all the issues that were going to come up at the Council. But they'd failed to tell me about the virulence of the fight between the Church's Biblical scholars and those in the Roman Curia who were trying to do them in. Maybe they were too close to the battle to see how newsworthy it was. Maybe they were holding back on me because they didn't feel they could assume responsibility for taking their private little war into the pages of *Time*. Or perhaps they didn't foresee how their Biblical Institute would be at the center of the first session's most dramatic debate.

As it turned out, someone who called himself Xavier Rynne broke much of the story in the October 20 issue of the *New Yorker*, in a long gossipy piece entitled "Letter from Vatican City." *Time*'s John Elson, son of the *Life* writer, Bob Elson, airmailed me a copy of the article and asked me what I knew about Xavier Rynne. He said there was a rumor going around New York that I was Xavier Rynne. I wish I had been. The article was journalism of a high order, contemporary history done with the sure touch of a modern Herodotus, and it was all about the Roman Curia's attack on the Jesuit professors of the Biblical Institute — and the counterattack, by the Jesuits and others trained by the Jesuits.

I went to the Biblicum, a rose-colored seventeenth-century palace at the foot of the Quirinal Hill, and, rather than bring Ben or Bill into this, I rang for Frank McCool, the vice-rector. McCool was a Bronx-born American, a graying man with a heavy paunch and a bit of an Irish brogue and a lot of sparkle in his cool blue eyes. I had a copy of the *New Yorker* in my right hand, tapped it on the palm of my left and said, "Is this stuff true, Frank?"

He didn't play games with me, didn't pretend he hadn't seen the piece. In fact, he said, he had had a lot to do with the article himself. He had given Xavier Rynne some of the material in it and he was making copies of it available to every English-speaking bishop he could collar, to get them ready for the conciliar debate on the whole scriptural question. I confessed that I didn't even know the state of the question. I'd seen T. D.'s copy of the *schema* on scripture but I really didn't have enough background to understand much of what was at stake. "We're talking as much about politics as we are about doctrine," said McCool. "And if you want to know what's at stake, it's the very existence of the Biblical Institute itself — and the entire future of scholarship in the Church."

He leaned back in his chair, lit a pipe and told me to get comfortable while he taught me a little history. "I don't know how much you know about the Biblicum," he said. "We've got more than 250 priests doing doctoral work here — from 43 different countries. We've only been in business a few short decades. But we've turned out more than 1200 graduates. They're doing fine work now all over the world, a lot of it in collaboration with Protestant Biblical scholars. We've helped create an intellectual revolution in the sacred sciences."

"And what," I said, "is so wrong with this?"

"There are elements in the Curia who think we're teaching heresy. That *schema* on scripture that you've read may look like pretty tame stuff to you. It's dynamite. Ottaviani and his crowd wrote it. If the Council Fathers approve it, we're dead."

"How?"

McCool proceeded to tell me all about the Catholic Biblical movement — which didn't really start until the beginning of the twentieth century, and then got an immediate setback when the heresy hunters of that period of the Church called the Modernist crisis went after Marie Joseph Lagrange, the founder of the Dominican's *École Biblique* in Jerusalem and the brightest Catholic Biblical scholar of his day. On June 29, 1912, the Holy Office came out with a decree forbidding Father Lagrange to continue teaching at the *École* and banning all his works in all the Catholic seminaries of the world. Obediently, he returned to France, and marked time there writing innocuous commentaries on the New Testament until his death.

Decades later, when a pope who had been a scholar himself came to the Chair of Peter, he decided to get Biblical scholarship in the Church moving again. That man was Pius XI, who approved the appointment of the German Jesuit Augustin Bea as rector of the Biblical Institute in Rome and charged him with the task of forming future professors of scripture in Catholic seminaries around the world.

For a time, the Institute made solid, if unspectacular progress, but soon after Pius XII came to the papacy, members of the Roman Curia began to play the old anti-Modernist game again and started attacking the orthodoxy of the whole Biblical movement. Pius XII answered these attacks with the encyclical letter *Divino Afflante Spiritu* (drafted by Father Bea). In that letter, the pope finally gave the scholars the charter they needed to plumb the depths of the Scriptures with all the scientific tools at their disposal. These included ancillary sciences like archeology, paleontology, Semitic languages, and ancient literature. In particular, the pope dwelt on the use of what he called "literary forms" and considered the particular type of "history" found in the bible.

To a modern, history is an account of events "just as they really happened." Biblical history is not that kind of history. It is "salvation history" — the story of God's self-revelation to mankind through various literary forms understandable to the men and women who lived during the times when that history was being written. These men and women were not abstractions and God did not deal with them as if they were. They existed in a real environment and God spoke to them there, in their own languages. So far, so good, in principle, and especially as long as the scholars confined themselves to interpretations of the Old Testament.

But when the scholars started applying literary form criticism to the New Testament, then they were in trouble. Example: The New Testament stories surrounding Christ's birth. Were they really true? Yes, said the Biblical scholars, but not exactly and literally true. McCool instanced the story of the Magi, the Three Wise Men from the East who came to Bethlehem bringing gifts of gold and frankincense and myrrh. Many Catholic Biblical scholars now believed that the Magi weren't historical figures at all, but characters in a literary form called a midrash, concocted by an inspired storyteller to get across an idea that was fairly revolutionary to observant Jews. The Messiah had come to save not only God's chosen people, the Jews, but the Gentiles as well (symbolized by the Magi).

"To some men in the Curia," McCool said, "this is heresy. And it isn't only the story of the Magi that bothers them. They don't like anything we're doing. They want to get rid of us." He showed me some evidence, a jaundice-colored thirty-six-page pamphlet penned in Italian by a professor at the Lateran University named Msgr. Francesco Spadafora. "When every single Council Father got his credentials here in Rome, he got one of these, too." McCool tapped the copy on his desk several times. "It's an outright attack on our whole approach here, our teaching of form criticism. In it, Spadafora urges the Fathers to make an explicit condemnation of form criticism — and of the Biblicum, too."

I asked McCool about one of Xavier Rynne's stories — that a consortium of conservative Italian prelates had already succeeded in getting two of the Biblicum's top men taken out of Biblical exegesis (that is, interpretation) and demoted to the teaching of ancient languages.

He nodded. "I wish you wouldn't make a big deal out of this," he said. "It's true, but we're trying to get these men reinstated and a lot of press isn't going to help them right now. We're trying to work on this quietly."

"But what did they do?" I demanded.

"Well, the charge is that Stanislaus Lyonnet has perverted the sense of original sin as taught by the Council of Trent. And that Maximilian Zerwick has denied the historicity of Matthew Sixteen, verses sixteen to nineteen."

I whistled. In the Vatican, Matthew 16:18 ("I will give you the keys of the kingdom") was the deed to the house, the last will, the ultimate warrant not only for all the Church's spiritual power, but for all the real estate that went along with it: St. Peter's, the Sistine Chapel, the Vatican Museum, not to mention the Vatican Bank and the millions of dollars it had invested with Merrill Lynch. Matthew 16 was real money. I said to McCool, "You talk about charges. Was there a trial?"

"No. We simply went to the Congregation of Seminaries and said Spadafora had gotten some bad information about Zerwick and Lyonnet. We thought that would do the trick. The next thing we knew the Holy Office sent us a note demanding the end of their exegetical careers."

I nodded and said this was a part I understood. It was another piece of a pattern that I was getting accustomed to. Some powerful men in the Curia were still fighting the old battle between the Church and science, for scriptural studies had become a science, allied, perhaps, with archaeology. For too long, they'd looked through the telescope of Galileo and saw only danger to the City of God. (And, in the case of Max Zerwick, danger to Vatican City as well.) "So what's the answer to all this?" I said. "What are you going to do?"

"The answer? The answer is the Council. Soon, they'll have this *schema* on scripture up for discussion. In the main, it's the work of Ottaviani and his crowd. If it passes, the Biblicum is done for. If it doesn't, well, we'll see if we can't get a new mandate from the Council to take its place."

"What kind of mandate do you want?"

"We want the Council Fathers to cast their vote for the scholars in the Church."

"And why is that so important?"

McCool paused for a moment. "We can't keep asking the people to swallow words they can't understand. This is what the Council is all about: we're trying to reformulate the faith in concepts that make sense to people today."

"O.K." I said. I was pleased because McCool had helped me play catch-up with this new rival of mine, this Xavier Rynne. I grabbed my trenchcoat. McCool walked me down to the nicely landscaped courtyard of the Biblicum. I stopped in front of the porter's lodge, hesitated, then had one more question for McCool. "This Xavier Rynne," I said. "You know who he is?"

McCool's blue eyes twinkled and then he threw back his head and laughed, showing me some fine gold fillings. "I don't really know," he said. "But you might want to talk to Frank Murphy."

"Murphy?" I said. I'd been to a party early in the summer that Bill McHale had thrown for the leading reporters living in Rome, but I didn't recall meeting a Frank Murphy.

"Frank Murphy is a Redemptorist priest," he said. "He's from the Bronx, as I am, but he's been teaching here for years. He lives over on the Via Merulana." He gave me a little wink. "Don't tell him I told you. Ask him his middle name. And ask him his mother's maiden name."

I smiled, happy to learn that perhaps my rival was no mere layman, but an obvious insider in Rome. It was no shame to be scooped by an insider. But I was surprised to learn that he was a Redemptorist. In my book, Redemptorists were a bit backward. They had a reputation for preaching a lot of hellfire and damnation, and at this Council, I saw a Redemptorist in action every day at the U.S. Bishops' Press Panel. He was Father Francis Connell, a likeable old fussbudget who was so full of distinctions and subdistinctions on the differences between mortal and venial sins that he reminded me of nothing so much as one of the Pharisees so scorned by Jesus.

Back in my office, I phoned Murphy at the Redemptorist College. He sounded a bit taken aback when I identified myself. I mentioned nothing about the *New Yorker,* or his suspected role in the "Letter from Vatican City." I simply invited him to come over the following Sunday night. He took down my address, asked me what part of Rome it was in and allowed that Monteverde Vecchio was quite a ways away. "Well," I said, "come if you can."

He didn't come that next Sunday. Mary and I had another surprise visitor instead — Father Gustave Weigel, the well-known Jesuit ecumenist whom I had interviewed in Woodstock, Maryland, before I had drawn my assignment to Rome. Now, here he was, come late to the Council to serve as a liaison with the delegate-observers for Cardinal Bea's Secretariat. Weigel was a cadaverous hulk, with a huge nose, baleful eyes, sparse dark hair plastered down on a mostly bald pate, and a deeply pessimistic view of life. "According to Weigel's law," he told me once, "everything in life has a way of turning out — badly." But he had a heart full of affection for those people who were real. That first night, he matched me martini for martini and our little daughter made an attempt to repeat his name. It came out as "Eagle." From then on, Father Gus was Betsy's Eagle.

༄

BY EARLY NOVEMBER, the Fathers were beginning to see their way. They had surprised themselves for voting in such overwhelming numbers in favor of the vernacular. Now as they turned to the *schema* on Scripture, they found themselves being lobbied by both sides. Cardinal Bea had done a special fifty-nine-page article trying to explain what the Bible scholars were up to — trying to make the scriptures more understandable to the people — then saw that it was translated into four languages and sent around Rome to a selected list of northern European bishops. Meanwhile, Cardinal Ernesto Ruffini of Palermo (himself a graduate of the Biblical Institute) had been giving speeches to Italian, Spanish, and Latin-American bishops urging them to pass the scriptural *schema* as written.

On November 13, Weigel warned me, "Tomorrow, the bare-knuckle fight begins." When I drove T. D. to the Council the next morning, I told him how much I'd like to get inside, just for this session. He said, "You may not have to get in. They may blow the roof right off St. Peter's." He told me to pick him up at 12:30, so he could give me his blow-by-blow account.

When that morning's session adjourned, I was standing just to the south of the basilica, right outside the Holy Office, and as I watched the bishops stream by I could see their faces glowing. Bishop Leo Dworshak of Fargo stopped and told me with a grin, "The *proelium Domini* (the battle of the Lord) has begun." Soon, T. D. came tottering along, wrinkling his nose and clutching a notebook. He'd filled several pages with his own account of the goings-on, and hastened to tell me about the assault on the Ottaviani *schema*.

T. D. said, "Old Ottaviani himself was here today. He introduced the *schema* with this opening, get this: 'The teaching of truth is always and everywhere the same....'" I laughed. T. D. had already told me that the motto on Ottaviani's coat of arms read *Semper Idem,* always the same.

We were caught in a little traffic jam, sitting there amid a chorus of honking horns while T. D. began his report. "I'm stunned," he said. "I didn't think these blokes had it in them. But they blasted Ottaviani to smithereens. The first intervention came from Lille," said T. D. — making his habitual identification of a bishop by citing the name of his see; here it was Cardinal Achille Lienart of Lille, in France. "Lille said the *schema* was hopelessly inadequate and that it failed to take into account the tremendous progress made in scriptural scholarship during the last forty years, by Protestants as well as Catholics."

T. D. also liked Cardinal Frings of Cologne. "Cologne was almost poetic. He said that truth is like music and that this *schema* belongs to the wrong class of music." (It is almost certain that the author of Frings' allusive intervention was his young aide, Joseph Ratzinger, an accomplished pianist, who would later take Ottaviani's job at the Holy Office under John Paul II.)

"Lienart and Frings?" I said. "They're both graduates of the Biblicum, aren't they?"

T. D. said that he thought that they were. "But I don't know what that proves. The next man to get up was Palermo." (He was referring to Cardinal Ruffini of Palermo.) "He was all for the *schema*. He said that this was the pope's own *schema*. How, therefore, could anyone presume to attack it?" T. D. consulted his notes again as we broke through the traffic jam and started to climb up the Janiculum. "Genoa said he liked the *schema,* too." Uh huh, I said to myself, Cardinal Siri would like it. "He likes it because it guards the Church against the danger of modern heresy."

T. D. continued. "The next six cardinals at the microphone all attacked it. Montreal said the *schema* was plagiarized from some out-of-date textbooks. Vienna said it avoided all the important questions. Utrecht refuted Palermo, said the Fathers were really showing reverence to the pope and the pope's Council by engaging in discussion. Brussels said that one part of the *schema non placet* and the other part *minus placet.*"

"Huh?"

T. D. wrinkled his nose. "One part of the *schema,*" he explained, "did not please and the other part was even less pleasing." He went on. "St. Louis" — Ah yes, I thought, Cardinal Elmer Ritter — "St. Louis said the *schema* did not fit modern needs and had a pessimistic, negative tone." T. D. looked over at me. "Ritter's right. We're talking about the Gospel, the so-called Good News. And Ottaviani makes it sound gloomy." He went on reading from his notes. "Then Cardinal Bea got up. By now, it was past 10:30, time for me to go to the coffee bar. I didn't make a move. And neither did anyone else. Bea said this *schema* didn't meet the needs of this Council, which was called to bring the Church up to date and to promote Christian unity. He said it would close the door to intellectual Europe and turn away the outstretched hands of friendship in both the Old and the New World."

T. D. said Maximos IV Saigh, the Melkite patriarch of Antioch, spoke in French (his usual open protest against the Latinization of the universal Church) and said the language of the *schema* sounded like "outmoded formulas of the Counter Reformation and anti-Modernism." T. D. said that maybe a dozen others spoke. "Many of them urged the Fathers to have confidence in the Church's scholars and theologians."

"Well," I said, "one swallow doesn't make a spring. But I think the men from the Biblicum did their job." I delivered T. D. to our door, then turned right around and drove back to the Council's press office to pick up the day's official communiqué. By T. D.'s account, this was the most exciting day of the Council so far, but the handout gave little hint of that, or of the fact that there was an overwhelming dissatisfaction with the *schema*. It read: "The various positions were outlined: the first favorable to the project, the second unfavorable, and the third asking for its reworking. All agreed that the work of preparation had been very accurate. All, however, admitted that the project on the whole must be perfected." That was all the communiqué said. Given the bias of the official press office, that is just about all it could have said. The top officials in the Roman Curia would have deemed anything more as treason.

During the rest of that week, the progressives kept blasting away at the Ottaviani *schema,* with Ottaviani offering only legalistic arguments on its behalf.

Of all the arguments I heard, I liked best the words of Bishop Charue of Namur, emphasizing the possible impact on the modern world of a biblical science that is really scientific. "The best means of entering the modern world," he said, "is to encourage the scholars." He added that if the Church did not do that now, it would regret the day "as much as it now regrets its silly position on Galileo."

♪

THAT SUNDAY NIGHT, I took no chance on Frank Murphy's not coming to the party. I phoned and asked if I could pick him up in my VW at seven o'clock. He said that would be fine — as long as I promised to get him home by ten. "We have rules here," he warned. He sounded severe over the phone. In person, he was a grinning, grizzled Irish pixie.

"What's your middle name?" I asked him as soon as he climbed into the car.

"Xavier," he said.

"What's your mother's maiden name?"

He said, "Rynne."

"Then you're Xavier Rynne," I said in triumph.

He laughed, "No, I'm not Xavier Rynne."

We played some verbal games. It was clear that, on a technicality, he wasn't the *New Yorker*'s Xavier Rynne, not all of Rynne. Later, I found some samples of Murphy's own prose style. It lacked the knowing sophistication of the *New Yorker*. In fact, it didn't even come close. Obviously, he had a collaborator who could write, which meant that Xavier Rynne was a composite creature: Frank Murphy supplying the gossip and someone else putting it in form.* But I could understand Murphy's reluctance to take

---

*In the spring of 1997, I visited Frank Murphy, then pretty much retired, at the Redemptorist house in Annapolis, Maryland. He made a clean breast, then, of the whole story behind Xavier Rynne. It seems that a New York book editor named John Chapin had been doing some editing at the time for the Redemptorists, and that he, Murphy, had given Chapin a look at his long, rambling story of the battle for the Bible that had been going on behind the scenes in Rome. Murphy was hoping to place the piece in a Catholic magazine, though he wasn't quite sure which magazine. Chapin quickly recognized that this was a story that was good enough for a wider audience, and phoned Robert Giroux, the Manhattan book editor who had discovered the Trappist Tom Merton many years before, and published Merton's *Seven Storey Mountain.* "I may have another discovery, for

any credit for this stuff. That could hurt him and his Redemptorists, too, when the Council was over and the Curia resumed control of the Church.

I remember that Sunday night in November, remember it particularly well because we had rented a piano that week. When Mary had discovered that one of our regulars, Archbishop Hallinan of Atlanta, loved to play, she came to me and said, "Bob, we've got to get a piano. What's a party without a piano?" Mary wanted to bring a little of Irish Milwaukee to Rome. Nothing like a piano, then, where people could crowd around and sing the sentimental songs that Irish folk (and their non-Irish friends) favor whenever they gather for a jar or two.

Mary and I had gotten a caterer to put on this week's buffet and when I arrived with Frank Murphy, I could see that the caterer had filled two tables with spiced baked hams and crusty beef roasts and turkeys barbecued to a dark gold. In our entrance hall, there was a table that served as a bar, stocked with local wines and Dutch beer, with scotch and bourbon and gin and vodka, mixes of all kinds and bags of ice and cases of glasses, and by 7:15, some American students from Loyola University of Chicago's Rome campus were already in place and serving drinks.

By 7:30, taxis were pulling up in front of Via Quirico Filopanti 2. We had a full floor in a new five-story villa, with huge picture windows looking out over Trastevere, and a triple living room. Now the place was beginning to fill with black cassocks and episcopal purple. Art Yzermans, priest-editor of the diocesan newspaper in St. Cloud, Minnesota, arrived with a theologian I had heard a good deal about but never met before. His name

---

you," said Chapin. "It will make a book. It might even make a piece in the *New Yorker.*" Giroux looked at Murphy's notes, and agreed with Chapin. "Put this in *New Yorker*-ese," he said, "and we will have something." The rest is history. The Chapin/Murphy team went on to do their chatty contemporary history of the Council in the *New Yorker,* and Giroux produced four best selling volumes of *Letters From Vatican City* for his publishing house, Farrar, Straus and Giroux. Xavier Rynne became a delicious piece of Council history.

There'd been a rumor going around Rome that I was Xavier Rynne. A good many folks, including Sen. Eugene McCarthy and Archbishop Pietro Parente, then the number two man in the Holy Office, asked me if the rumor was true, and Parente didn't believe me when I denied it. More than thirty-five years later, I discovered on a trip to Asia that a number of Jesuits in Sri Lanka and Indonesia still believed I was Rynne. Now I am tempted to conclude that Murphy himself had been the man whispering my name on the Roman gossip network. He was the only one who had anything to gain. He was on the faculty of Rome's ultraconservative Lateran University, where he picked up some of his choicest items. If his colleagues there ever found out that he was a pipeline to the *New Yorker,* there would have been hell to pay.

was Hans Küng and he had already written a best-selling book translated into many languages on his hopes for a truly reformist Council.

Küng had verve and Teutonic good looks; he didn't wear a cassock but a tailored black suit, not a round Roman collar but a white cotton shirt with a dark tie, and his golden hair sat in high waves on his head. I was surprised at his youth (he was thirty-five, I discovered, just a little older than I) and I was glad that he was not intimidated by this mostly English-speaking crowd. In fact, his English was pretty good, though he was inclined to have trouble with his J's.

Soon, T. D. Roberts came out of his room, introduced himself around and began talking to Küng immediately about his favorite subject, Ottaviani's Inquisition, euphemistically known as the Holy Office. "Now take Parente for example. Archbishop Parente, I should say. He's the assessor of the Holy Office, whatever that means. Sounds rather like a tax collector, doesn't it? Well, at any rate, Parente gets up in the Council this week and says that the Church needs no reform, that it is already without spot or wrinkle." T. D. worked his nose. A zinger was coming. "Well, I say she's still got bulges in all the wrong places. And one of them is the Holy Office itself."

Hans Küng laughed appreciatively and Art Yzermans, who had joined the group also chuckled. Thus encouraged, T. D. continued. "Now the trouble with the Holy Office is that it insists on doing everything in secret. To the modern Western mind, there's something radically wrong with that. Justice must not only be done, it must also be seen to be done. The old star-chamber kind of justice does not wash."

"Wash, wash?" asked Küng. "What is this 'wash?'" T. D. explained. "Oh," said Küng showing his dimples. "Oh, yes, wash. Yes, you are right. That kind of chustice does not wash. Not anymore."

T. D. wrinkled his nose, ready to deliver another quotable one-liner. I moved off because others were arriving, most of them my clerical regulars. Tom Stransky came with Jim Sheerin, the Paulist editor of the *Catholic World,* and Gregory Baum, a German Jew who had fled to Canada with his parents before the war and converted to Catholicism. Bob Tucci arrived with his opposite number from Paris, Robert Rouquet of *Etudes,* and Bob Graham of *America.* I turned around and found that three of my better sources had suddenly materialized: Msgr. Fred McManus of Boston, an expert in liturgical matters, who drank only Coca Cola, and George Higgins, a labor priest from Washington, D.C., who drank only scotch.

Jorge Mejía, an exuberant priest-journalist from Argentina, introduced a Latin American contingent that included the darkly handsome Ivan Illich of Cuernavaca, looking like he had stepped out of a painting by El Greco, along with Betsy Hollants, solid and fiftyish, one of the lieutenants in the peculiar culture war that Illich was fighting out of Cuernavaca. Then along came Leo Alting von Geusau, director of the Dutch Documentation Center in Rome, with one of his aides, a buxom blonde named Jeanne, and two topnotch laymen, Jean Vogel, my Parisian friend from *Informations Catholiques Internationales,* and Jan Grootaers, a correspondent for *Die Maand* of Brussels.

The rooms became alive with chatter and laughter and the decibel level rose as the familiar faces appeared at our front door. There were also a good many faces we did not know, but Mary and I had no difficulty making each of them feel immediately welcome. We steered them toward the bar and over to the buffet table and nature took its course. Soon they were deep in conversation with people they had read before, but never dreamed of meeting. "I've heard of your work in Cuernavaca," I overheard Jim Sheerin saying to Ivan Illich, "Now tell me, just what do you have against Yankee missionaries?"

Archbishop Hallinan and Bishop Robert Tracy arrived together, and Mary kissed both of them on the cheek and showed them the piano. Soon, Hallinan was at the keyboard, and Mary and a small crowd (including Frank Murphy) were singing, "My Wild Irish Rose" and "Sweet Rosie O'Grady" and "Rose of Washington Square." The party had begun.

Gus Weigel arrived with a bishop in tow who was new to me. "I taught this young man," he said proudly, "and now look at him. He's on the Theological Commission, keeping Cardinal Ottaviani in line."

The bishop, who was at least a head taller than Gus, was Mark McGrath of Panama. He laughed a modest laugh over Gus's introduction, but Gus knew what he was saying. Others told me that McGrath was elected to Ottaviani's Commission precisely because Council progressives got out the word that McGrath stood for growth in the Church, in its understanding of itself, in the development of doctrine. McGrath told me more about himself. He had an American father and a Panamanian mother, and he was a citizen of Panama. He was also a member of the Congregation of the Holy Cross and a graduate of the University of Notre Dame, which his congregation had founded in Indiana in 1842.

In came a professor from one of Notre Dame's old rivals on the gridiron, Albert Outler from Southern Methodist University, one of the Protestant observers. I introduced him to McGrath and soon the two of them were comparing the relative all-round punting, passing, and running skills of SMU's Doak Walker and ND's Paul Hornung. And here was another observer, Robert McAfee Brown, the Presbyterian from Stanford, wearing a tweedy jacket and bow tie, and the Lutheran observer, George Lindbeck, and his wife, Vi, who had become more than occasional Sunday night drop-ins.

Now McGrath and the three Protestants shifted their focus from football to the week just ended at the Council. They spoke like equals, each adding a bit of his own understanding to the play and by-play between Archbishop Parente and Cardinal Gilroy. "When Cardinal Gilroy cited the rules right back at Archbishop Parente," Outler was saying in his broad Texas accent, "it wasn't much of a move, but it was significant, if you knew what was happening." Outler was a New York Yankee fan, and he used a baseball metaphor. "It was a bit like watching Gil McDougald edge in two extra steps at third. To someone not familiar with baseball, a meaningless move. But to an aficionado — " I nodded and smiled, and Outler shifted quickly to the nub of his story. "For a non-Curial cardinal to speak right up and correct a high official of the Roman Curia — on a matter of protocol — well that means that even the cardinals and the archbishops from the boondocks bear watching now."

McGrath nodded. "We're finding our way," he said.

When Frank McCool came in the door with the contingent from the Biblical Institute, some of us gave him a round of spontaneous applause. He blushed and waved a hand in front of his face.

"Please, please," he protested. He whispered to me, "Make 'em stop it, Bob."

I turned to the crowd. "Frank's embarrassed," I said. "He wants to give all the credit for the week's victories to — " I paused for effect. " — the Holy Ghost."

"Yea, Holy Ghost," shouted Mary. She assumed a cheerleader's stance, feet wide apart, hands raised. "Gimme an H. Gimme an O." Laughter and cheers from the Americans present. Puzzled smiles from the others. Mary went over and kissed McCool, leaving a scarlet imprint of her lips on his cheek. McCool growled, but he must have loved this special mark. He wore the lipstick for the rest of the evening.

When the huzzahs had died down, Mary went back to the piano and I turned and shook hands with Bill Moran, who had been laughing over this as I had. He said he wanted to introduce me to a new arrival at the

Biblicum, fresh from his studies at the Biblical Institute in Jerusalem, a Jesuit named Malachy Martin.

"Malachy Martin?" I said. My California Jesuit friend, Ben Franklin Meyer, had told me a bit about Martin. He was an Irishman, and one of the good guys, recently arrived to help in the politicking around Rome designed to save the Biblicum from the conservatives who wanted to shut it down.

"Like us," said Bill, "he drinks martinis, too."

"I'll get your first one," I said to Martin. "After that, you're on your own."

I wanted to hear Martin's story. But, as soon as he got a drink in his hand, he drifted over to the group around the piano, implying that he'd rather sing than talk. He had a fine Irish tenor voice that didn't tire, even when the other voices flagged, and he did a winning solo rendition of "Annie Laurie," rolling his eyes up toward the heavens every time he hit a high note and lowering his lashes modestly when the group insisted on applauding him.

At forty-seven, Martin cut a fine figure of a priest. Dark hair turning gray, aromatic pipe in his hand, nice tailored suit. I took a personal liking to him. The fact that he had joined McCool and others who were fighting for the life of the Biblicum was a plus. Perhaps an hour later, he came up and whispered conspiratorially in my ear. "You don't know, Bobby, how important these Sunday nights are becoming to the progress of the Council."

I might have dismissed this remark with a modest nod and changed the subject. But I was curious, about Martin and about the basis for his remark. "Who says so?" I asked.

He grinned. "I do."

"And how long have you been at the Council?" I said.

"About three days." He hailed one of our waiters and asked for a martini on the rocks, with a twist. "But every cleric I've met is talking about these parties. They're saying this is where ideas are incubated, friendships struck, new national alliances formed, strategies laid, plans formed for each coming week."

I put on a skeptical air, and moved to the *ingresso* to say goodbye to someone who was leaving the party. But I was impressed with Martin's friendliness. Even if he was exaggerating, I was flattered to hear what people were saying.

When Frank Murphy saw me near the door, he came over and gave me a merry look and cleared his throat. Ah, yes, I had promised to get him home by ten o'clock. I jingled my car keys in my pocket and slipped out the door with Murphy and drove him back to the Via Merulana. It didn't take more than forty minutes, roundtrip, and I was glad to do it, glad to get some more time alone with Murphy, because he was able to summarize some of the gossip he had picked up that evening at the party.

When I returned (unnoticed, I thought), I joined a small group that included Vi Lindbeck and Mary. Malachy Martin was still there, and he was telling stories. "The lady asked me what Christ meant when He said that in heaven there'd be no marrying and no giving in marriage." He took his pipe out of the side of his mouth and pointed the stem sternly at Mary and said, "And I told her, 'In heaven, Madam, we'll have promiscuity, pure promiscuity.'"

Mary laughed, a little too loudly, but when I laughed, too, she noticed that, at last, I had returned from my foray into the Roman night. She took me into our bedroom and put a hand on each shoulder, looked me in the eyes and said she was furious with me. "You've got an obligation to your guests," she said, "and you're no chauffeur. You're trying to do too much for others and not enough for yourself. In the future, let them take a cab."

I put my arms around her and kissed her on the forehead. "Mary, you're right," I said. "You're absolutely right. In fact, right now, I'm going to do something for myself. I'm going to build a great big Dagwood sandwich and have a bottle of beer."

We moved back out to the party. Mary grinned. "Okay. That's better. When you've got your sandwich, come on over here. It's storytelling time. And you've got to hear Bishop Cowley." Leonard Cowley, the hefty, happy auxiliary bishop of Minneapolis, had a half-million jokes, and he could tell them in a dozen different dialects, but I never found time to sit down and listen. There were too many good conversations going on all around me, and many of them were damned important, too. In many of them, I heard ideas that would appear on the Council floor in the weeks (and years) ahead. My salon had become a garden of ideas. Like a bee, I flitted from flower to flower to flower, until the last guest had departed, which was well after midnight.

Among the last guests to disappear was Malachy Martin. He took me aside again to whisper to me, to tell me that he was well-connected inside the Vatican, that he was a personal friend of Loris Capovilla, the private secretary of John XXIII. I asked him how this could be. "If you've been in Jerusalem and Capovilla's been here —"

Martin dropped his eyes. "I've been stationed in Jerusalem. But I've been coming to Rome — all unbeknownst to my own superiors — at the special insistence of you know who. Now you cannot ask me how I know this, but this very week, Capovilla was busy making many quiet phone calls to the Council Fathers, subtly dissociating the pope from Ottaviani and his *schema*. He called one Irish bishop I know and afterward the Irish bishop told me, 'We've had a mistaken idea that Cardinal Ottaviani represents the Holy See. My God, now we'll have to revise our ideas of what the Holy See is.' "

I was intrigued with this. Not only did Martin seem to have a special relationship with the pope, he also seemed to have the lowdown on Rome's higher ups, and he was more eager than any of my sources to tell me things he probably shouldn't have repeated at all, least of all to a newsman. He said that after Ottaviani got his big setback last week he told one of his aides (who told Martin), *Sumus semper sub Petro et cum Petro, etiam in summo periculo.* "We're always under Peter and with Peter, even when he's in the greatest danger." This was heavy stuff. If Martin knew aides of Ottaviani who'd tell him this, and if Martin would tell me, Martin was a guy worth cultivating.

৵৮

NOT THAT I GOT all that much reporting done at our Sunday night soirees. I didn't move through the party with a tape recorder or a notebook. Most of the time, I was too busy just running around making sure everyone's glasses were filled, saying hello, saying goodbye, saying come back next Sunday night. I did get a feel for the Council's movement, of its weekly shifts in mood, of who the movers and shakers were. And I gained a familiarity with them that made it possible for me to interview any of them during the week with more than a remote hope of getting honest answers.

With that kind of gyroscope, I had a way of steering through the seas of misinformation and disinformation about the Council that was filling the right-wing Italian newspapers, funneled to them, I suspected, by members of the Roman Curia. My inside information also tended to keep me in the magazine almost every week. Foreign correspondents don't get regular space in a newsmagazine unless they have something significant. With my special edge, I had important news from Rome. And when I didn't have earth-shattering news, I suggested profiles on important individuals who had never rated more than a line or two in *Time* before, men who epitomized the two vying forces at the Council.

Time ran my profiles on Karl Rahner, a German Jesuit who had raised so many questions about the faith in more than seven hundred books and articles that the Holy Office had demanded he submit all of his pieces to the Jesuit general in Rome before he could publish, and on Cardinal Alfredo Ottaviani, secretary of the Holy Office.

"Last week," said the article in *Time,* "as the Vatican Council's forces for change demonstrated their swelling strength, even Ottaviani's supporters realized that *Semper Idem* is a hopeless cause."

Calvin Trillin, who was subbing that week for my religion editor, John Elson, wrote the piece with his usual panache, and never for a moment challenged my reporting. He gave me more credit than some of my friends and co-religionists, like Senator and Mrs. Eugene McCarthy, for instance, who were visiting Rome because they were both fascinated by the Council and wanted to see what was happening. When they came over for one of our Sunday nights, the Senator accused me of manufacturing the entire piece on Ottaviani. "You went too far on that coat of arms," said McCarthy, who had once studied to be a Carthusian priest.

"What? What?" I demanded. "Went too far?"

" '*Semper Idem?*' " he said. "You fabricated that." I shook my head vigorously and laughed. The Senator was shocked. "You didn't? My God!" His wife, Abigail, said, "This is too good to be true."

I found that Karl Rahner was almost too good to be true. Though he was on Cardinal Ottaviani's hit list, he had become one of the major weapons of the Council's liberal wing, and it was he who had written a *schema* on Scripture that was far more modern, far more ecumenical than the preconciliar version, which had been shelved after heavy attacks on it by the liberals.

Father Rahner and Gus Weigel and I had *cannelloni* together at a fine restaurant called Tullio, not far from the Piazza Barberini. We talked in Latin (with Gus serving as a sometime interpreter when my Latin faltered) and I got more than a passing personal glimpse of Rahner and Rahner's down-to-earth theology. Rahner was something of an elf. He smiled a lot and he ate heartily, but when he spoke he did so with intensity. He told me it was the theologians' job to keep asking questions. "Each generation must keep rethinking the problems of theology for itself. Sure, we have a long line of dogmatic definitions. But we have to ask what those definitions really mean. We must rethink everything. A holy boldness is needed."

Later on in the interview, he demonstrated the difference between his approach and that of the old Roman school, which had everything codified, ready for Catholics to memorize — and obey. For Rahner, nothing was writ in granite for the modern man or woman. "The theological problem today," he said, "is to find the art of drawing religion out of a man, not pumping it into him. The Redemption has happened. The Holy Ghost is in men. The art is to help men become what they really are."

At lunch, I found another evidence of Rahner's down-to-earth approach: he became as excited as I when we discovered that they had some extraordinarily good ice cream for dessert.

"Why," I said to myself, "Karl Rahner is just like me. He likes ice cream, too."

16

In late December, newsstands all over the world featured my second cover story on Pope John, *Time*'s Man of the Year. I was darned pleased with it. Ed Jamieson, the writer in New York working with my files and those of a good many other *Time* correspondents around the world, had succeeded in summing up much of the first session's spirit. Nothing had been decided with any finality. And yet a new language, a new spirit had taken hold inside the Council. Toward the end of the first session, the liberals managed to ding another Ottaviani *schema*, one that was simply a standpat restatement of centralized, monarchical church authority. They blasted its substance — and its style. Bishop Emile Josef De Smedt of Bruges, Belgium, zeroed right in on the tone of the whole thing, shot through with "triumphalism, clericalism, and juridicism."

Time reported (from my file) that De Smedt's intervention brought the loudest applause of the whole first session and was itself a demonstration of a new spirit in the Church. Jamieson wrote: "The bishops, who had long considered Rome the sole source of power and authority in the Catholic world, gathered together for the first time in their lives, discovered that they and not Rome constituted the leadership of the Church."

To Jamieson, it looked like a majority of the bishops were ready "to adapt the Church's whole life to the revolutionary changes in science, economics, morals and politics that have swept the modern world; to make it, in short, more Catholic and less Roman." The notion was an expression of my own hope. In fact, in mid-November I crossed the line between participant and observer, by writing Cardinal Suenens a long, earnest note, urging him to expand the conciliar agenda, move the Council from strictly churchy questions to matters of moment to the world at large. I like to think my letter helped galvanize Cardinal Suenens of Brussels into action. (Historians could check it out by looking at Suenens' correspondence and working papers during November 1962.) Just before the end of the first session, Suenens, backed by a consortium of liberal cardinals, succeeded in introducing a new *schema,* on the Church in the World, which he billed as an inspiration of Pope John himself: to give the world a new sense of its unity as a human family.

"That sense (said our cover story) is at the core of the Christian tradition, whose God lives in history and invites the family of man to help him form it. If the invitation goes begging in a world besieged by tension and seduced by its own accomplishments, Christianity must share the blame." If our prophecy was true, it even looked like T. D. Roberts was going to get the subject of war and peace and The Bomb to the Council floor.

Dick Clurman was proud of my work and wrote from New York, "You're getting applause and compliments from all your colleagues in this building, itinerant clergymen (including Cardinal Spellman) and just about everyone else who's crossed your path in the past six months." He gave me a big raise.

And then Gus Weigel told Betty Bartelme of Macmillan that she ought to try to persuade me to write a book on the Council. Miss Bartelme phoned me from New York. She didn't have to urge much. I said I'd do the book if I could get the time off from my duties in the Rome bureau.

In February, Macmillan sent me a book contract along with what was then a good advance (for someone who'd never written a book before). What was more important, Clurman gave me six weeks off, with pay, to get the job done. Six weeks didn't give me much time, but I knew I could do it, if I worked hard. At first, I tried writing my book at the office, and then at home, but there were too many phone calls and too many interruptions.

As the Vatican correspondent, for instance, I had to take time out to do things no other could do. Like, invite Pope John to attend a gathering in New York for *Time*'s fortieth birthday party. Harry Luce had decided to honor everyone who had ever appeared on the cover of *Time.* Ed Jackson, the man who had come in to take over as the new, permanent bureau chief, could have done this himself — if we had only wanted to make this a pro forma invitation.

We didn't want it to be pro forma. We were serious. And so, in a series of notes and meetings, I really tried to persuade Cardinal Bea and Msgr. Eugene Cardinale, the Vatican's chief of protocol, that Pope John could make an outstanding Catholic witness by breaking precedent and traveling to New York. The pope's closest advisers in the Curia ended up telling him, "This just isn't done. Popes don't travel abroad and especially not to gatherings of a mere secular nature."

On the very next day, however, the pope had his chauffeur drive him to Fiumicino, where he secured permission from the airport authorities to let him sit in his limousine next to a runway. For an hour, he watched the jets take off — and, I suspect, fantasized going to the Time Inc. party in New York. Later in the spring, he would become too ill to travel. But in February 1963, I was told by Msgr. Capovilla, Pope John did want to go to Harry Luce's party. And his Curial advisers wouldn't let him.

These distractions weren't helping me get my book written. I had to find a quiet place to work. I did the most natural thing in the world, for me. At the invitation of Father Ralph Wiltgen, a Divine Word missionary from Chicago, I went to his order's college in Rome, lived there and wrote my book. I came home every day at lunchtime and on other odd evenings for an occasional dinner party, but I wrote no less than fifteen hours a day and got the first draft finished in six weeks.

In the process, I got unexpected help from Malachy Martin. He had become a regular at our smaller dinner parties; he was a great storyteller and a man with such an unclerical approach to life that I could include him in any kind of gathering, no matter who was on the guest list — movie producers, film stars, cabinet ministers, members of the diplomatic corps, editors of *Time* or *Life* visiting from New York. And with Mary he was totally charming.

I was anxious for Martin to see the beginnings of my book, and pleased, after he saw a draft of my early chapters, when he said I was doing something important. He said he thought he could help me as a kind of research assistant. I was under terrific deadline pressure. I took his offer and he started feeding me dozen-page memos on the history of the Church (a subject I was weak on) and imaginative descriptions of key Council figures (he called them "pen portraits") which I adapted for use in the book. One night, I had had a sudden inspiration: to use the familiar image of Peter's bark as an extended metaphor for this Church of 1963, groaning and rusted after a few centuries in dry dock, now getting ready to "move out on to the seas of the world." When Malachy saw that, he went to the Gregorian University's library and dug up an appropriate piece of history that helped the extended metaphor.

It was the story of a young Florentine painter who brought his masterpiece, *The Bark of Peter,* to Pope Adrian VI, the last non-Italian pope in history, in 1528. According to Martin's memo, Pope Adrian himself was featured in the painting, holding a book that was carried by angels blowing eschatological trumpets. "The waters beneath the ship were calm, but all around, the waves were whipped up in fury and full of drowning sinners, heretics, and schismatics. The pope sat on the deck of this bark, eyes closed, hands clasped in prayer, surrounded by his Curia, and his guards, while the faces of the faithful peeped out of square portholes below. Adrian cried out at this monstrosity, 'No, no this is not my ship.'

"The startled painter hastened to explain, 'This is the bark of Peter,' he said, 'high above the stormy seas of heresy, preserved from contamination by the angels of light.'

" 'No, my son,' replied Adrian, 'you do not understand. Perhaps we ourselves have understood only lately. The dimensions are wrong.' "

"The painter's patron, a rich Florentine merchant, broke in and told Adrian respectfully that the Master, Giacomo, had trained the lad and really ought to know what the dimensions should be. Adrian answered sadly: 'No, no. Put my ship upon these troubled waters. Fill the sails and dip the rudder in the sea and let me steer my bishops and their flocks. We must calm these waters and be saved with these.' He knocked his fisherman's ring against the writhing figures in the water. 'And these, and these, and these.' Some days later, Pope Adrian died. Some say he was poisoned."

For my purposes, Malachy's story was perfect and I used it right at the beginning of my book to lead into an introduction of Pope John XXIII, the 262nd successor of Peter, "who would be, according to the ancient prophecy of Malachy, shepherd and sailor, which can be translated 'fisher of men.' "

For research help like this, I was grateful. And when Malachy told me he needed money for a special trip, so hush-hush he couldn't tell superiors about it, I gave him several hundred thousand lire, about $500.

"I can't spell out the details of this trip, Bobby. Not just yet."

I laughed and said, "It's okay. Tell me when you can."

✍

BY THE BEGINNING of April, I had finished correcting my galleys. Macmillan scheduled the book for an August 26 publication and then

Macmillan reported that they'd also sold the British rights to Burns & Oates, official publishers to the Holy See in London.

That didn't mean I could coast along. In April, Pope John released his most major encyclical, *Pacem in Terris*. I had extra reporting to do on the pope's approach to peace. For one thing, I had to ferret out the man who'd drafted the encyclical for the pope. That wasn't very difficult. Msgr. Cardinale told me that if I wanted "the best commentary on the encyclical's meaning," well then, why didn't I try to talk to Msgr. Pietro Pavan?

Msgr. Cardinale was then the chief of protocol for the Vatican secretary of state. It was a high post, and he sometimes served as "acting substitute" in the Secretariat of State besides, the very job that Msgr. Giovanni Battista Montini (who was soon to become Pope Paul VI) had held before Pius XII had appointed him the archbishop of Milan. Winning Cardinale's support helped me at every turn. This polylingual diplomat (he was an Italian who had been raised in the United States) not only gave me quick answers to quick questions about papal directions when I needed them, steering me to authoritative sources in the process, he also steered important sources to me.

I still have a copy of a confidential memo written by Donald B. Straus of New York, then board chairman of the Planned Parenthood Federation of America, which described his visit to Rome in February 1963. It was then that he learned from Msgr. Cardinale, among others, that the Church had no quarrel with Planned Parenthood over its goals, only wanted his assurance that the organization wasn't pushing "all kinds of contraceptives without regard for moral considerations." To Straus's surprise, Cardinale volunteered the information that "in many parts of the world, overpopulation is a grave threat to civilization." He also said that "anyone who has heard confessions and who has no useful advice to give women is faced with a grave spiritual problem. Rhythm is no solution...."

Straus wondered whether some of the liberal views expressed by Msgr. Cardinale and others couldn't be exported to the United States. "Specifically," wrote Straus, "I wondered if the word could be passed along that discussions with Planned Parenthood representatives did not amount to consorting with the devil." Msgr. Cardinale found Straus's question "very amusing." But when Straus asked whether it was possible for the Vatican to promulgate the liberal views he had just heard from Cardinale "without reference to Planned Parenthood," Msgr. Cardinale said such action would be premature.

It was not premature, however, for Msgr. Cardinale to tell me, a *Time* correspondent, about Straus's visit, nor for Msgr. Cardinale to suggest to Straus that he talk to me, "a man with great insights into these questions." In fact, although I had been a part of the informal, reformist discussions on birth control which were being held by bishops and theologians around my dinner table, I had no special insights into the reformist temper of certain members of the Roman Curia itself regarding the matter. What Msgr. Cardinale was doing was leaking the information to me (albeit very indirectly) that something special was going on inside the Vatican. I didn't know it at the time, but Pope John XXIII was setting up a commission even then "to test the Church's doctrine" (the words were Cardinale's) on birth control.

☙

AND THEN Pope John started dying.

When I heard the news, I was in New York with Mary and Betsy to receive an award from the Overseas Press Club "for the best magazine reporting of foreign affairs." I picked up the plaque and took the bows, then jetted right back to Rome, scrapping our plans to do some serious shopping in Manhattan, so I could be in on one of the biggest stories a Rome reporter ever has, the passing of papal power: death, burial, conclave, white smokes, a new successor to the Big Fisherman.

We arrived in Rome late at night, with Giulio meeting us and whisking us through customs at Fiumicino, stopping off to deposit Mary and Betsy at Via Quirico Filopanti 2, then heading straight to St. Peter's Square where thousands were kneeling and praying while Pope John lay dying.* One old Roman told me that people hadn't poured out in this manner for this kind of vigil when Pius XII was dying. This was a sign, he said, that John XXIII was someone who was truly special — "a saint."

I smiled at the word, because I had a feeling it would take Roncalli a long time to win canonization. Rome still requires a saint to "perform" a number of miracles during his lifetime and after his death before it will declare him a saint. It also hesitates to elevate those who were not unequivocally orthodox. Pope John XXIII was not the kind of saint who worked miracles in his lifetime and I thought he would be less inclined

---

*Amid the throng, I spied a man in a trenchcoat about fifty yards away. I didn't know him, but I wanted to, and strode in his direction, as he did in mine. I stuck out my hand. "I'm Bob Kaiser from *Time*," I said. He said, with a laugh, "I'm Larry Collins of *Newsweek*."

to work them after his death, as the Roman officials would insist he do in order to win his Roman "wings." (I was wrong. On September 3, 2000, Blessed John XXIII was, as they say, "raised to the altar.")

Nor was he all that tradition-bound. He was rather more like those saints who created new Christian lifestyles while they were alive, who were prophets of what the Church needed to be and needed to do at a given point in time — but who had also gotten zapped by the official Church for their trouble. Some of them, of course, won canonization — eons later when those with 20–20 hindsight could see how important they were for the life of the Church at critical times in its history.

Nothing makes more news in Rome than the death of a pope and the reelection of a new one. I was so busy these weeks that I had my secretary block anything but emergency phone calls — and I still didn't finish an average day until 3:00 A.M. I had two *Time* covers in a row (one on the death of Pope John and one on the election of his successor, Cardinal Montini of Milan, who took the name Paul VI), and text pieces to do for *Life* and precious few moments for Betsy, or for my mother and stepfather, whose visit couldn't have come at a worse time, or, for Mary either, who was now six months pregnant.

I had been exposed to the old Catholic doctrine that "the primary end of marriage is the procreation of children" — just enough exposure to believe, at least subconsciously, that I had done my holy duty by Mary and that, since we couldn't or shouldn't have sex, we needn't even cuddle or fool around a little bit. At that time in my life, I could have written (as James Thurber did) an uproarious, unconsciously funny essay entitled, "Is Sex Necessary?" In fact, one night Mary and I were out to dinner with my folks, and Mary was complaining to me about her problems with the new drapes in the apartment, the probable pregnancy of our maid (who was unmarried), and the plumbers, who hadn't come to fix one of our bathroom sinks, though they had been called three days before.

I glared at Mary. I was tired and hungry and said I didn't want to hear about all this domestic *quisquillia* (a word we used in the Novitiate for "garbage"). "What do I have a wife for?" I said. I turned to my mother. "Why," I huffed, "do I even *need* a wife?"

This was unfair. Mary deserved a lot of credit for making my life wonderful and for putting up with temperamental me, this often absent husband, this budding author, this instant Church historian, this theologian in short pants, this coruscating correspondent, this Richard Harding

Davis of the Via della Conciliazione. And then she had to play hostess for a succession of houseguests.

First, there was Father William Van Etten Casey, a Jesuit from Holy Cross College who stayed with us for three weeks in May on his way back to the United States after a year's stint as president of the American School of Biblical Research in Jerusalem. Then we had three separate, two-week-long parental visits in a row, first from Mary's mother and father, then from my mother and stepfather, and then my father. I rented a summerhouse at Lavinio, at the seashore, a move that would give Mary more domestic garbage to deal with. Out at the beach, of course, Mary and Betsy could be free from Rome's noxious summer air pollution, but Lavinio was a good two-hour drive from Rome. Sometimes I wouldn't show up until dawn and sometimes, too tired to face a two-hour drive at three in the morning, I wouldn't show up at all.

When the last of our families had jetted home, Mary was at the shore with Betsy and our two maids. Bennett Bolton of the Associated Press, his wife, Barbara, and their two tots lived in a summerhouse next door. Jack Shea, a political attaché at the American Embassy, and his wife, Mary, and their children had their summerhouse nearby. There was even a small, extempore Jesuit community that started to camp in our villa. John Felice, who headed the Rome campus of Chicago's Loyola University, and Ed Lynch, a California Jesuit recently assigned to Vatican Radio, were frequent overnight visitors; so were John Long and Ben Meyer and Malachy Martin. Often enough, all of them would be there at the same time.

Mary really didn't need me, did she? Well, it didn't matter if she did or not, I wasn't much available. I was wrapped up in my Vatican coverage for *Time* and *Life,* and working on the galley proofs of my book. I also had to repel an attack on me by the Holy Office.

On Saturday, June 8, I received a phone call from Monsignor Henry Cosgrove, a tall handsome cleric from Brooklyn who was assigned to the staff of the Holy Office in Rome. Sanche DeGramont, the bureau chief of the *New York Herald Tribune,* had already told me that the monsignor was making phone calls all over town to complain about "the vicious press campaign against Cardinal Ottaviani — with *Time* magazine leading the way." And now Msgr. Cosgrove was calling me. Specifically, he said *Time's* report of a scene at Pope John's deathbed was not true. (We had quoted Ottaviani saying, "To many, it appears to be the hand of God.")

Msgr. Cosgrove said that the cardinal wanted some kind of retraction in *Time.* "Even if I was thinking those thoughts," the cardinal had told

Msgr. Cosgrove, "I wouldn't have said them then and there with other cardinals present. This is a lie and a calumny. The implications are too much. This has gone much too far."

"Oh, oh," I said to myself. I knew I was in trouble, because, of course, I hadn't been present at Pope John's deathbed. I'd gotten the story from Malachy Martin, who said that Msgr. Capovilla, Pope John's secretary, had told him. The magazine normally closed at midnight Saturday, but when the pope died early Sunday morning, it was still Saturday night in New York. The editors decided to keep the magazine "open" Sunday so they could produce a Pope John cover story. I had had to work all day Sunday, with Elson and the editors standing by for my files, and under that deadline pressure, I made an attempt to call Capovilla to see if he would confirm the story. I couldn't get him on the phone — and made the snap decision to go with the Ottaviani quote anyway.

Now, with Msgr. Cosgrove challenging me, I wished I hadn't. There was little doubt in my mind that, after the beating Cardinal Ottaviani had taken in the first session of Pope John's Council, he was not exactly stricken by the pope's passing. And the cardinal had almost admitted those feelings in his very denial. But if he didn't utter them as I had reported he had, then I had goofed. I had had enough experience around the Vatican to know the difference between genuine and diplomatic denials. In a diplomatic denial, officials tipped their hands by the blustering overuse of adverbs like "absolutely" and "completely" and "categorically" when a simple "not true" would do just fine. Now, I was inclined to believe Monsignor Cosgrove. I asked if Cardinal Ottaviani wanted to see me. He said that maybe that would be a good idea, then said he didn't believe the cardinal would want to be put in the position of defending himself to me.

I told him I would consult with my editors. I sent Clurman a confidential cable telling him what had happened and urging that *Time* stand pat. I report now with shame that I hid behind the standard journalistic immunity.

I KNOW OTTAVIANI SAID WHAT HE SAID BUT I WILL NEVER REVEAL MY SOURCE, I said. And, then, I suggested this: SINCE OTTAVIANI AND COMPANY HAVE USED THE NOTORIOUS HOLY OFFICE TO SCREW INNUMERABLE DEFENSELESS CLERICS ALL THE WAY UP TO ARCHBISHOPS (I was thinking of T. D. Roberts), I ADVISE TIME INC. GIVE THEM A TASTE OF THEIR OWN MEDICINE, THAT IS, INSIST ON COMPLETE ANONYMITY OF SOURCE, REPORTER, WRITER AND EDITOR.

I strongly suspected that I'd been had by Martin, a man whom I thought was one of my best friends. After all, he had helped immeasurably with my book and entertained our folks with Irish (and other) songs and folk tales and even predicted the sex of our unborn child one evening by pulling a long strand of Mary's hair, tying it to her wedding ring and suspending the ring above her tummy to see whether it turned clockwise (in which case it would be a boy) or counterclockwise (a girl). There was an undeniable intimacy about our relationship and a conspirational air about it, besides: when I was writing my book, Malachy signed his lengthy memos "Pushkin," after the Russian poet.

But I had to cover my ass. I told Jackson, confidentially, that my source was Capovilla. He was happy enough to believe that; after all, Msgr. Capovilla was a credible source and, in the journalism business, there were some things that were, practically speaking, uncheckable but believable. What it came down to in the final analysis was good common sense: consider your source, consider his believability.

"O.K.," said Jackson. With a canny instinct, he added, "But we've got to watch out for some of your friends — Martin in particular. I don't trust him. While you were still in New York, he phoned me to report that Pope John had gotten up out of his sickbed to sit in a chair and smoke a Camel. I didn't believe that story for a moment. I think Martin just makes things up. I think the man's crazy." I nodded, not agreeing, not disagreeing. Whether Martin was crazy or not, I knew — now — that I'd be crazy to take his stories on faith any longer.

∮

I THOUGHT I'D HEARD the last of the Ottaviani matter, but then, I didn't have much time to worry about it. I had to go out to Lavinio, pick up Mary, and take her off with me to Istanbul, where I had a scheduled interview with Athenagoras, the Orthodox Ecumenical Patriarch. But Msgr. Cosgrove wouldn't be put off. When I returned a little more than a week later, he was calling again. I told him *Time* could make no retraction. "I knew it," he snapped. "*Time* has never admitted it was wrong about anything." He said he was going to write to Mr. Luce (which was a lie: he had already mailed a letter to Luce three days before) to tell him the cardinal never said what we said he said, or at least he didn't say it at the pope's bedside. The cardinal admitted that he may have told some people that the Holy Father's passing was the will of God, but his position now was this: "If at any time I ever said anything like that, this was not my meaning, not the implication that was made in the *Time* story."

I asked Msgr. Cosgrove if the cardinal felt he was being put on trial in the pages of *Time* without being allowed to defend himself. "Of course," he said. "If he makes a public statement, he only compounds the situation."

I played the smart ass. I said, "Now the cardinal knows how various theologians feel when they are delated to the Holy Office and condemned without a trial." We got into a long conversation then about Holy Office procedures.

Msgr. Cosgrove took immediate refuge in the Holy Office's rules of secrecy. "There's nothing that Cardinal Ottaviani or any of us can do about it," he said. "The pope is the official prefect of the Holy Office. He makes the rules, and we follow them." I maintained that the work of the Holy Office was not done by the pope but by the cardinal and his staff, and that if the cardinal wanted to change the rules, his opinion would have a great deal of weight.

We were getting pretty far afield from Cardinal Ottaviani's original complaint. Now the monsignor would put the conversation on another, more personal level. "The cardinal is not really an ogre," he said with more than a touch of earnestness. "He is an honest man. We don't all agree with him. I disagree with him myself on a lot of things, and he knows it. But he's trying to do the right thing." Now his voice was pleading. "The cardinal and I both wish you would stop telling lies about him and painting such a black picture."

I admitted that *Time* didn't present a very nuanced view of the cardinal and said that I might be able to do something about this in the future.

Maybe that mollified Msgr. Cosgrove and his boss. At any rate, the monsignor wrote a second letter to Luce, to tell him that the cardinal had reconsidered his protest and wanted to "withdraw his request for retraction in the pages of your magazine. He does so because he feels that it is not desirable to draw further attention to the matter at this time." Msgr. Cosgrove suggested that *Time*'s reporters be requested to check with him "when it is a question of stories pertaining to Cardinal Ottaviani."

In a note dated June 24, Luce assured him that *Time* would take great care in future stories about the cardinal and said he was surprised to learn that no one in the Rome bureau had spoken with Cardinal Ottaviani. I got no reprimands from anyone, but I did get a copy of Luce's letter, which was all the notice I needed to be as careful and as fair in dealing with Cardinal Ottaviani as I was in dealing with Cardinal Bea. Up to that time, I had no good source in the Holy Office. Now, at least, I had Msgr. Cosgrove, a man who said he had been a reader of *Time* for many years.

In the fall, however, I would learn that Msgr. Cosgrove's team played the game according to an old slogan favored by Irish politicians in Boston and New York, "Don't get mad, just get even." The Holy Office would have a surprise for me.

17

Now I was in my pride-that-goeth-before-a-fall period, the intrepid foreign correspondent off on his ego trip. There I was, riding into London from Heathrow Airport in a limousine with Archbishop Roberts, who was almost as excited about the impending publication of my book as I was. A traffic jam in the city brought the car to a halt, and T. D. pointed to a newsstand. I looked out to see the face of Pope John XXIII staring at me on a large poster. "THE MOVE TO THWART POPE JOHN," said the poster in big black letters. "Exclusive to *The Observer* — by Robert Blair Kaiser."

T. D. wrinkled his nose and grinned. "That poster's all over London. It's in all the tube stations, too." He looked so proud, because, among other things, he was the "Uncle B." in my dedication — To Uncle B., Pushkin and Eagle. "The book," said T. D., "has already made quite a stir here."

It hadn't made much of a flutter in Rome. The *Observer* had started carrying excerpts from my book in June. But the paper just lay there in a pile at the news kiosk on the Via Veneto, along with the *Times* and the *News of the World* and no one seemed to be around to comment on it. Sanche and Nancy DeGramont had gone off on vacation. The special seventeen-man-and-woman crew of *Life*, who had finished their all-out coverage of Pope John's funeral and the coronation of Pope Paul VI, had packed up and returned to New York. Most of my Jesuit friends were away for the summer. Frank McCool was in Chicago, Ben Meyer had a new assignment in California, and Malachy Martin was going off to Beirut for a couple months of special research. When I took the Sunday papers out to Lavinio, neither Mary, nor the Boltons nor any of the Jesuits who were still around found anything remarkable about my being in the *Observer*.

I had shrugged that off. They had all read my book in galleys. It was old stuff. Besides, Betsy was clamoring for my attention. She hadn't seen me in days. And she had a new trick to show me. She took my hand, climbed up on the garden wall of our villa, stood there stiffly for a moment, then plummeted headfirst into my arms with a squeal of terror and delight. "Who taught her this?" I asked Mary, pleased but just a bit jealous because I already knew the answer she would give me.

"Malachy," she said.

I wondered about her tone. It was almost defiant. And I wondered about the wisdom of having my most rambunctious friend Martin as a houseguest. I said nothing. Mary was eight months pregnant now, and it had been a hectic summer for her. She had struck a little girl on the road, driving with Malachy through a small town on the way to Lavinio one day, knocked her out of her shoes. She hadn't hurt the girl, but couldn't stop blaming herself, had not been sleeping well, and had deep circles under her eyes. When I said goodbye to her at Fiumicino Airport, she seemed troubled at my departure.

"Don't worry," I laughed. "A few days in London, a week or so in New York and I'll be back — before the baby comes." Mary didn't smile, she just stuck out her lower lip and nodded silently.

T. D.'s limo stopped at a magnificent house on Grosvenor Square and he took me in to meet a dear old friend, a tweedy widow, who, in fact, was the owner of the limousine. She fussed over both of us a bit and then had tea brought in by a, yes, by God, a butler wearing tails.

She had the latest reviews of my book ready in a pile for me to read. "General surprise," she said, "that the official publisher in England to the Holy See would do this book. One of these fellows says it's a new kind of Church that can allow this."

I couldn't help skimming the reviews. Douglas Brown of the *Sunday Telegraph* said my "brilliant piece of reportage" only reflected *Time's* "accustomed irreverence." John Raymond of the *Sunday Times* said the book showed how Vatican II blew a hole in the Counter Reformation.

The reviewers were intrigued at the hints of scandal inside the Vatican. To think that some of the pope's own cabinet had been trying to derail Pope John's Council! Paul Johnson of the *New Statesman* wrote that the machinations of the Roman Curia were sometimes amusing, and sometimes dispiriting, but always fascinating, that I had presented a view of ecclesiastical behavior that many would prefer to keep hidden, but that it was exactly this kind of secrecy which I deplored and which I had deliberately breached. Father Bernard Basset of the *Catholic Herald* said "those who love the Church will rejoice that an American layman is saying in public what so many have thought and whispered in secret for so many years." The length of the notices said that editors were taking the book seriously, which made it worth all the hard work for me.

T. D. and his friend said I could take the papers with me. I nodded, folded them in my lap and glanced at T. D., who was looking as happy as if he had written the reviews himself. In fact, I thought, maybe he had had a hand in arranging them. He was a quotable guy and thicker with the London press than I would have imagined from his more retiring attitude in Rome.

"Paul Johnson is an interesting chap," said T. D. "Fallen away Catholic. Fine writer himself. You'll be meeting him and some of the others, I suspect, this evening." Ah yes, I thought, my publisher's party. "You'll like Paul Johnson."

I did like him. I tended to like most reporters and journalists because, we had a common quest, common curiosities in this chaotic world we were covering. Johnson came right up to me, with the familiarity that reporters assume with one another. "Your book tells me," he said, "that the Roman Church may have a future after all."

I laughed and said, "Yes, this Council has moved the Church ahead centuries. From the sixteenth to the eighteenth." Johnson did the proper double take. I added, "It's not my line, it's Gus Weigel's."

"Weigel?"

"American ecumenist. Jesuit. *Peritus* at the Council. Works with Cardinal Bea at the Secretariat for Promoting Christian Unity." I didn't tell him that he was the "Eagle" of my dedication.

"Oh, yes, Weigel." With a self-deprecating laugh, he said, "It was only recently that I realized who Cardinal Bea was. Now, in order to be *au courant,* I'm going to have to memorize the names of all the Council *periti?*"

"No," I said. "There are a couple hundred of them. Don't try to memorize them. Just keep reading *Time* for notices on the important ones." I said this with a wide grin, trusting that he would recognize the braggadocio as a put-on. When a reporter stops to think, as he can rarely afford to, he doesn't really believe that most reports of world events are more than an approximation of what is actually happening. The press often reflects reality no better than the clay wall of Plato's cave. It was intriguing, however, to note how *Time*'s reports affected those who read them—like the men and women in this room.

I sipped a sherry and met them, one by one, with T. D. or Tom Burns, my dapper English publisher, making the introductions. I remember one noble, the Earl of Longford, and one Member of Parliament, Norman St. John Stevas, and there were a good many names I cannot now remember. They all made me feel good about being the bearer of good news — that their Church was at last becoming more relevant to the real world.

We had dinner later, at Burns' club, the Garrick, which had a smell of spice and fine leather and a squadron of red-jacketed waiters — Burns, John Todd, another book publisher, T. D., and I. I can make an approximate reconstruction of the conversation we had.

It was Todd, I believe, who gave me a short course in the sociology of English Catholicism: "The Catholic intelligentsia here, you see, have been fighting a losing battle for decades with the English hierarchy, who used Pius X's *Pascendi* as a stick to beat our thinkers over the head with in the early part of the century. Now, if we can believe your reports, we have had a Modernist on the throne of Peter for the past five years."

About four weeks before, Tom had been told by a high British ecclesiastic not to publish my book. He went ahead and did it anyway (after getting roaring drunk in anger) and he was pleased by the new standing this had given him in the London publishing business. Now, he wasn't sure he liked this view of Pope John. He sputtered a bit over his glass of Pouilly Fuissé and said, "The pope a Modernist? Not really?"

I said, "For what it's worth, Tom, there was a time early in Roncalli's career when the powers in Rome suspected he was, and that he was probably in a place where he shouldn't be — teaching in a seminary near Val d'Aosta. He got a warning from the Holy Office, a private *monitum*. A few months later, he was given a diplomatic assignment in Turkey, where, they thought, Roncalli's Modernism (if that's what it was) could do the least harm."

Todd said, "What does that mean to us? A man who may have been a Modernist forty years ago just happens to be pope today. Does that mean that sweet reasonability can prevail and Catholics can think for a change?"

There was an angry edge to his voice, but Tom Burns didn't hear it and countered with a question. "Can't they?"

"I hope they can," said Todd.

"But you don't have high hopes?" I said.

"I think Mr. Todd is not happy with the conclave's choice of Montini," said T. D.

I said I didn't think it mattered who the pope was now. "I don't think Paul VI could stop now what was started at the Council, even if he wanted to, which I don't think he does."

"That's irrelevant," said Todd quietly.

"Irrelevant?" I said. "Well, I'd say the pope's attitude—"

Todd stopped me. "No, you're right. The pope's attitude *is* relevant. Far too relevant for far too many Catholics. It shouldn't be: that's my point. I'm talking about growing up, I'm talking about psychological maturity, I'm talking about using our own consciences. We've rarely told ourselves that we can work things out for ourselves. If there was ever any doubt, we trained ourselves to ask Father Brown, or Father Smith, or Father Jones. So we never ended up wearing our own thoughts. We wore the thoughts of others—whether they fit us exactly or not." He shook his head sadly. "I'm afraid that we've looked like a sorry, rag-tag lot."

The rest of us were silent for a moment. Deep down, I knew that I was still caught in that bind. My book, purportedly signaling a revolution in the Church, simply tried to make an old set of tailors look foolish and give new fashionability to another group of tailors. The new arbiters of Church fashion were more liberal, to be sure, but they were still telling me what to think. I said, "I believe maybe we all have some intermediate stages to go through. Growing up isn't all that easy."

The waiters were now bringing on the coffee. After he had finished doctoring his brew with cream and sugar, Todd said, "Yes, I expect so. I am talking about growth. And growth takes time. I shouldn't be so impatient. But damn it! I am!"

Burns grumbled a bit about Todd's imagery. "I say, we're talking about the informed Catholic conscience, aren't we? Why compare it to a suit of clothes?" He tugged at his own camel's-hair lapel. "Clothes! Of all things! They change with the season. I, for one, am proud that the Church was built on a solid foundation of truth. From that, it can take a stand on— anything."

"Yes," said T. D. "the Church, insofar as you can tell by listening to its official spokesmen, is never at a loss for an authoritative opinion on anything. Pius XII was an expert on everything from astronomy to zoology. He ranged far beyond his competence. He even gave a good bit of advice to Italian midwives."

Burns sputtered. He himself had published every papal utterance of Pius XII. And made a lot of money on the series, too. Before he could speak, T. D. put up his hand, like a policeman signaling stop. "Tom," he said soothingly, "I don't think any of us questions the teaching authority of the pope — although I sometimes wish Pius XII had done more teaching and less — pontificating." He laughed. "Yes, good word. Pontiffs pontificate."

"How do you mean?" asked Burns.

"I mean that teaching is not simply a question of making statements, writing encyclicals, bulls or *motu proprios*. Even popes have to listen. If he finds he's not getting across even to his students, he's got to try another tack. Otherwise, all he's doing is — "

"Spouting off?" I said.

"Uh, well," stammered T. D. "I think a lawyer might say, 'Making a record.' So that, generations from now, theologians can cite that record and say, 'The Church has always taught.' "

I said, "In fact, the Church has not 'always taught' a lot of things. The trouble is that today, when the pope says anything it's all too official." I looked directly at Tom. "And ought not to be bound up in buckram volumes."

Burns began to growl. T. D. stopped him. "It's nothing against you, Tom. All of us have paid far too much attention to what is sometimes called 'official.' In my own case, it only took a few 'official' frowns from the Holy Office to put me into a tailspin for several years."

We all knew what T. D. was talking about. I said, "You mean you should have ignored the Holy Office's *monita?*"

T. D. paused. Finally, he said, "Yes. But I couldn't. Oh, Rome didn't say I couldn't write anymore. And, God knows, I had more that I wanted to write. It's just that an opinion — dashed off, no doubt, by some ill-trained monsignor in Ottaviani's office — made me feel disloyal if I did."

T. D. took a deep breath and held up his hand, begging to finish what amounted to a kind of confession. "That feeling prevailed," he continued, "until last fall when I learned many of my brother bishops felt as I did. Only then was I free again, to speak, to write. But — and here, I think, is what Bob is insisting on — the dismaying thing is that I needed some kind of endorsement, if not from the Holy Office, then, at least, from my brother bishops. Bob is right." His shoulders sagged a bit. "We are still children at heart, waiting to be told that what we know is right is right."

Our talk went on until they closed the club, with Tom Burns arguing that children do not, in fact, grow up, without some informed guidance and John Todd holding that there had been so much informed guidance in the Church that few Catholics had taken the trouble to grow up. T. D.

was doodling on the back of an envelope, making notes on a piece he wanted to write on this very subject in the *Month*. Toward the end, I could hardly keep my eyes open.

Tom Burns drove me to the London Hilton in his chocolate-brown Mercedes. "You're already registered," he said, "and your bags are in your room. Just go in and ask for the key."

"A great day, Tom," I mumbled. "Thank you." I walked as quickly and as steadily as I could to the front desk. When I found my room, I wanted to phone Mary and tell her what was happening in London. But it was 2:00 A.M., too damn late. I'd call in the morning.

18

In the morning, I couldn't get through to our damned beach house at Lavinio on the damned Italian phone system, and I couldn't keep trying because at ten I had a meeting at my London hotel with Walter Wanger, the movie producer. Coming off *Cleopatra* in Rome (starring Elizabeth Taylor and Richard Burton), Wanger had found an advance copy of my book and fallen in love with my portrait of Pope John. He wanted me to write a feature-length documentary film he would produce as *The World John Loved*, a title taken from the last line of my book. "So," I said, "after working with Taylor and Burton, you need —" He interrupted me. "I need to do something, something good." I understood. As the acting bureau chief of the Time-Life office in Rome, I had had to chronicle the mad passion of Taylor and Burton every week for the People section of *Time*. Not my favorite kind of story. Informing the world about the best pope in history, however — that was worth doing. Now the producer of *Cleopatra* wanted to do something that made him feel worthwhile, too. How could I say no?

I wondered if doing a documentary would jeopardize my job at *Time*. I liked working for *Time*. I was so pleased with the Rome assignment that if Harry Luce hadn't been paying me, I'd be paying him. Since Wanger and I were both heading for the U.S., I suggested that I ought to get my chief-of-correspondents' advice in New York, and maybe find an agent, too.

"You need an agent?" he said.

"So, could we firm things up in New York?"

"Yes. But if you really want to do this, don't let an agent get in the way."

I nodded, soberly. I didn't have the slightest idea what he was talking about. Then I had to hurry over to my London publisher's office to be interviewed by a man from *Newsweek*. This was a delicious turn of events.

Once, I couldn't get a job with *Newsweek*. Now, here was a reporter from *Newsweek* interviewing me. The reporter was Ward Just, a bright, friendly guy who went on to write very good Washington novels.

"How'd you bring this off?" he asked. He was holding my book. I told him how — how the book was a spinoff of my heavy reportage for *Time*, how the Church's "open" faction wanted me privy to the power struggle behind the scenes, how Dick Clurman had given me six weeks off to go off and write it. "Six weeks?" he demanded.

I smiled. "Six weeks was enough." I told him I'd gone to the Divine Word College on the outskirts of Rome and worked fifteen, sometimes eighteen hours a day on it.

"And got it done it six weeks?" I nodded. "In a monastery?" He shook his head and made a note. Clearly, he admired the Spartan determination of someone who could produce a book in six weeks. I didn't tell him that it was Ignatian, not Spartan. I didn't tell him that I'd been a Jesuit, still felt like a Jesuit in the old Ignatian sense, one who wore no special habit, one who could become completely at home as an Indian bonze or a courtier in Peking. Or a foreign correspondent for *Time*.

"What did your wife think of that?" he asked.

I paused. It was odd. I didn't know the answer to that question. Mary hadn't said anything, one way or the other. I hadn't remembered asking her. I'd just assumed she wouldn't mind. Mary had Betsy, a vivacious two year old, to keep her company, and two maids, and her friend up the street, Barbara Bolton, whose husband worked at the Associated Press.

I mumbled something about the time I did spend with Mary — going home for lunch every day, going out to parties on Saturday night, to Santa Susanna for Mass on Sunday, strolling the Via Veneto, buying the Sunday papers, browsing them with Mary at one of the sidewalk cafes — before I plunged back to my little cell and my notes and my typewriter. "Naturally," I said, "my wife didn't like my being away all that much. She's a real trouper." I added — it was a proof that our marriage was okay — "We're expecting our second child sometime in late August."

The *Newsweek* reporter smiled and folded up his spiral notebook and stood as Tom Burns swooped into the room. "Got enough, old chap?" asked Burns. "We've got to get our author over to the BBC and ATV."

Ward Just assured him that, indeed, he had enough. He was fascinated by the political overtones of the Vatican Council, a gathering of the Church's elite. He told Burns, "Kaiser is covering the Vatican just about the way I'd cover Capitol Hill in Washington. It seems like such an obvious thing to do."

Yes.

⌘

ONCE, WHEN I WAS SIXTEEN, I had found the waves at Corona del Mar in Southern California exactly right for body surfing. It was a hot, cloudless day in mid-July, and there was a slight rip tide that sucked me effortlessly out to where the waves were forming so perfectly and breaking with such power that I could ride them in as far as I cared to go. That was pure pleasure, the closest I had ever come to knowing what Aristotle meant when he defined pleasure as "unimpeded activity."

In quite a different, but analogous, sense, now, I felt pleasure. The rip tide was just right and the waves were breaking beautifully for me, and, riding down a London street in Tom Burns' Mercedes, dressed in my secular "habit," my trenchcoat, I felt good. *Newsweek* didn't interview authors unless they were hugely successful. And now, though I was working for a rival publication, *Newsweek* had interviewed me. I asked Tom if he could tell at this early date, publication day, July 29, 1963, how the book was doing. Tom grinned but kept his eye on the road. "We went into our third printing last week."

"Before publication?"

"Right. Just to fill advance orders from the booksellers."

"How many copies in a printing?"

He said he wouldn't tell me. "You see, dear boy, if I were to tell you, then you might start expecting a large sum of money from me next winter."

I told him he'd already paid me an advance of five thousand pounds on the British rights, and that was more than I'd expected to make on the book, in toto. "I don't really care if I ever see another, uh, brass farthing from the book. I just want to know, need to know, have a right to know how many copies of my book you have in print." My emotions were rising.

"Easy, dear boy, easy," said Tom. He was a good driver and he seemed to enjoy weaving his way through the heavy midday traffic. "Our first printing was five thousand copies. Our second was seven five. Our third was ten thousand."

"So you've printed twenty two thousand five hundred copies?"

"Yes."

"O.K., Tom." That was enough for me. I'd made my point. All I wanted from my publisher was the truth. I didn't give a damn about the money.

Probably never would. Abruptly, I switched the conversation. "What's going to happen at ATV?"

Tom said the TV people wanted me for one five-minute interview and then some radio chaps from the BBC would talk with me for at least a half-hour. As it turned out, Tony Firth, the TV man, had questions that were altogether primary and after I gave my tentative, primary answers, the time was up and I felt that ATV's viewers were going to be cheated. I had so much to tell them. But the radio interviewer brought a chunk of understanding to the interview. He had a cleric with him, a Catholic chaplain from Cambridge. The three of us taped a satisfying discussion that BBC would later broadcast all over the world for a full hour.

The chaplain was under the thumb of the conservative English hierarchy and he had to take a cautious, adversarial position with me. I liked that. It gave me a chance to meet all the standard objections to change in the Church. Only after the program was all over did I express some reservations about my performance — that I must have sounded more like an advocate for change in the Church than an objective reporter. Well, no matter. I was only being honest. And who was objective anyway?

On the sidewalk in front of the BBC's gray stone building. I munched on an ice cream bar and spoke with the cautious chaplain while a young woman wearing a monogrammed jacket stood by with the young man who had interviewed me on BBC Radio. She was an attractive brunette with high cheekbones and a high bosom and she seemed not to notice me. In my state of exhilaration, I decided I needed this woman to notice me. I couldn't bear being ignored. I turned to her, fixed my eyes on hers and started interviewing her. I learned her name, rank, and serial number at the BBC and drew from her her own thumbnail biography. Meridee Barnett was only a few years out of Cambridge, had worked for the BBC as a documentary researcher for five years and then graduated to the rank of producer.

"O.K.," I said. "That's your two-minute history. Interesting, as far as it goes." I guessed that she was someone else's girl, but that didn't stop me. I pulled a copy of my book from my briefcase, inscribed it to her with some words that made her laugh, and took her hand in mine. "I want you to join me for the theater and supper tonight."

She said she'd like that. I told her to meet me at the Hilton at seven, she did, and we took a taxi to see *Oh, What a Lovely War,* a pacifist musical recommended by my pacificist Archbishop T. D. Roberts, though he hadn't seen it. He hadn't seen any play in fifty-four years. English clerics were forbidden to go the theater — part of that old keeping-the-world-at-arms-length attitude. Meridee had already seen it once, but wanted to see it again anyway, and afterward we dined at an Indian restaurant in Soho. In the balmy night, we walked hand in hand all the way back toward the Hilton, and I asked her about her hopes, her fight to make it in British television. "It is a struggle," she said. "But I am going to show them, all of them."

"You sound almost desperate," I said.

"Not desperate, just determined."

"Why so determined?" She shrugged and we walked for a time in silence. I tried to prime her. Mock serious, I said, "Because you come from poor, but honest stock?" She shook her head. We walked along, and she was still silent. Finally, I said, "Look, I'm not prying. At least, I hope not. It's just that I'm a reporter and I'm curious about people — and particularly about people who want to win."

"Well, in that case," she said, "if it's just your professional curiosity, go to hell." She wasn't angry. She had a provocative smile on her face.

Now I was on the defensive. "Uh, no," I stammered. "I mean, I, I really care. I mean, I care. It's just that — "

"It's just that your reporter's role makes it easier for you to ask questions — and remain a bit detached from the answers you're afraid you might receive?" It was a question and a statement. I didn't know how to reply. I was amazed at this young woman's directness and told myself I wished I could be this way, too. "No," she said, "we don't go up Oxford Street." She tugged me up another sidewalk. "This way."

"Look," I said. "Forget my reporter's role. What is it with you? I want to know."

"Oh," she said. "it isn't all that strange. You don't need to be Carl Gustav Freud to understand this. It's just that my father's frightfully rich and I have this overpowering desire to show him — and myself — that I can do things on my own. Without his help."

I nodded. I had enough information, but I had to ask another question to distract myself and her from the fact that her last words (about her father's being frightfully rich) had given me a sudden erection. "What does your father do?"

"Steel. He owns steel mills in Birmingham."

"Birmingham?" I said idiotically. "You from Birmingham?" What difference did it make where this woman was from? In my oversexed distraction, I needed to say something to fill the space. I hoped Meridee wouldn't notice. I tried to employ an old trick, once suggested as an antidote to "impure thoughts" by my Master of Novices: I cast all the fat people I knew as members of a mythical football team. I put Bishop Wright at center, Frank McCool at right guard, Vincent Yzermans at right tackle.... At the same time, I couldn't help wondering at the connection in me between money and sex — in me, who had once taken a vow of poverty and still acted as if money were the least important thing in my life.

Meridee told me about her childhood. She didn't spend much time in Birmingham. She went to school in London, to an exclusive convent school run by Anglican nuns. At this point, I was grateful she chose to chatter on. And more grateful still when we arrived at the Hilton and she agreed to come into the bar for a nightcap. We settled into a soft, red leather booth and ordered stingers from the waiter.

When the stingers came, Meridee said to me with a mischievous grin, "You all right — now?" I wondered, with a slight panic, if she had noticed me back there. She answered my unspoken question by lightly putting her hand on the inside of my thigh and giving me a soft, tentative kiss. Well, now I knew she had noticed and my heart leaped when I realized she was not only not offended, but a little excited herself. I kissed her back. Our kisses became one deep, passionate embrace. When we came up for air, she sighed, "I want you to fuck me."

"Oh," I said, completely surprised. I'd heard women use that word before, as an expletive and in anger, but never in this nice, passionate manner. I tried to recover, didn't know what to say, what I should say. Silently, I looked into her eyes. Lying to myself, I told myself that this had gone further than I had intended, that I'd better be cruel in order to be kind — though I took secret satisfaction in thinking that I was being more cruel to myself than to anyone else.

"Meridee," I said, "you are being direct with me and I love you for it. Let me be direct with you. I'm married. My wife's expecting a baby in a few weeks. This wouldn't be fair to her. I want to. I'd better not. I'd hate myself. Maybe I'd hate you, too. And I don't want to do that." As I uttered this priggish little speech, I was aware that I'd hate myself more for going to bed alone that night, hate myself for denying myself — and for denying Meridee. Damn me, I was incapable of admitting that. I thought I'd turned my back on the masochism of my Novitiate days. Obviously I hadn't.

Now, Meridee was kind enough and clever enough to accept my abnegation with a laugh. "I was only testing you," she said, patting her hair and taking out a little mirror. "As, perhaps, you were testing yourself."

"Did I pass the test?" I said, with a forced little chuckle.

"You passed your own."

"Did I pass your test?"

"No," she said, her eyes wide and searching. "You're a chap who feels one thing and does another. I'm not quite sure why, Bob. Some day you might find out. I certainly hope you do." Her mouth smiled, but her eyes didn't, though she touched my hand gently, as if to take the edge off her sharp words.

I smiled and nodded. "Maybe you're right." I rose and so did Meridee and together we walked toward the front door of the hotel where I asked the doorman to get the lady a taxi.

♪

IN NEW YORK, I had some radio interviews, arranged by Macmillan, part of the advance promotion for my book, whose pub date was still a couple of weeks away. I found Macmillan had done little else. "No parties?" I said to my editor. She seemed embarrassed and proceeded to invite a small group of *Commonweal* Catholics over to her apartment for cocktails. New York was not London, where Tom Burns, the Lord High Publisher himself, had taken a personal interest in my book, sold excerpts to the *Observer,* and helped get it reviewed in all the best places.

Here, of course, the pub date hadn't come yet. There was no mention of my book in the New York papers, because the papers were on strike. Nor in any magazine. There were no publisher's parties, there was no TV, certainly no women offering to go to bed with me. I thought of Christ's complaint about the people of Judaea: no man is a prophet in his own country. American readers, it seemed, were more intrigued with the mysterious and pseudonymous reporter for the *New Yorker*, Xavier Rynne, whose collected pieces were now between hard covers and already in the bookstores. So who was interested in my account? Not even, it seemed, the P.R. people at my publishing house.

Time's P.R. people set up a number of radio interviews for me and asked if I wanted to fly out to Chicago where Murray Gart, *Time*'s bureau chief, had booked me on Irv Kupcinet's television show. When? Saturday afternoon. I said I would come to Chicago, but I had to be in New York for a meeting on Monday with Walter Wanger and my new agent, who was going to ask Wanger for $25,000 for film rights to the book, plus $1,000 a week for a minimum of twelve weeks work by me. In 1963, that was big money. And he was going to suggest I receive five percent of the producer's profits as well. I was stunned. What had I done? When I returned to New York, I found Wanger balking at my agent's demands. "Look," I said to the two of them. "Work things out and let me know. My wife's going to have a baby, maybe tomorrow. I have to hustle back to Rome."

I cabled my office on Via Sardegna to see if someone could find Mary and tell her I'd be home late on the 12th. I hadn't been able to get her on the phone. Once, I made a connection to the villa in Lavinio, but Rosa, the maid, said that *la donna* had *uscita*. Exasperated, I demanded to know where she had gone to and Rosa said, *"Alla città."*

But if Mary had gone to the city, she certainly wasn't at home. I had tried there many times and gotten no answer. Now, I'd try one more time. It took me a half-hour to get the Rome operator. And then, happy surprise, it seemed that Mary was at home, for the line was busy. I waited five more minutes, tried again, and was lucky enough to get right through. No one answered the ring.

"Goddamn," I said in a fury. "Goddamn."

19

I landed at Leonardo da Vinci Airport at midnight, made my way through passport control, and saw Mary outside the customs barrier, great with child. Her arms and legs were bare. With her short summer haircut and light gray maternity dress with its wide black stripes, she looked like an escapee from the California Prison for Women at Tehachapi. Malachy Martin was right behind her. He was not wearing his cassock, but a pair of khaki pants and a light blue shirt with epaulets on the shoulders. The tan of his face was emphasized by the frosty whites of his cool blue eyes.

While the customs officers were making little chalk marks on my bags I watched Mary and Malachy with their heads inclined in earnest conversation. For an instant, I stiffened. I thought of two other moments this past summer when I had seen them with their heads together. It happened first when I was returning from a trot on the beach with our infant daughter on my shoulders. Another time I had driven to Lavinio early one afternoon and had come upon them unexpectedly on our patio. On both occasions, they had put on smiling faces as soon as they saw me. I had wondered about that then; I felt a pang of resentment now. I asked myself why Mary hadn't gotten someone else to come with her to the airport, or why she had come at all.

Of course, I told myself, she'd come because she'd missed me. I'd been away for days and I hadn't written or called much at all, not knowing how wives need to have their careering husbands keep "in touch." A *Time* magazine correspondent in Rome should have been more worldly-wise, more woman-wise, than I. But I was still a Jesuit at heart: I'd been a Jesuit for ten years, and the training had taken such a hold on me that I still followed the Jesuit code. I was still working "for the greater glory of God and the good of souls." Wives had never been part of that equation.

Once I had freed my bags from the eyebrows of the customs agents, I slipped through the gate and took Mary in my arms. I noted she was trembling. "What is it?" I asked.

"The baby," she said. "He doesn't want to come out."

I was speechless. What did Mary mean? Do babies have free will in such matters? For a moment, I consulted my memory, asking myself whether St. Thomas had written on the question. Was there an article in the *Summa Theologica* headed *Utrum sit liberum arbitrium in fetere humano?* I dismissed the thought and simply held Mary close and told her everything was going to be all right. I kissed her ear.

Malachy had hung back. Now he came up to the two of us, but he didn't speak, perhaps not wanting to intrude. He was very close to being our family priest, one of our best friends in Rome, and I tried to make him feel welcome. "Mal," I said, repeating by rote an archaic expression I hadn't heard for years, "you're a sight for sore eyes."

What the hell did I mean by that? There was a tight feeling in my chest. I knew I had told him a lie. I didn't appreciate his coming at all. I wondered why he wasn't in Beirut. He had been planning to go to Beirut. Then I told myself I shouldn't feel this way. After all, I had left Mary in a delicate condition. What the hell did I expect? That she drive out to Fiumicino by herself? I turned to Mary. "You shouldn't have come. You should have phoned the office and had Giulio come for me."

Mary made an effort to smile. When she was happy, her crossbit smile was a winning one, if only because it was, well, different. When she was sad, however, her smile became more of a twisted grimace. "I wanted to see you," she whimpered. "It's been weeks."

Malachy grabbed my largest bag and whispered in my ear, "Go easy. She's having a hard time of it right now."

I didn't know how I could react to that there and then. How was Mary having a hard time? It really wasn't any of Malachy's business at all, was it? And if Malachy knew something about Mary that I didn't know, that only helped underscore my guilt at taking my trip to London and New York.

"Come on," I said. "It's past midnight, almost one. We'd better get going." It was an hour's drive to the beach from the airport. I picked up my briefcase and a shopping bag full of presents for Mary and little Betsy and the maids. I even had one for Malachy.

We walked out into the night's humidity before Mary spoke. "We're not going to the beach," she said. "I moved back to Rome on Tuesday."

"Oh," I said. "You did?"

"I wanted to be close to the hospital."

I said nothing.

"I didn't want to be all the way out in Lavinio."

"Uh huh," I said. "What about Betsy and the maids?"

Mary pointed me toward our VW parked down the curb and said, "They stayed at the beach." She paused. "It's so hot in town."

"Sure," I said. I couldn't argue with her. Her story made sense. Keep Betsy with the maids at the beach. Nine months pregnant, Mary had best be close to Salvator Mundi Hospital.

Mary handed me the keys to the VW. I eased my bag into the back seat, stuffed the other things on top of it, leaving room for Malachy to climb in there, helped Mary get in front, closed the door gently and went around to the driver's side. Mary didn't reach over and unlock the door. She was sitting there, staring straight ahead, smoking a Marlboro, when I got behind the wheel. I started the car, released the brake, turned on the lights, and put the car in gear.

We were a mile down the road when Malachy, finished with the business of filling, tamping, and lighting his pipe, tried to break the tension. It was ninety degrees Fahrenheit outside and humid, but there was a spiritual chill inside the VW. "Tell us about London and New York, Bobby. Did they lay the world at your feet?"

I could see that Malachy was just trying to make conversation, but even so, there was an edge to his question, almost as if he were needling me. According to St. Matthew, it was the devil who, tempting Jesus, took him to a mountaintop and showed him all the kingdoms of the world and the glory of them. I resented the implication because there was a kernel of truth in it: that I, a new, celebrated author of the first book on Vatican II, was the recipient of recent worldly temptations.

I replied evenly, "New York was hot and muggy and not too interested in me." I added quickly, "But London was great." Though I had already written Mary about it in one letter, I told her how glorious a reception the people in London had given me and my book. "I got major, excited reviews in all the London papers. And my name writ large in all the subway stops." I didn't mention the tempting, beautiful producer for the BBC who wanted me — or report that I was too timid to honor her offer.

Malachy said he had heard about the London triumphs. He'd even gotten a note from a priest-friend in Ireland, telling him that my book on the Council was sold out of every store in Dublin. "The Irish clergy are in a tizzy. The Irish bishops even discussed it at one of their meetings."

Mary laughed. "The Irish bishops!" She said this with an air of contempt. I grimaced. Mary didn't know a single Irish bishop, but she'd learned from Malachy what an illiberal lot they were and now she held an all-too-confident scorn for them. I said nothing, concentrated on the road, let Malachy do most of the talking and got to our home on Monteverde Vecchio in forty minutes. I told myself, again, that no reasonable man should have negative feelings about Mary and Malachy. Malachy was a Jesuit priest. He had his vows. He wouldn't do anything bad with Mary. What I needed was more faith.

I threw my things down in the middle of the living room. I was glad to be home. Feeling better for that, and ready to show some faith — and hope and charity, I wondered if anyone wanted a drink.

"Yes," said Mary. "A martini." I did a mental double take. Mary had always preferred Scotch.

"A martini for me," said Malachy. "With a twist."

"A twist for me, too," said Mary.

I went to the kitchen, noted the sink was full of dirty dishes, grabbed an ice tray, and took it to the bar. I delivered the drinks, then went back to the bar to mix scotch and Drambuie for myself. "I've got things from New York," I shouted. "Want to see them?" I walked over to my bags and pulled out two dolls for Betsy and two cartons of duty-free Marlboros for Mary, and a stack of twenty LP records as well. I had the latest Richard Condon novel for Malachy, who had become a Condon fan after I had given him *The Manchurian Candidate* one night during a dinner party at our villa. He had taken the book back home to the Biblical Institute and stayed up until 3:00 A.M. to finish the thing — and then turned right back to the beginning and started all over again.

"I bought two suits at Brooks Brothers," I said. "What do you think?" I flourished each of them in turn. They were just two plain, unremarkable Brooks Brothers suits. What could anyone say about them? Mary said nothing. Malachy said nothing.

Mary took one of the records and put it on the hi-fi. It was an original cast recording of the Broadway musical *Carnival,* but The Grand Imperial Cirque de Paris was a little too grand for me. "Not too loud, Mary," I said.

"It's one thirty in the morning." She shot me an angry look and turned down the volume.

Mary came back and poked in my bag.

"What's this?" she said, pointing down to a hank of hair sticking out of the shopping bag. Her tone was accusatory.

"Well, uh," I stammered. "Just a little joke. They had these wigs at Bloomingdale's — "

"So you got me a blonde one? Great! Am I supposed to wear this thing?"

I was abashed. It wasn't an expensive wig, just a toy. Why the hell did I even get it? "It was there on a counter," I said weakly. "I just thought." I paused. I didn't know what I thought.

"Just a slip, huh? Like a slip of the tongue?" said Mary. "I wonder what Freud would make of this?" She dandled the blonde wig from the end of her index finger and twirled it. Then she put it on, at a crazy angle, crossed her eyes and grinned. I laughed. Malachy laughed. Mary stopped grinning. "Would you like me better as a blonde, Bob? Would you?"

"Of course not," I said, raising my voice a little as I admitted to myself that I probably wouldn't mind if Mary were a blonde, a brunette, and a redhead successive nights of the week. And what the hell was wrong with a little variety, now and then — or even all the time? Then I realized that what I really preferred was a Mary who would be herself. More and more, at parties, I'd been hearing her declaiming about the Council as if she understood what she was talking about when, actually, all she was doing was repeating something, word for word, that she'd heard me (or Malachy) say at a previous dinner party.

I stomped off to our bathroom, noticed a little brush that men used for scrubbing their fingernails. It wasn't mine. I had a hunch it was Malachy's. I'd seen it when he was staying at our beach house in Lavinio. I poked my head in the guestroom and found a bunch of Malachy's things scattered on the bed, along with a huge traveling bag.

I returned to the living room, made myself another, more generous Rusty Nail and then came back and gave Malachy the keys to the VW. "Time for you to go home," I said. "Take the VW. I'll get Giulio to pick me up in the morning."

Malachy said that it was a little late to be walking into a Jesuit house of studies. "They think I'm in Beirut. I haven't got back from Beirut yet." He looked at me wide-eyed, eyebrows raised, lips pursed, and then forced a bit of air through those lips to make a popping sound, which meant, finally and emphatically, "That's the way it is." The popping was like an exclamation point. Most people were content to use exclamation points in notes and letters and rarely in any other written work. Malachy had his own patented oral exclamation points to underline key elements in his picturesque speech and patter.

"You've been staying here?" I said, trying to sound matter-of-fact about it. He nodded and popped his lips. "Okay," I said. No more, just, "Okay." I didn't like this. I told myself they couldn't be intimate—not understanding, then, that spouses don't have to be sleeping with someone else to be unfaithful. As happily married couples all know, they do hundreds of things together that seal their intimacy: they talk and laugh, and dance, and play with the kids. They shop together, they cook together, they entertain friends, watch television, read in bed, lie on a beach together in silence. But if one of them is doing these things with someone else....

I took Mary by the hand. "Come on, Mary," I said, "let's go to bed."

"I haven't finished my drink yet." She looked like she was stuck in her chair for the rest of the night.

"Bring it with you." My voice was insistent. I gave her hand a little tug. On the record player, a raucous voice from *Carnival* was singing, "The dirty rat, he treats me like — a wife!" I went over and turned it off, then returned to Mary's side. She looked at me wryly, then rose and we went off to our bedroom. Malachy was over at the bar, making himself another drink.

I closed the bedroom door. Suddenly, Mary started to weep. "Oh, Bob, I've been so lonely. I didn't want you to go away and then you went away and then everyone else staying at the villa went away and I was so lonely."

I held her and cooed, "There, there. Of course. Of course."

"You didn't phone and you didn't write."

"I phoned. I just couldn't get through the goddamn chaos of the goddamned phone company, and when I did, I couldn't find you. I wrote you—three times—care of the office."

"I never got the letters. Malachy went in to the bureau to get the mail several times. And there was never anything from you." She started sobbing harder.

"Oh, Mary, Mary." Now I was weeping, too. "I'm sorry. I'm sorry. I love you so much." I turned out the light, climbed on to the bed and pulled Mary back into my arms. I whispered silently, "St. Joseph, pray for us." I hadn't said "a pious ejaculation" since my days at the Novitiate of Los Gatos.

My Novitiate was like a U.S. Marine Corps boot camp. Its discipline was supposed to make us into the kind of men who could take orders, so that, later on, we'd be the kind of shock troops our superiors (or even, in special cases, the pope himself) could send anywhere in the world, on any mission. It was also a life that seemed designed to keep us psychologically immature. Of course, this is one reason I joined the Jesuits in the first place: to keep from growing up, like some latter day Peter Pan.

I was still immature. I had had a Puritanical upbringing, and for ten years in the Jesuits, I was trained to think of sex as something dirty and dangerous and women as nothing but temptations to my holy vocation. Even after I was married to Mary, sex to me was more of a legitimate release than a way of creating an intimate communion with someone I really loved and wanted to be a part of and make a part of me. Mary was more of a symbol to me, a proof that I'd overcome "my flight from woman" than someone I could share my thoughts with, or my deepest fears or feelings.

And it never occurred to me that Mary had any real womanly needs beyond motherhood and shopping. I didn't know how to make her come, much less let myself let go with any great passion. I liked sex, but not too much, because (second-guessing the Creator) I thought too much sexual pleasure was bad.

Now, bound no longer by my Jesuit vows, I lay in silence with my wife. We were as close-fitting as two spoons, Mary's back to my front, and Mary sobbed quietly before she went to sleep. I was thinking about the Novitiate, and about Joseph, the guy who had had all kinds of doubts about his Mary, a young woman who had started to look suspiciously pregnant before they had come together.

I had a primal dream. I was in a large room, kneeling on the floor in the middle of a circle of my fellow Novices. One of them was unmistakably Malachy Martin, who stood and announced to the group that I had been rejecting him. He then proceeded to remove his cassock, lay it down on his chair, walk over to me, kneel down, and put his arms around my neck. Just as he was about to kiss me, I woke up.

Now what, I asked myself, was this all about? A Freudian psychiatrist would undoubtedly call this a homosexual dream. If it was, however, I didn't see it as a sign of my homosexuality, but of Malachy's. My dream was a warning, telling me what I hadn't noticed when I was awake. Malachy wanted me.

I sure as hell didn't want him. By now, I had no special fondness for Malachy Martin, this priest-poet-professor of the Society of Jesus. As a matter of fact, he'd become such an intruder in my life that I was beginning to curse the day he first walked into our Roman villa. Now, after the dream, I was staggered to think he might be trying to get closer to me by seducing my wife. I told myself this was a crazy thought.

But it didn't look quite so crazy the next morning, when I came upon two oil paintings in the guest room where Malachy had slept. One was a chain of nine nudes, frolicking hand in hand, in a circle. One was a nude study of a brunette with a twisted smile, like Mary's. I studied them more closely, looking for a signature. There was none.

20

I had been gone too long. Now at last, I was at home and glad to be here for the birth of my son. But almost a week passed, and still no baby. Mary was beginning to get more and more anxious. And so was I, not only because the kid didn't want to make his entrance, but because Malachy Martin didn't want to make his exit. He was still camped in our apartment and he was not ready to go back to the Biblicum just yet. As gently as I could, I questioned that decision. "I have my reasons," he said with a dark look, hinting something sinister.

"In that case," interrupted Mary, even more concerned about him, it seemed, than I, "you can stay."

Five more days passed. Still no signs of labor. Dr. Mario Pignanelli, Mary's obstetrician, said, "If the baby doesn't come this weekend, we'll have to induce labor." By Sunday night, Mary was ensconced in Salvator Mundi Hospital, relieved that at last the uncertainty was over. The baby would be born at ten o'clock in the morning.

"You may as well go to dinner," Mary said. "Go ahead. I'll see you in the morning." I hesitated. "Go on," said Mary. She smiled. "Take Malachy."

ॐ

MALACHY MARTIN AND I dined out-of-doors at a trattoria in Trastevere, where he told me the latest news on "the Jewish *schema.*" Malachy had inherited an Irish ancestor's gift for storytelling and in each of his yarns, he always found a good role for himself, perhaps too good. Invariably, he was the sleuth and the hero of each tale, a black-cassocked Sherlock Holmes. Various other Jesuits — John Long, Frank McCool, John Felice, Ed Lynch — served as his Dr. Watson. His efforts always proved beyond a shadow of a doubt that someone, either the anti-Semitic Roman Curia or Catholic prelates from the Arab nations or a combination of both, was trying to sabotage Catholic-Jewish relations by scuttling "the *schema* on the Jews."

This was a conciliar document that was supposed to exonerate modern-day Jews for having killed Christ. The ecumenical intent was clear: Cardinal Bea wanted the Council to make it impossible for anyone, ever again, to justify their anti-Semitism with some pseudo-theological, much less Biblical, reasoning. My own Jewish friends at *Time,* all highly acculturated, didn't quite understand what all the fuss was about. They insisted they weren't there when Jesus was crucified on Golgotha and they didn't need "exoneration" from the Vatican Council or anyone else. But if the Council wanted to make a statement, that was the Council's business. I took pretty much the same position, and I was puzzled when Malachy Martin kept trying to make such a big deal out of "the Jewish *schema.*"

Now here he was again, Malachy-one-note, telling me a story about a phony telegram from Bea's office to the American Jewish Committee in New York, and another about forged letters, supposedly sent from Bea's office to the Council's Central Commission.

"Forged?" I said. "By whom?"

Malachy lowered his eyes. "The usual place," he said.

"The Curia?" I said. He nodded. "Where in the Curia?" I said. He shrugged, paused for a moment, as if he were trying to assess the prudence of letting me in on this. I shrugged, too. Since I made my truce with Cardinal Ottaviani, I knew I'd have to check and double check on everything from this source: I couldn't afford to be a conduit for any more of Malachy's tendentious tales. "It's still early," I said, giving up on the Jews for the nonce. "Let's go to a movie."

We saw a dubbed version of *Some Like It Hot,* with Jack Lemmon and Tony Curtis and Marilyn Monroe. I'd seen it before, but it was an escape, at least, from the overdose I was getting of Malachy Martin. Not even this movie could provide that for me. Halfway through the picture, Malachy started making puzzling noises when Miss Monroe appeared on the screen wearing a white jersey frock that concealed nothing. I couldn't figure out what was wrong and tried to peer at him in the dark without seeming to peer. Nothing wrong, I discovered. Just the natural result of a cleric contemplating the bust of Marilyn. Those noises were the noises of Malachy breathing hard. I had read the word "panting" before, and had seen a dog panting. I had never seen a man in heat. Now, by God, here I was watching one of my friends, a Jesuit, panting after a blonde sexpot. On a movie screen. I tried not to think about it.

We got back home around eleven. I made an immediate move to retire and was already in my nightshirt when Malachy knocked on my bedroom door. I didn't respond, but walked over to the door instead and opened it a crack, bracing my foot behind it. "Yes?" I said.

Malachy was standing there in his shorts. He said, "I'd like to talk a bit." He tried to push open the door.

"Nope," I said, continuing to block the door with my foot. "I'm tired."

"A nightcap would help you relax. Let's have a little nightcap."

"No, thanks." I shook my head, slammed the door and turned the key in the lock and tried to read myself to sleep.

Just before midnight, Mary phoned. She told me she'd started having labor pains, the doctor had come over and found that the baby's heart was racing. Dr. Pignanelli wanted to operate within the hour.

I put on a pair of pants and a sports shirt and emerged from my room to find Malachy sitting on the floor in the living room with his legs crossed, Indian-style. "You meditating?" I said, smiling at my own private joke. I had never caught Malachy Martin engaged in any kind of prayer. I had never even seen him reading his Divine Office. He looked up and frowned, because I am sure he caught the veiled sarcasm, but he did not respond. "I'm going to the hospital," I told him. "The doctor's going to take the baby tonight."

He wanted to come with me.

"Oh, you don't have to do that," I said. I was hoping he'd stay out of this. I wondered to myself why the man didn't just stay home and masturbate or something. No such luck. He had his clothes on and was in the car before I was. On the way to the hospital, he chattered like a chickadee. I wasn't even listening.

At Salvator Mundi, I hurried up to the third floor and asked a nurse about Mary. She evaded my question. "Dr. Pignanelli should be back here." She consulted her watch. "In a little while."

"Fra poco?" I said sardonically, making a subtle, angry jibe at the vague phrase the Italians used all too often when they intended taking their own sweet time. I clomped down the hall to Mary's room. When I opened the door, I found Malachy leaning over Mary's bedside. I gasped.

He straightened up, tiptoed over to me, took my elbow with one hand and eased me out of the room. "She's asleep," he said portentously, as if he'd just been privileged to announce the secret of King Tut's tomb. I stiffened, shook him off and put my right hand in the middle of his chest. "Just — stay — away," I said fiercely.

"All right, Bobby," he said, popping his lips once, then again, for emphasis. "All right." He pulled out his pipe.

I went back into the darkened room. Mary was breathing heavily through her mouth and when I touched her brow, she seemed feverish. I put my ear and a hand down to her swollen tummy. I couldn't hear or feel anything that was significant to me. I kissed her on the cheek and then said a silent prayer. "God," I said. "I hope the child is okay. I hope Mary is okay. Make them okay."

Fifteen minutes later, Dr. Pignanelli came into the room and turned on the overhead light. "Ahh, Mr. Kaiser," he said. "Good. Good. I may need you in a moment or two." He took a stethoscope out of his jacket pocket and listened for a moment to whatever was going on inside Mary's womb. He shook his head. "Yes, definitely," he said. "The baby's heart is still racing. It will fibrillate even more during the next contraction. I'll need your permission for the surgery."

"Is it dangerous?"

"The baby's heart cannot stand a normal delivery."

"And Mary? Is surgery dangerous for her?"

"Any surgery is 'dangerous.' But this Cesarean should be no more dangerous than a tonsillectomy." He waved his hand, revising that statement. "Only a little more dangerous. But Mary is in good health, she is young, what? Twenty six? I recommend it."

"Then go ahead."

The doctor moved to the door. "Come," he said. He led me down near the nurses' station. "Please wait here in this lounge," he said. "I will call you when it is all over."

I nodded and shrugged, went over and sat down. One of the nuns came over to me with a clipboard, pointed to a form, and gave me a ballpoint pen to sign. I signed it without reading it as Dr. Pignanelli and two attendants hurried by with a shrouded figure on a gurney. I clapped my palms to my eyes and lowered my head. I heard footsteps approach. I didn't turn.

"It looks bad, Bobby," said Malachy Martin.

I glared at him. "How the hell do you know?" I rasped. Martin blinked furiously and popped his lips, but said nothing. "What the hell do you know about it?" I asked, my voice dripping with disgust. "Are you a doctor?" He stared at me. Hell, I thought, he doesn't even look like a priest.

He looks more like a zookeeper standing there in his sneakers and his wrinkled khakis. I shook my head, closed my eyes, and let my head fall back on my shoulder.

I may have been half-asleep. Suddenly, Dr. Pignanelli had a hand on my knee and he was smiling. "It's a boy," he said. "Mary's fine, and so is the baby. He was all twisted around, with his head up and his rear end down and his feet sticking straight out."

"All right!" I said, elated. I shot a look of scorn toward Malachy Martin, still sitting across the hall from me. "Can I see Mary?"

The doctor nodded. "She's asking for you."

Mary was smiling. "It's all right, Bob," she said. "I'm all right. The baby's all right." Her speech was slurred, an aftereffect of the anesthetic, but her voice was strong, triumphant. "Everything's going to be all right."

"Oh, Mary," I said. My eyes were wet and my voice was choked.

Malachy Martin pushed in between us. "Yes," he said, just as if Mary had been talking to him. "I told you so. I said everything would be all right."

I sagged a bit. Was there no end to this guy's moonshine? The best thing I could think of was to get him out of here, take him out. "Come on," I said, controlling my voice as well as I could. "Let's let Mary get some sleep. Let's all get some sleep." I put my face close to Mary's. "You really O.K.?"

"Yes, yes, yes," she said, almost laughing.

"Good. Good." Mary was high on something, I thought. On what? On life, I guessed. On new life.

"But, Bob?

"I don't want to name him John Paul." She made a face. "I don't like the sound of John Paul. John Paul Jones died of syphilis in a Paris hospital. Let's call him T. D."

Now it was my turn to laugh. "T. D. For Tommy Roberts? Sounds good. Great." I kissed her on the lips and turned to Dr. Pignanelli. "Can I see T.D?"

"Yes," he said. "I'll take you." He waved his hand, with a motion that means "bye-bye" in the United States, but "come" in Italy.

I regarded the baby through a plate glass window in the nursery. A nurse brought him close to the glass and I could see that he was beautiful. He wasn't all red and wrinkled, like most newborns. He was a peach, with a halo of fuzz, a golden peach.

It was a moment I wanted to savor in silence but Malachy was right behind me, chattering again. I didn't even listen to him and drove him back to our apartment, only a few blocks from the hospital, said good night and tumbled into bed.

When I awoke, my Jesuit friend was packing his things. He was going back to the Biblicum. It took both of us heaving together to wrestle his huge bag into the back seat of the VW, and then we motored through the streets of Trastevere, over the Ponte Vecchio, past the stark monuments of the Forum, circled the Coliseum, and stopped just past the Trevi Fountain at the front door of the Biblicum.

When we got his huge bag out of the car and on to the cobblestones, Malachy said, "Thanks, Bobby." His voice was abstracted.

I turned and climbed back into the car. *Fa niente*, I said. I turned the key in the ignition. "It was really nothing." As I drove off, I could see Malachy in my rearview mirror, still standing next to his huge bag and staring down at the cobblestones.

21

I didn't have any more time to think about Malachy Martin, because, all of a sudden, the second session of the Council was upon us. Now, in September 1963, thanks to Pope Paul VI's promise to continue the aggiornamento begun by Pope John XXIII, the world was pretty much convinced that something historic was happening in Rome, a sea-change in the life of one of the world's great, unchanging institutions. I wanted to chronicle this history — and keep two steps ahead of my press colleagues, who were arriving at this session in seemingly greater numbers than a year before. The official press center seemed more crowded. Most of the newcomers were reporters of real quality.

Newsweek had hired Dick Senier, a bright young man with a seminary background, to help Bill Pepper in Rome, and they had a new religion writer in New York named Ken Woodward, a Notre Dame grad. The *New York Times* sent in Milton Bracker, a Jew who was too good a reporter not to get excited about the new things happening in Rome. The *Chicago Daily News* assigned a veteran foreign correspondent, George Weller. John Cogley, an editor of *Commonweal,* had taken up residence in Rome with his family. Monthly magazines had commissioned some tweedy intellectuals to observe, to put things into historical context, yes, and to do some reporting of their own, too. One of them was Michael Novak, a young academic out of Harvard, who phoned me the day he arrived in Rome to tell me he would appreciate any guidance I could give him. He was in Rome on assignment by *Harper's.* I had heard of Novak, knew that he had strong liberal Catholic credentials and asked him and his bride, Karen, to lunch so I could meet them both.

We dined in an outdoor garden at Gigi Fazzi, near the American Embassy, and I laughed when he told me that the editors at *Harper's* wanted him to find out "the secret of Kaiser's mysterious influence at the Council." No secret: I invited Mike and Karen to see for themselves — by joining us at our Sunday night buffet supper, the day that little T. D. was baptized by Archbishop T. D. Roberts, not in St. Peter's, but at St. John Lateran. ("There," said Roberts with a flourish when he was finished pouring the water. "You're the first Kaiser to be baptized here since Charlemagne.") At Via Quirico Filopanti 2, the Novaks would see that Mary and I simply loved to entertain, and that we enjoyed putting together an ambience that could draw the Council's newsmakers and their friends.

The ambience: a high-toned word for good food, good drink, and informal ways that made people feel they could come and relax and stay as long as they wanted. The Sunday evenings had begun in the first place with T. D. Roberts and an all-star cast of Jesuits, who kept inviting more and more of their friends. Quickly, our home on Monteverde Vecchio became a center of the Council's progressive wing, those who were pushing hardest for updating everything, and doing so with a high hilarity. (Strange: Iñigo de Loyola was best known as a leader of the Counter Reformation, and now his troops were taking a leading role in bringing it to an end.)

The Sunday nights were filled with good stories, but, as a host trying to make sure everyone was happy, I usually ended up listening to none of them. Instead, I flitted from group to group. I rather enjoyed knowing that Weigel and McManus and Diekmann and Danielou and Küng (and our seventy-five other intimate friends) wouldn't be having all this fun if it weren't for me and Mary — and my *Time* magazine expense account.

The cast of regulars had expanded. There were more of the Protestant observers, and their wives, "the separated sistern." I did not invite my rivals from the English-speaking secular press, but laid out welcomes for Francis Xavier Rynne Murphy (who was wearing a very fine, tailored suit now, not his old tattered cassock, and traveling in taxis), Ed Duff, a Jesuit working for Religious News Service, Gary MacEoin, a former seminarian and a prolific freelance writer, Donald Campion, Daniel O'Hanlon and Robert Graham, Jesuits from *America* magazine, and, of course, Michael Novak and John Cogley, who had become my two best friends at the Council. Henry Fesquet of Paris's *Le Monde* and Jean Vogel from *Informations Catholiques Internationales* were back in town, and to our Sunday nights they brought in a few more friends from the foreign press: Gunnel Vallquist, a blonde journalist from Stockholm who would later become a member of the Swedish Academy (which handed out the Nobel Prize), and a Belgian, the Jesuit Piet Fransen, a man who always seemed to have a cigar in his mouth.

Prominent Catholic liberals kept showing up, men and women who had come to lobby the Council for one pet project or another — Ivan Illich and Betsy Hollants from Cuernavaca, Mexico, Gordon Zahn, the Christian pacifist, John Todd, the publisher from London, and others who just came to look and listen: Paul Horgan, the novelist, Frederick Franck, the artist, and, from Naples, Bruno Scott-James, the man who was Morris West's model for the burnt-out monsignor in *The Devil's Advocate*.

Archbishop T. D. Roberts was our houseguest again. Two or three nights a week, we'd have a sit-down dinner for eight people who could stimulate one another. One night was not an untypical mixture. We had Otto Preminger and his wife (he was making a movie in Rome called *The Cardinal*); Jules Leger, the Canadian ambassador to Italy, and his wife; Archbishops Denis Hurley of Durban, South Africa; Eugene D'Souza of Nagpur, India; Harold Henry of Kwangju, South Korea; Bishop Sergio Méndez-Arceo of Cuernavaca, Mexico, with his private theologian, Gregoire LeMercier, prior of the Benedictine monastery in Cuernavaca. And, of course, Archbishop Roberts.

LeMercier was by far the most interesting man at that dinner party. He was a tall, graying man with a military bearing, who had grown up as an intellectual in his native Belgium, but somehow found his way into the Benedictine Order, escaped Europe during World War II, came to the U.S., and eventually founded his monastery in Mexico. One night, he had a vision of the Blessed Virgin Mary — and woke up the next morning blind in one eye. Instead of consulting a holy confessor who could help him discern the religious significance of this, he did what any good intellectual would do. He betook himself to a psychoanalyst in Mexico City, to see what was going on. In analysis, he learned so much about himself that he suggested his whole monastery go into group analysis. Most of his friars agreed to do so, so they could become better Benedictines, by getting to know themselves. With the help of Sigmund Freud.

When LeMercier told his story, Preminger shook his head in wonder. Most of the civilized world had thought the Church clearly opposed to the very idea of Freudian analysis. Now here was a Benedictine monk telling him that his whole monastery had embraced it. Preminger said, "You have a Catholic psychiatrist?"

"No," smiled LeMercier. "In Mexico City, I found Gustav Quevedo, an atheist and a Jew. He turned out to be just fine. He also brought in a woman to help him."

"A woman? Among all your monks?"

"She turned out to be just fine, too. Better, even, than a man. A lot of our monks found, in group analysis with her, that they'd come to the monastery in flight from women."

"What did they do then?" asked Preminger.

LeMercier said that many of them left the Order. "If they didn't really belong there," he said, raising his palms, "I couldn't expect them to stay."

"And the Vatican?" said Otto, trying hard to keep his monocle from falling out. "The Vatican just let them go?"

"The Vatican couldn't stop the men from leaving."

I broke in. "Tell them, Gregoire, about the process that the Benedictines — and the Vatican — set in motion because of all the movement." In fact, LeMercier would soon go on trial before the Holy Office.

LeMercier smiled and looked around the table with his one good eye. "Ah," he said, "that is a story not yet ended. Let's wait and see how that comes out."

I turned to LeMercier's bishop. "Where do you stand on all this, Don Sergio?"

Méndez took a sip of wine, blotted his lips with a napkin. "With Gregorio's help," he said, "I am preparing an intervention for the Council. I think it's time we baptized Freud."

At this point, Mary started nursing the baby at the table, damned if she'd miss any of this talk. Preminger looked confused. The other prelates, who had already learned not to be shocked by anything they saw or heard at our dinner table, only smiled and moved on to the next topic. One of them wondered whether we thought the Council should take a new look, at last, at birth control. Preminger raised another expressive eyebrow. Archbishop Roberts said it was high time. The Legers seemed especially pleased to see how this Church of theirs was destroying old stereotypes.

∽

SUNDAY NIGHTS, of course, we still had our buffet supper for sixty or seventy: all the old gang from the first session: Gregory Baum, Tom Stransky, John Long, Jorge Mejía, Leo Alting von Geusau, Roberto Tucci, Vincent Yzermans, George Higgins, even Malachy Martin, who, despite my cool attitude toward him now, couldn't stay away from the action.

He himself was at the center of one imbroglio at a party early in the fall. I watched as Gus Weigel took Malachy aside, upset with him. Weigel had given a story to the *New York Times*. The story had quoted Weigel saying that the *schema* on the Jews would probably be tabled during the second session, and Weigel had been called on the carpet by Cardinal Bea for telling the *Times* what was, Bea knew, not a true story at all. No one was asking to table the *schema*. I knew Martin had been Weigel's source; back in mid-August, Malachy tried to sell the story to me, but I wasn't buying. Now Weigel was complaining to Martin, "But you told me...." Martin said something I couldn't hear. He did so very solemnly, popped his lips for emphasis, then giggled. Weigel shook his head. "Well, I don't see how Bea and Willebrands could tell me just the opposite then, and in such emphatic terms."

Martin and I hardly exchanged two words together. I had stopped using him as a source, simply because I couldn't trust him any longer. Sir Frank Willis, a distinguished gentleman from England who dabbled in art history, came up to me one day at the U.S. Bishops' Press Panel and told me that he'd been trying unsuccessfully to find the painting I had described in the beginning of my book, the painting of Adrian VI on the bark. Could I give him my reference?

I asked Malachy Martin, my original source, for the reference, but he only smiled. Sir Frank didn't give up easily. He approached me several times during the next few weeks; I had no answer for him. Months later, he wrote me from England to tell me that he had consulted with an expert in Florentine art who told him that he doubted there was such a painting. During the reign of Adrian VI, there was no "master" in Florence named Giacomo. My guess: that Martin made the whole thing up.

I also knew, now, that he was planting more false stories about "the Jewish *schema*." His reports about opposition to the statement, relayed to me by Mike Novak or John Cogley, never seemed to check out. I knew that Martin was manufacturing them, but I had to wonder why. I suspected he wanted to keep the statement in the news, so that, in face of aroused public opinion, the *schema* would remain an important issue in the conciliar aula. But what was Martin's special interest?

I figured it out when Martin showed up the next Sunday night with a pair of important American Jews, representatives of the American Jewish Committee. But of course: Martin was their lobbyist. These Jews were using him, and paying him well for his help, which they thought they needed because they were reading all these stories in the *New York Times* (planted by Malachy Martin!) saying the schema was in trouble. During the summer, I had noted that Malachy always had a wallet stuffed with hundred-dollar bills. Now I knew where he was getting them.

During the second session, there were some other new faces. John Courtney Murray, the New York Jesuit who had been specifically disinvited to the first session, was here now as a *peritus* to none other than Cardinal Spellman. Spellman was no liberal, but he had become one of my better sources before and after the conclave that elected Giovanni Battista Montini, Pope Paul VI, and I found that, in Rome, at least, he was not the ogre of legend. There were times when, alone, he would stroll over to my office on the Via Sardegna simply to chat, or bring me a document. Furthermore, he had aligned himself with those Council liberals who wanted the Council to baptize America's religious freedom and make it a part of Pope John's aggiornamento. That was why Spellman brought in Murray, the *Time* cover boy whose learned articles had outlined the underlying theology of the U.S. Constitution.

I had every reason to like Murray. But I didn't. He was intelligent, he had a sense of humor, he was a friend of my friend Gus Weigel, and he was very close to the Luces. (In fact, Weigel told me that several years before, the Luces, Weigel, and Murray had experimented with sacred mushrooms together under the clinical direction of one of the nation's leading psychologists.) It soon became clear, however, that Murray, like many a New York Province Jesuit, thought of himself as someone above the rest of us. He was as tall as Andy Heiskell, Time Inc.'s board chairman, carried himself like General Douglas MacArthur, and spoke with a deep, upper class New York honk. He had a tendency not to converse so much as orate; he was like an up-to-date reincarnation of St. Robert Bellarmine, as played by Sir John Gielgud.

Still, I welcomed Murray's presence at these Sunday nights, because he drew a number of U.S. bishops who might not have come if they weren't sure Murray would be there. I'd been told that many of the American bishops were uncomfortable at Via Quirico Filopanti 2, even some of the more liberal U.S. bishops, afraid Kaiser might quote them in the pages of *Time,* a worldly and, therefore, anti-Catholic, journal.

I didn't let the gossip bother me. I was able to recognize a snub when I saw one. At a reception given by Loyola University of Chicago one night at the Hilton, I moved into a receiving line to introduce myself to Chicago's

Cardinal Albert Meyer, only to have him turn aside with a look of dismay. The hurt didn't last more than a moment. Cardinal Jan Alfrink of the Netherlands was standing right next to Meyer in the receiving line. When I told him who I was, he said, "Not the Bop Kaiser who wrote the book?" He hugged me and called over to several other Dutch bishops. "Here! Come over here and meet Bop Kaiser."

The Dutch bishops embraced me, but some English bishops were as wary of me as many Americans. In London, someone had given orders that my book not be displayed in the windows of the Catholic Truth (!) Society on Ashley Place. Moreover, at a reception in the English College, one English bishop was moved to apologize to Msgr. Cardinale for my book, published as it was by one of their own Catholic houses, Burns & Oates. "Sorry about that book by Kaiser," said this bishop to the monsignor.

Msgr. Cardinale, third in command in the Vatican's Secretariat of State, had been the source of some of my best stories. He wasn't sorry about that book by Kaiser. "Ohhh," he said. "Bob Kaiser's book. A beautiful book. A lovely book."

"Uhhh, yes," said the bishop, backpedaling furiously. "A beautiful book."

England's ranking prelate, Archbishop John Heenan, had even given me a fine notice in his own paper. Thanks to him and other reviewers, my book had held the number-one spot on best-seller lists in London and Dublin for weeks. And my name became notorious in the British Isles. One newspaper sponsored a limerick contest on the Council and the winning entry went:

> There was a *New Yorker* named Rynne,
> Whose reports when in doubt he kept thin.
> But Bob Kaiser of *Time,*
> Thought conjecture no crime,
> And every doubt Rynne left out, he put in.

The author of that jingle may have been thinking about some of the (largely undocumented) muckraking I did on the Roman Curia. Now, I imagined, the Curia was getting even. I learned on October 1 that a Church official had sent someone around to all the bookstores in Rome and had them put copies of my book under the counter, along with Xavier Rynne's, and Hans Küng's.

Whoever the church official was, it was a counterproductive move. Hundreds of newsmen were roaming the city, looking for their own muck to rake over, and one of them soon traced the order to a priest in the Rome Vicariate who admitted he had his orders from the Holy Office. He said he hadn't banned the books; he didn't have that kind of power. He'd just asked the booksellers not to display the books, not sell them to seminarians.

I couldn't believe this. The Holy Office was only helping to prove what its critics had been asserting all along, that it had too much power, that it hid behind its own rules of secrecy and ignored due process, and that it tended to treat members of the Church like children. The seminarians sent by their bishops to Rome were the cream of the crop, a group whose faith in the Holy Spirit, if not the Holy Office, could hardly be shaken by Kaiser or Küng or Rynne.

The Holy Office action only helped give more bite to Pope Paul's own words to the Curia just before the opening of the second session, that the Curia needed reform, now. Members of the Roman Curia had been quoted in the press; they weren't against reform in principle, but like the Southern whites then faced with demands for integration, they'd been saying that now was not the time.

George Armstrong reported in the *Guardian* that, despite the ban, I was among several hundred journalists who were received on October 1 by the pope and given his blessing. After the papal audience, he wrote, many of my colleagues in the hall hastened over to tell me the Holy Office ban could only boost sales in Britain and the U.S. Armstrong concluded: "Mr. Kaiser may be the first author to be banned by the Church and blessed by the pope on the same day."

I imagine this report boosted sales somewhat. POPE BANS 3 AUTHORS, cried a page 1 headline in the *London Daily Express*. In the U.S., *Commonweal* wrote a wry editorial hailing the Holy Office on its move. "Many of us have been worried that a spirit of Catholic liberty was rearing its head. We feel more secure now."

I was not pleased. I still cared too much about the approval of others, and if I got one negative review, I wanted to fight back. I received a note from an Irish pastor in County Antrim who said my book "will do harm both inside and outside the Church." I wrote to him and said that "others here in Rome this fall — including cardinals, archbishops, bishops, abbots, and theologians — believe the book is doing a great deal of good, especially with non-Catholics. If that is so, all the better. I could never content myself with speaking to the saved." He thanked me for my courteous reply, said he was seventy-three years old and respected my "honest attempt to arouse all concerned to greater pastoral efforts."

Gus Weigel warned me of the criticism that would be coming my way. "Strong prejudices show up in your book," he had written in the summer from his home in Woodstock, Maryland. "They do not offend me, because the same prejudices are my own. But you will have to pay the price of your courage and candor."

Of course, he was right. The *Denver Register* said I was "a profoundly ignorant man" who had produced "worthless scuttlebutt about the Council." The *Register's* reviewer, Msgr. John S. Kennedy, who was widely syndicated in the U.S. Catholic press, called it "a cheap and vulgar sensationalism of what actually happened." That bothered me more than it should have. Msgr. Kennedy, after all, wasn't there at the first session of the Council.

I had more than enough support from those who were there. Bishop Emmett Carter of London, Ontario, who later became the cardinal-archbishop of Toronto, wrote Msgr. Higgins, "I am reading the last pages of Kaiser's book. . . . I admire him and I honor him. It is quite obvious that the inner core of the Curia is both ruthless and dangerous. I for one did not rejoice at the presence of Cardinal Ottaviani and some of his friends. I do not rejoice now at their continued presence in Rome, where their counterattacks are likely to prove more effective than all our oratory."

Shortly after the book ban, Msgr. Luigi Ligutti, an American priest who had pioneered a special pastoral ministry in the rural Midwest but who was now living in Rome, asked me to visit him at his home on the edge of the city, a home he had built with his own hands. He seemed concerned about a rumor he had heard: that the people in the Holy Office had tried to get me fired. I assured him that *Time*'s editors were backing me one hundred percent.

"That's good," he said. Then he launched into a delicate matter. Someone very high up in the Vatican liked my book very much, so much that he wanted to see it translated into Italian and published in Milan, if I would bowdlerize it a bit. What did he mean? "Well," he coughed. "There were some references in it to Cardinal Ottaviani. There was a terrible reaction in the Holy Office to your description of the cardinal's eyes."

In retrospect, I didn't much like it myself. He was talking about one of Malachy Martin's pen portraits that had appeared in my book: "Ottaviani's eyes. One half closed, the effect of an ailment, lulled one with the half-formed idea of myopia and at the same time pulled one up with the jerking impression of a weary eye peering through barred shutters; the other eye wide open and staring in downright challenge, in silent reproof." The pen portraits may have been fun for Martin, but none of them really belonged in my book: they weren't mine. A more courageous editor, seeing them for what they were, tasteless purple patches, would have cut them out of the manuscript.

I told the monsignor that I'd welcome a chance to rewrite the whole book. I had done it in an awful hurry, in six weeks. But I was still too busy to do any extra work now. I had turned down a chance to write Wanger's documentary movie about Pope John, because I wanted to go on covering the Council for *Time*. And I was so busy doing that I hardly had time to read all the book reviews that were coming in now from the United States.

Msgr. Ligutti said I didn't understand. "This person who wants to see the book in Italian," he said, "is very high up in the Vatican."

I regarded him for a moment with a raised brow. Did he mean the pope? But of course he did. Ah, the monsignori of Rome! Now I fully kenned the meaning of the phrase "a fine Italian hand." Still the blunt American, I asked the monsignor if this was "someone at the very highest level."

He nodded soberly. "But you can't say—"

I interrupted him and held up my hand. "It's okay," I said. "I won't tell a soul." (And I didn't, even though I was tempted to tell the likes of a Msgr. Kennedy.) "But I *am* busy. Let's wait. I'm going to do another book at the end of the second session. Maybe we can do something then about a revised Italian edition. Of both books."

I walked a little taller after this covert endorsement of my take on the Council from Pope Paul VI himself. I would need the boost later on. I really didn't need it then. Around the city, I started noticing that people were pointing at me in restaurants, news photographers at the press center were snapping my picture, and TV cameras at the American Bishops' Press Panel would whirr when I stood to ask a question. That was no cure for my colossal egotism, and I began to think of myself as some kind of big shot — just about the time that I got a phone call at the office from a visiting journalist, Meridee Barnett of the BBC. She was in Rome to do a special feature on the Council. She wanted to interview me and she wanted me to point her to some other good sources.

She showed up at the *Time* office on Via Sardegna, and I took her out to one of the nearby sidewalk cafes on the Via Veneto, where we sipped *negronis* for an hour and watched the *passegiata,* the Romans' informal, 5:00 P.M. strolling parade, while I regaled her with stories of conciliar Rome. I arranged to meet her and her camera crew the next day at noon in St. Peter's Square, and I gave her the names and phone numbers of others who might help her do a good report. Among them: the name of Malachy Martin. I didn't tell her what I was after, but I had a hunch about him that I wanted to test. "Ask him to have dinner with you," I said. "At the BBC's expense, naturally."

She agreed and phoned the next afternoon to say she'd be having dinner with Martin at nine that evening. "Good," I said. "I'll be working late. I want to come by the Excelsior at eleven or so, so I can get your impression of him." Meridee started to object — no wonder, because she knew I was using her for something she didn't understand — but I shushed her and said she owed me one.

It was 11:15 P.M. From my office, I phoned Meridee in her room at the Excelsior. No answer. So I walked to the hotel, two blocks away, and waited off to the side of the portico so I could spot her as she returned from dinner. She sauntered up shortly, dressed in a smashing little black cocktail dress, and spotted me. "He doesn't act like a priest," she said.

I asked her what she meant. She could not, or would not, explain, and she seemed angry at me, and stalked off to the lobby. I didn't follow her. Her move confirmed — what? Nothing certain.

I confirmed something disquieting in myself, however, on the very next day. I found that I, myself, was feeling attracted to Meridee more than I should be. We were having lunch together at Piccolo Mondo, a popular midday spot for English-speaking expatriates in Rome, not far from my office. (There was no meeting of the Council that day and no news conferences.) And I gave her a look as we sipped the last of our Montrachet that said I was now ready to accept the invitation she had given me back in July in London.

She was not ready now. She said, "You didn't want to go to bed with me then because you were married. You had children. Well, you are still married. You still have children."

I started to say that things were different now.

She interrupted. "No, I don't really think they are. You suspect Father Martin is having an affair with your wife, don't you?"

"Well," I said. "Not really. They —"

"Well, then, how are things different?" I hesitated. I stammered. Meridee, the direct one, zeroed in on the truth. She said, "The difference is that you're horny now, hornier now than you were back in July, right? Your wife's just had a baby? She's not feeling very amorous these days?"

I nodded, meaning yes. Meridee was right. "I'm sorry," I said. "You think I'm just using you, then?"

"No," she said. "When lovemaking has been good for my lover, it's always been good for me, too. Sex isn't a football match, with one winner and one loser. It's a love match, with two winners."

I smiled. That was nicely put. "So?" I said, with that look in my eye again, implying that I'd like to engage in a love match like that, with two winners. She frowned. By now, we were out in the street, heading toward the Via Veneto. I tried to deflect her from saying an immediate no by pulling her aside from an oncoming group of tourists who had just gotten off a bus. We moved on down the sidewalk. We found a curbside table and ordered *negronis*.

Finally she said, "The chemistry was right in London, in July." She paused, measured me, then shook her head. "It's not now. There's something going on inside you that frightens me. I think you're in the middle of some kind of fight right now. Maybe with Father Martin. And I don't like fighters. I like lovers."

I nodded. "I'm in the middle of a fight, all right, but not with Father Martin. I'm too busy for that. I feel like I'm covering a war. Journalists who cover wars — those who survive — say they never know any thrills, ever, that can quite equal the intensity of that experience."

Meridee regarded me for a moment. "Bob," she said. "Half the time I think you are full of shit. But, in this, I believe you."

It was nice to be believed, even if only half the time. I smiled, threw some lire down on the table and escorted Meridee up the Veneto, said good-bye to her in front of the Excelsior in the Italian manner, with a kiss on both cheeks (God, she smells good, I said to myself) and walked a short block to my office, where I had to finish a file to New York.

I would never see Meridee again, but I would think of her often. She had a directness that I had envied. It wasn't just that she had a fine mind (which she did), it wasn't just that she had fine body (which she did). In thinking back on her, I do not remember a woman "of parts," just a smooth wholeness.

Her integrity saved me at a time when I could have plunged into a casual evening of sportfucking, something that some warriors (and some war correspondents) have felt they needed, to divert themselves from the intensity of the battles they so much enjoyed. And I didn't really need that, I told myself, because I had a pretty young wife at home and two beautiful children.

22

Returning to Mary was not easy now, because she was keeping her distance. As before, we were together almost every evening, entertaining some of the actors in the conciliar drama, either at a Roman restaurant, or in a more relaxed fashion at home. Mary started attending the U.S. Bishops' Press Panel in the afternoons and sitting with me. We didn't have much chance to talk. Away from home, we were always surrounded by others. At home, T. D. Roberts, my archbishop-in-residence, was always around. The only time Mary and I had alone was bedtime. And then, Mary didn't want to talk. It was "too soon after the baby" to make love and our cuddling amounted to a kiss and a peck, no more.

This bothered me, but I told myself that time would take care of whatever it was that was ailing Mary, something that Dr. Pignanelli chose to call "postpartum depression." At any rate, I couldn't sit around and stew about it. I had a job to do, I had to cover the Council, and that was very much like covering a war: intense, demanding, from early in the morning until (and through) the late Roman dinner hour, and emotionally draining, because I was so involved. During the first session, I had cheered the victories of those who were trying to create a new, open Church that was more interested in serving real people than in maintaining a fortress against error. During the second session, I was appalled when the old entrenched powers (though they were in a tiny minority) seemed to be reversing the tide.

The victories of the first session and the defeats of the second meant more to me than they would have to an objective reporter. However, I was not working for the *New York Times,* whose reporters were told not to take sides in any fight. I was working for *Time,* whose correspondents and editors were encouraged to report the facts as fully as they could, and then make judgments on who seemed to be "right" and who "wrong." To help me make those judgments, I had a background, and sources I trusted — though I was learning to be careful about one of them.

In my interpretive journalism, I was coming down in favor of the liberals, and the editors in New York were following my lead, as anyone reading *Time* could plainly see. I felt no compunctions about sharing the hopes and fears of the Council liberals, any more than war correspondents (or sports columnists) feel guilty about the feelings they have for the welfare of the armies (or the teams) they traveled with. Clurman, my chief, understood, but he sent me and Ed Jackson a little reminder: "We have clearly opted in print for the reformation of the Catholic Church undertaken by Pope John, and now presumably being carried forward by Pope Paul. My caution is this: we should not make our stories and our reporting so one-sided that we become naked partisans in this rather than skeptical spectators."

That was good advice, but advice that was terribly hard for me to follow. If I incorporated my own skepticism in my *Time* files, I feared it would be all too easy for a writer sitting on the twenty-fifth floor of the Time-Life Building in New York "to get it wrong." I did resolve to be more fair (something that would be easier for me, now that Martin was no longer bombarding me with his juicy tales). I resolved to keep reporting all of the sides in the conflict I was covering. But I couldn't help practicing some advocacy reporting on the side of the Church's reform, which I felt was a service to the people at large, and a faithful reflection of the huge Council majority, which had also opted for the reform.

I also took some personal satisfaction to think that I was instrumental in winning over my magazine to the global vision I had long ago adopted from Teilhard de Chardin and Cardinal Suhard. By making information available to an international community of men and women who had an uncommon say in running the planet, *Time* was contributing to a better world, by opening up channels of communication that had long been clogged. That was a worthy cause.

I have since discovered that the greatest reporters in the history of American journalism did not hesitate to take sides in a worthy cause. Lincoln Steffens helped plan strategy for early-twentieth-century civic reformers in St. Louis, Cleveland, and Boston, and he tried to serve as a mediator between the unions and the Los Angeles Establishment in the trial of the McNamara brothers, who had blown up the *Los Angeles Times* in 1910. Walter Lippman wrote speeches for President Woodrow Wilson, then turned around and praised those offerings in his columns for the *New York Herald Tribune*. Most of the best reporters I know, given the chance, will try to make history as well as report it. At the Council, I helped make it, mainly by reporting it, but also by providing a place on Sunday nights where key figures in the Council's liberal wing could meet, count their defeats and victories each week, and make their plans for the next battle. I couldn't help but sympathize with my own crowd of bishops and theologians. I found that other journalists and even some Protestant observers were also active cheerleaders for the forces of reform. Sometimes, two or three of my Sunday night crew would retire to a back room and write up notes for speeches they intended to deliver on the Council floor.

Involved as I was, then, it was no wonder that the conciliar play and counterplay was more than a mere drama to me. I'd been watching the Council Fathers translate their emerging insights about the new open Church into concrete conciliar decrees that would serve as a good charter for the Church for the next fifty years, a Church of love rather than a Church of laws. But I could see another group at the Council, no more than 10 percent of the Fathers, who not only opposed this shift, but were quite capable of slowing it down, even while the Fathers were still in council. What would happen when the bishops went home? Would the Roman Curialists take over again? (I called them Roman, but the word was a code for an attitude. I knew Italian members of the Roman Curia who were open to change, and priests assigned to the Vatican from Philadelphia to Cochabamba who were closed to it.)

ぴ

FOR WEEKS, the Council turned into a not-very-well-organized high school debating contest. "Talk, talk, talk," said T. D. one night, "Why don't we get on with it?" He said he was starting to spend most of his time at the Council in the Bar Jonah or the Bar Rabbas. He was getting tired — and so were many other bishops, which is one reason why the Curialists were willing to let things drag: Archbishop Pietro Parente, an official of the Holy Office, had already said in an unguarded moment, "Councils come and go. The Curia remains forever." Maybe the weary bishops would start going home — and leave the Roman Catholic Church to the Romans. Why, after all, was it called Roman?

I could understand this feeling. The members of the Curia were predominantly Italian. The pope was Italian, and probably always would be.

At this Council, the Italians outnumbered every other national body. Perhaps the Italians couldn't help feeling that those who wanted the pope to share his authority with the rest of the Church were, implicitly, threatening to diminish them in some way. Thus, for a time, there was a certain amount of obstructionism at the Council from the Italian episcopate, simply because they were Italian. In mid-November, a whole parade of Italian bishops spoke to warn their brother bishops against the pernicious danger of this new thing called ecumenism. The very idea, that some Council liberals would say that Protestants and others who didn't acknowledge the primacy of the pope were part of the Church!

There was, inevitably, an anti-Italian backlash. For the most part, that backlash was a muted thing, virtually unnoticed by the press, until Bishop Steven Leven of San Antonio, Texas, concocted a zinger of a speech and gave it on the Council floor. He said the bishops seeking an accommodation with all Christians were not the ones who were disloyal, and he took obvious aim at the Church in Italy. "It is not our people who miss Mass on Sunday, refuse the sacraments and vote the Communist ticket. Our Catholics are good Catholics, loyal to us bishops, to Holy Mother Church and to the Holy Father. We have not lost the working class."

At our next Sunday night soiree, many raised their glasses to toast Bishop Leven. And Gus Weigel recited a limerick to celebrate this Texan who'd ridden into Rome from San Antonio:

> There was a bishop from Texas named Leven,
> Who had this six-shooter, or seven.
> He took out his gun,
> And when he was done,
> He'd sent many a dago to heaven.

Bishop Leven's talk had been pretty much ad hominem, and tough on the Italians, but it did help brighten things up a bit for the bishops, who were getting weary.

❧

I WAS GETTING WEARY, too. One morning, I decided to sleep in and let the day overtake me slowly for a change. About nine, I got Betsy up, changed little T. D.'s diaper, and was playing with the kids on our terrace when Malachy Martin drove up — in Mary's Fiat 500. He wasn't wearing his clerical robes, and he was whistling and acting as matter of factly as the milkman, say, on his daily rounds. Until he saw me looking down at him. His face darkened, but he could hardly turn around and go away. He came up and rang the bell (although he could have easily opened the gate himself, since the gate key was on Mary's key chain). I let him in and told one of the maids to get the padre a cup of coffee. The other maid went into our bedroom to tell Mary that Father Martin was here.

Malachy and I were making an effort at polite conversation when Mary emerged in her robe, still languorous from sleep. I gave her an unfriendly eyebrow, which she may or may not have noticed, and then I left for my office. Now I knew what I had to do. I phoned Martin that afternoon at the Biblicum and asked him if he'd mind coming to my office at seven. I was fortifying myself with a double Johnny Walker on the rocks before he arrived and then, as soon as he did, told him, "I want you to stay away from my wife." I didn't ask him what he was doing with Mary's Fiat, or how often he had been using it, or how often he'd been seeing Mary, or where, or how long he spent talking to her on the telephone every day. Mary had picked up one of his mannerisms, popping her lips at the end of a sentence, for emphasis. It was such a little thing, and yet, and yet, combined with other things, Mary's lip popping was a tip-off that, while I hardly saw Martin anymore, Mary was probably seeing a good deal of him.

Mary was reading *The Feminine Mystique* by Betty Friedan, about the problem that didn't have a name. The problem was that men wouldn't allow women to be — what? Autonomous? Well, hell, who was autonomous? I guessed that I was as guilty as any man of lumping his wife into the category of "*my* wife" — as in *my* house, or *my* car, or *my* dog. But I'd given Mary two maids, and she was leading a life that she told everyone she knew was damned exciting. I guess I just resented the fact that comments in Martin's handwriting were scattered here and there in Mary's copy of Friedan, along with a good many underscored passages that put the knock on husbands in general.

I didn't mention these little things to Martin; in themselves, they were ridiculous charges. I did tell him that Mary was becoming more and more hostile to me and more friendly to him, that I suspected he was directing this little farce and that I wanted it to stop. I got up, walked over to the bar in my office, and helped myself to another drink.

He pretended to be aghast, laughing and frowning in equal measure and protesting that he hardly ever saw Mary. He happened to have Mary's car, he said, because she had seen him by chance early yesterday evening getting drenched in a downpour on a Roman street corner. She had taken him to our home, then given him the car so he could get back to the Biblicum without getting drenched again.

I didn't bother asking him why she didn't just drop him at the Biblicum. "It's not a good situation," I said, shaking my head, and then I tried to make it even plainer. "I want you to stop playing around with my wife. Or else."

He laughed and said I was crazy. I wasn't crazy, but I was drunk, and when I started roaring at him, he didn't argue any further. He picked up and left, without another word.

Curiously enough, Mary didn't say a thing about any of this to me. I had expected her to confront me, complain, cry, shout at my idiocy for telling Martin to stay away from her — anything except what she was doing, which was simply ignoring me. Maybe I was wrong. Maybe the only one who was wrong was me. I was never the candy-and-flowers type, but I knew I wasn't paying Mary enough attention. At bedtime that night, I tried being more lovey-dovey. She didn't like that. She was too tired to talk, and she didn't want to make love. "I don't want to get pregnant," she said. Well, I could understand that. I didn't want her to get pregnant either. I wasn't giving enough time to the kids we had. Did I want another child right now that I wouldn't have enough time for? No.

"Would you consider taking the Pill?" I asked, lying there flat on my back in the dark. Mary knew what our theologian friends had been telling us about the Pill, that it might not conflict with the Church's ban on artificial contraception. I waited a time for her answer. Finally, she said she'd talk to her doctor about it.

"How about rhythm?" I said.

"Rhythm doesn't work," she said.

Now, I thought, we are like almost every other American Catholic couple we know, caught in the middle of the dilemma the official Church did not seem to understand: how could couples, literally, make love and avoid having more children than they could handle?

I went to sleep thinking of this, and woke at about four in the morning telling myself that, of course, I was already privy to a big news story and had done nothing with it. The Church was in the process of changing its teaching on birth control, and no reporter had written a line about it. No, it wasn't an official position yet, but I had heard a good deal of revisionist talk at my parties. Here at the Council, I had seen a lot of "official"

Catholic ideas and Catholic attitudes undergo change before my eyes. If frozen Catholics attitudes on birth control would start melting under the great reforming heat of this Council, then the Council would start meaning more to American Catholics. Later that morning, I cabled John Elson, my religion editor in New York, told him what I'd been hearing from my theologians in Rome, and suggested doing a story in *Time*.

He replied that if I were going to do the birth control story right, I ought to give more time to it than I could afford during my coverage of the Council's second session. "Do it later," he said.

23

The Sunday night following my stern session with Martin, hardly anyone showed up for our Sunday soiree. I phoned four of our regulars and asked them what had happened. They said that they'd gotten the word that our parties were off.

"Gotten the word? Who said so?"

In each case, there was a kind of stuttering, embarrassed pause, then, "Malachy Martin."

"Did he say why?"

In each case, I was told, Malachy said Mary had reported that I was "working too hard." The Sunday nights were taking a toll on me.

I tried not to let my anger show. I said to my friends, "The Sunday nights don't hurt a bit. They're fun. They help me unwind. Come on over. And pass the word around."

Mary sat there on our bed while I made the calls, looking more and more uncomfortable by the minute. When I was through, I turned to her. "I'll bet you didn't order any food or anything, right?" She did not reply. "You just cancelled our party without telling me?" Still no answer. "You and Malachy Martin? Well, you've both got one goddamn lot of nerve. Just what in the hell are you and Malachy trying to do?"

Apparently, Mary decided that a good offense was the best defense. "You're getting paranoid," she said. "I was just trying to make your life a little simpler."

"You were?"

"Yes."

"Malachy Martin had nothing to do with it?"

Mary didn't reply. She stood up and started for the door. "If people are coming after all, I'd better try to get some things ready." She glided out of the room, as if in a trance, and I went into the bathroom to brood.

I can't believe it, I said to my reflection in the mirror. For one thing, I couldn't believe that it was Mary's idea to start disinviting people to our Sunday night soirees. Mary enjoyed them as much as I did, maybe more, because I was generally the worrywart, always trying to make sure everyone had enough food and drink, while, more often than not, Mary was involved in fond banter with her favorites, or making friends with some of the newer faces in the crowd. On a recent Sunday night, Father Robert Drinan, dean of the Boston College Law School, a Jesuit we had met during our brief sojourn in Boston, showed up with a little house gift for Mary. Mary gave him the lipstick-on-the-cheek treatment, to the delight of those who were glad to be part of an inner circle of friends who could exchange affection in a manner so open, and so free.

No, I thought, this had to be Malachy's action, the action of an envious man. In effect, I had tossed him out of my inner circle. Now, the son of a bitch was trying to destroy it. What could I do about him? His move seemed so laughable and so unimportant to me then that I told myself not to worry about it. I think I even heard my Novice Master's voice telling me: *AGE QUOD AGIS*. Do what you're doing. And so I resolved to do it, and go on doing it.

૪

LIKE EVERYONE ELSE in the world, I remember where I was when I got the first word about the assassination in Dallas: I was having dinner with John Carmel Heenan, Archbishop of Westminster, and perhaps twenty other bishops at the English College in Rome. I had been trying to accept no invitations that did not include Mary. This was one I couldn't pass up. It was a kind of signal to me that, at last, I had won a measure of acceptance from a group that had been inclined to scant my work. I was almost certain that my champion there was Archbishop Heenan himself, who, as a member of Cardinal Bea's Secretariat, worked every day with some of my best friends at the Council.

Toward the end of the dinner, one of the college's porters appeared at Heenan's side and whispered into his ear. "Oh, dear," said Heenan. He stood and tapped his water glass for silence and told the others that John Kennedy had been shot in Dallas, Texas. He wasn't expected to live. Then Heenan turned to me, reached across the table to take both my hands in his and express his profound sorrow. He said he would celebrate Mass for President Kennedy in the morning.

I was the only American there. Each of the bishops, in turn, came up and offered his condolences to me, as if I were a member of the Kennedy family. One of the bishops imagined that Robert Kennedy would succeed John. I smiled sadly and told him that we had no royal family in the United States, but, if we did, it would indeed be the Kennedy family.

That was a dark weekend. We didn't bother trying to get the word around. We just made no plans for one of our usual Sunday nights. A handful of our regulars came anyway, to drink and nibble on what we had to eat and mourn with us for our slain president, and for a nation that could kill one of its finest leaders. T. D. Roberts, who was in India when Gandhi was assassinated, seemed uncommonly quiet. Later that evening, he took me aside and said I was working too hard. He advised me to slow down. "I will," I said, "in just a few more days." I pointed out that the second session would be over in less than two weeks.

He wondered whether I still intended doing another book — on the Council's second session. I nodded and told him I had a contract. He sniffed. "I'm wondering if you need this pressure."

I shrugged. Then I began getting more advice from others, my friends, who urged me to slow down. John Courtney Murray asked me to go to lunch with him and he asked me to consider how I was pushing myself.

"I'm probably a bit shell-shocked," I said. "Or maybe just tired. My real problem is that I think Mary is having an affair with someone we both know pretty well."

Murray frowned and said in his upper-class New York honk, without even asking me for details, "Baaawb, isn't that a bit paranoid?"

I shook my head. "Yes. I guess it is. After all, this guy is a Jesuit priest."

Murray didn't seem at all curious about that, either. He wasn't curious because, of course, someone else had already told him about my paranoid suspicions.

♫

AFTER MY LUNCH with Murray, I attended the press panel, then drove Gus Weigel to his pensione. I was uncharacteristically quiet. When he asked me what was wrong, I didn't have the heart to tell him about my deepest (and now most paranoid) fears. I told him I was just tired. He hugged me and said, "Stop running. You hear me? Stop running."

A day or two later, I got a visit in my office from Vincent Beuzer, an Oregon Jesuit whom I had known slightly when I was studying in Spokane. He was now working on his doctorate at the Gregorian University and he wanted to tell me about the course in psychiatry and religion he was taking there from an American layman named Frank Ayd. Dr. Ayd, he said, was a brilliant psychiatrist from Baltimore. Vince said I ought to do a story on him.

"Yes," I said. "That sounds like a possibility." A marriage between psychiatry and religion. With all I had to do, I didn't put the story high on my list of priorities. Still and all, I had an idea that it wouldn't hurt me to see Ayd. If I was paranoid, I'd certainly like to deal with it. The thought crossed my mind that maybe someone was using Beuzer, all unbeknownst to him, to get me into the hands of a shrink. I rejected that thought, because it was a paranoid thought. I resolved to go and see Ayd. I just wondered when I'd get the time. I was pretty damn busy. I was still running.

24

O n December 2, word came through to my office: Cardinal Ottaviani would give me an audience at three in the afternoon on the morrow. "Ah," I said. "At last." Though I had been spending most of my reporting hours with the group flying the banner of the aggiornamento, it was clear that Cardinal Ottaviani was the one making the news now, for I had it on good authority he was the one most responsible for slowing down the pace of change in the conciliar aula. He was making news in much the same way that Congressmen with seniority make news in Washington, by chairing important committees and blocking those pieces of legislation that might pass if only they could get on the floor of the House or Senate.

I was ushered into the waiting room of his offices on the second floor of the Palazzo Sant' Ufficio, smiled when I saw the legend, *Semper Idem,* on the cardinal's coat of arms, and was given a seat in a room filled with tapestries and Renaissance art. Msgr. Cosgrove led the cardinal in, holding him firmly by the elbow.

I rose. We traded greetings in Italian. I called him *Eminenza.* He called me *caro Kaiser,* "dear Kaiser," and invited me to sit close to him. I was surprised to find that he was all powdered up and perfumed, and surprised again to find his eyesight so poor. I'd seen his batty eye in photos, but I had forgotten the poor man was practically blind. No doubt he, too, was surprised with me, surprised to find that a man representing *Time* in Rome spoke such poor Italian. When I'd first arrived in Rome, Sophia Loren had kidded me about my "Yankee accent." It wasn't only the accent. My Italian was basic then, and, now, after more than a year and a half in Rome, it was still basic.

Basic or not, I plunged right into my interview by asking the cardinal why the Holy Office was so anxious to keep scrutinizing (and persecuting) good, reputable theologians who were only doing what they were trained to do: to come up with new theories and new explanations and new theologies to help their contemporaries understand the Christian story.

He immediately launched into a monologue on the Holy Office and its methods, which had been drawing fire on the Council floor in recent weeks. The cardinal said that the Holy Office's means were beyond question because its ends were pure. He used last year's Holy Office *monitum* (or warning) on Pierre Teilhard de Chardin as an example, occasioned by the publication of Henri de Lubac's then-current work on the thought of the Jesuit paleontologist-philosopher. The Holy Office had to take a stand against Teilhard because "the faith isn't some fantasy, and it does not consist in.... " He hesitated, groping for the right word. "It does not consist in poetry, no matter how beautiful it is." He paused a moment, then launched into another thought. "The faith is not in France," he said, gesturing toward the west, "it is here." He pointed down to the marble floor beneath his slippered feet. "Here in the center of Christendom."

I noted that Teilhard had been dead now for fifteen years. I said some of the Council Fathers were more worried about the high-handed methods the Holy Office was using to condemn others who were still alive. I recalled that some Fathers, led by Cardinal Frings of Cologne, had asked openly for some updating of Holy Office procedures, and that this suggestion had been resisted by certain members of the Curia, including Cardinal Ottaviani himself.

The cardinal smiled patiently, indulgently. *Noi siammo gia aggiornati.* "We are already up-to-date here." And then he went on to explain how the Holy Office now dealt with theologians who were teaching heresy: "We don't — " I thought he was going to say we don't burn heretics anymore. "We don't condemn anyone anymore. We just write letters."

"Letters?" I said.

"Letters to the theologian's bishop. Or to his religious superiors. They, in turn, advise the theologian privately not to write or publish anything further along the lines that seem offensive to us."

Apparently, the cardinal could not conceive of any kind of due process that would take place before the private little letters were sent off from the Palazzo Sant'Ufficio. Due process, to be sure, is an Anglo-Saxon concept, something which I was told sounds strange to the Roman ear. Granting certain rights to an offending theologian before he is told he is "in error" may sound reasonable to much of the civilized world, but it was a notion that didn't click with Cardinal Ottaviani. He said I didn't understand: the Holy Office had its own ways, far more charitable ways than anything I could find in a court of law in England or America. And did I forget? He, Cardinal Ottaviani, was only the secretary of the Holy Office. "The Prefect of the Holy Office," he said, "is the Holy Father himself."

"And he's infallible, right?"

The cardinal paused, waffled a bit, admitted that the pope's infallibility was only operative when he spoke *ex cathedra*. The cardinal said he was talking about "the ordinary magisterium of the Church." The word "magisterium" means teaching power. I got the impression that we were talking less about teaching and more about power. The Holy Office had the power over any theologian, because the Prefect of the Holy Office was the pope himself who had some special gifts, aside from his infallibility, that somehow derived from his being the successor of Peter. It was in this role, as successor to Peter, that the pope had power, over all the Catholics in the world, over the bishops, and, of course, over theologians, too. (This was the meaning, I guessed, of Matthew 16. "I will give you the keys of the Kingdom.") The cardinal admitted that this was a very monarchical view of the papacy, but it was the way he saw matters.

I asked him why he was slowing down the Council's pace. He said he had to be sure that the Council was doing the right thing before he let something pass out of his commission to the Council floor. He explained that he held a particularly unique position relative to the Council: though a Council Father like the others, he was somehow outside the Council, and above it, because he was acting for the pope. I could hardly wait to tell my Council liberals that Ottaviani, their nemesis, considered himself "above the entire Council." More than two thousand bishops on one side, and Ottaviani on the other. He thought he could veto them. Neat.

I left the Palazzo Sant'Ufficio looking for Giulio, my driver, found the bureau's big, dark-blue Fiat parked over near one of the Bernini colonnades, climbed into the back seat and started scribbling some notes on what the cardinal had told me. Mike Novak, for one, would like to know about this encounter. He was going to be doing the book on this session that I had decided not to do. Maybe he could use this scene between me and this cardinal, this cardinal who was so proud and so unashamed in his service of a papacy that would serve the world "with truth."

✸

MARY WAS ON THE TELEPHONE when I got home. I started playing with the kids, and wondered when — and if — Mary would spring some kind of birthday surprise for me. During our five years together, Mary and I had made it a point of celebrating birthdays. Mary loved presents and always had to open them right away. I hadn't cared much for presents, but I liked dinner parties, and now, when Mary and I were having our troubles, I would have liked something special. This night, Mary had planned nothing, had not invited any of my friends over, did not even have a cupcake or a candle for me, much less a kiss or a card. Finally — at bedtime, naturally, what other time? — we had a row. "You know what day this is?" I demanded after we had gotten into our nightshirts. She said she didn't. "Think about it," I said.

"Your birthday?" she said. "No. Your birthday isn't until — December 3."

"Well, today's December 3," I shouted. "How could that little fact escape you?" I never got an answer because T. D. Roberts heard me shouting. He came knocking at our door and peeking into our bedroom "to see if everything is all right." He was obviously solicitous about Mary, not about me. Did he think I was going to beat her? Ah, the hell with it, I said to myself. I'm probably off my rocker. I turned out the light and tried to go to sleep, and so did Mary. I'm afraid I kept her awake with my musings, paranoid no doubt, about Malachy Martin.

"Mary," I said, "I'm not sure Martin is what he seems to be. He's a charming guy. Now I'm starting to wonder."

"Oh, God," Mary groaned.

"Okay, that's paranoid, I know." I paused and reflected for two, maybe three=minutes. Then I added, had to add, "Michael Novak and I have both heard stories about some hanky-panky in the Council regarding the *schema* on the Jews. When either of us try to find out the source of the stories, we find they always lead back to Malachy Martin. We think he's inventing these stories, just to keep the Jews all fired up. We think the man is actually working for the American Jewish Committee."

"What's the matter with that?" she asked.

"Well, if he's a paid lobbyist, at least he ought to register, so people will know where he's coming from."

"Oh, God," Mary groaned.

"And I think he got Gus Weigel in trouble with some of those phony stories."

"Bob," she said. "I'm trying to get some sleep."

"Okay." I lapsed into silence. After more reflection, I had to add, "Have you ever wondered why he is always with Zachariah Schuster? He used to get spending money from me. He doesn't get it from me anymore. I think he's getting it from the American Jewish Committee."

"You don't know that. You're just guessing."

"Yeah, that's not fair, is it? But I think he's keeping the pot boiling just to make himself more indispensable to the Jews."

"Are you going to shut up?"

I did — for awhile. I couldn't help adding, "You know, the *New York Times* has been going big on this story. The man who has been doing these stories, Milton Bracker, came up to me the other day with a big smile on his face and said, "Hey, now I know one of your secret sources. I phoned the Biblicum today and asked for Padre Martin, and the porter said, '*Chi è? Signor Kaiser?*' " I hadn't phoned Martin in weeks, but the porter knew this voice was an American voice and assumed Milton Bracker was I. Ironic. Doubly ironic. As a correspondent for the slanted weekly newsmagazine, I knew I couldn't give Martin credence any longer. Now the objective newspaper of record was using him as a prime source.

Mary started to whine, because I was keeping her awake and God only knew when the baby would wake up and want to be fed.

"Okay, okay, I'll shut up." But I didn't get any sleep. I was busy thinking, thinking, thinking.

⁂

MAYBE JOHN COURTNEY MURRAY thought he was being funny. I failed to see the humor. It was during the cocktail hour at one of our smaller dinner parties, and he was telling my three-month-old son that his daddy was "all upset because some people didn't like his book." I stood there watching this scene, sipping a double martini on the rocks and wondering why Murray was trying to play psychologist. It seemed to be a preamble of sorts, for in a moment or two he was taking me aside to tell me that he'd arranged for me to check into the Institute of Living in Hartford, Connecticut, on December 9. Gus Weigel would be flying to New York on December 6, and I could go with him. It was all set.

"You talk to Dr. Ayd?" I said.

He hesitated a moment, then nodded. Gee, I thought, the great John Courtney Murray, with all the important things he has to do, can still take time out to look after me. I was flattered and impressed.

Perhaps a week before, I had finally gone to see Ayd. He was a tough-looking little guy, a middleweight, I'd say, with a Marine haircut. I didn't pretend I'd come there on a story. "My friends are telling me," I said, "that I need a rest and a checkup." He asked me how I felt and I promptly proved to him that I was a nutcase by plunging into a rambling, almost incoherent monologue about my deteriorating situation at home. For some reason, I felt that the doctor could get a better fix on me if I didn't choose my words carefully. I should just let my stream of consciousness overflow its banks. Then the doctor could see who I really was. I was genuinely concerned about my paranoia.

Ayd had seemed concerned, too; not about my paranoia, because I didn't mention Martin, but about my mental condition. "I never met you before, but, from what I've heard of you and your work, and comparing that with your story now, I'd say you're on some kind of downward slide. Maybe you're just tired."

I nodded.

"But maybe," he added, "maybe there's more." He suggested he would see if he could get me into some Swiss clinic, for some checkups and tests.

I asked him why I couldn't do the tests in Rome. He said there was nothing in Rome that could equal the diagnosis I might get in a real clinic. I said I'd think about it. I didn't really want to go away. I didn't want to leave Mary and the kids. I couldn't tell the doctor why, I couldn't tell him my worst fear, because I wasn't sure at this point that I even believed it myself.

✑

STILL, I WAS SURE of one thing: that I didn't want Martin around anymore. Mary knew this and understood, and she must have conveyed that message to Martin, because he'd stopped coming around, at least when I was there. And so Martin simply wasn't with us for our last dinner party of the season. I moved over to the bar and made some small talk with Gus Weigel, drained my glass and built myself another martini and looked questioningly at Gus. He took my dare.

"Nobody can outdrink me," he said. "Not when we're drinking martinis." I think he was right. I couldn't outdrink him. But I could keep up with him. We touched glasses and I said, "I guess we'll be going back to New York together."

He didn't seem to know what I was talking about.

· 215 ·

"On December 6?" I said. "Murray said he'd made a reservation for me and everything."

"Oh, yes," said Gus. "Yes, that's right." He went over to talk to Murray.

At dinner, Murray was explaining about his *schema*. There were dozens of others working on the *schema* on religious liberty, but, to Murray, it was "his." Gus and I, seated next to each other, were still on the martinis, but I was turned away from Gus, trying to listen to Murray. Gus tapped me on the shoulder and gave me a bleary look. He said in a low tone, "Don't listen to everything that guy says. He doesn't know what he's talking about."

I laughed and said to myself that this was just the Beefeater's gin talking, not Gus Weigel. Murray was probably right. The trip to Connecticut was what I needed. Some rest, some professional diagnosis. But Murray's amateur diagnosis (delivered to my three-month-old son!) didn't make any sense. I'd resolved my early upset over the book banning. I could hardly expect the book banners to like what I had written; much of it was an attack on them. Still, dozens of those in the conciliar community who mattered most to me had gone out of their way to thank me for it. And, I'd almost forgotten: according to Msgr. Ligutti, the pope himself wanted to see it published in Italian.

ঞ৮

GIULIO DROVE ME and Gus Weigel to the Fiumicino airport. Mary and Betsy and Archbishop Roberts came along. No one said much. In fact, they all looked gloomier than I. "Hey," I said. "No big deal. I'll be back sooner than anyone thinks."

"Of course you will," Mary said. Roberts gave her a baleful look. He did not wrinkle his nose. When they called my flight, we all moved to the gate together. I gave Betsy a big hug and Mary kissed me warmly. It was the first real kiss I had had from her in months. I wanted so much to think that she meant it that my heart skipped a beat, and I thought to myself that, well, maybe I *was* crazy, and that I had mistrusted Mary for no good reason. "She really does love me and will always love me," I assured myself, "and this is why I am going away, to get better, and come back and be a good man for my woman." I strode toward the doors of the jet with a spring in my step.

Gus wasn't springy, and he didn't talk much on the plane. When he did, he made it clear to me, without giving me any details, that he had been very unhappy about the way he, personally, had been treated of late by the people at Bea's Secretariat, and that the source of his problems with them dated back to the tendentious report on the Jewish *schema* that Martin had given him last summer, disinformation he had innocently handed on to the *New York Times*.

When we reached New York, Gus climbed down the stairs of the jet, knelt on the tarmac, kissed "the good old U.S.A.," stood up and gave me a broad smile.

I did some Christmas shopping the next day, scared up a pair of tickets to the Giant's game on Sunday and persuaded Donald Campion of *America* to join me at the stadium. On Monday, John Courtney Murray showed up at my midtown hotel, the Dorset, in a chauffeur-driven Rolls — it belonged to a Mrs. Murray, he said, no kin — and we motored up to Hartford. There were high fences and barbed wire all around the place, which surprised me. "What is this?" I said.

"Well, Baaawb," he honked. His tone was somewhere in between a rebuke and a nervous laugh, that I should even have to ask. "It's the Institute of Living."

I uttered a silent goddamn. Murray had said he was taking me to a clinic, and here I was being chauffeured to an insane asylum. I wanted to scream, but I quieted my anger by recalling the great note I had gotten from Clurman two days before. My chief told me not to worry, that "a lot of *Time* and *Life* people get battle fatigue if they are any good."

Murray introduced me to the Institute's director, Dr. Francis Braceland, and to the man who would be working with me, Dr. Austin McCawley. We chatted a bit. One of the doctors asked me how old I was. I said, "Thirty-three." I paused. "Just the right age to be crucified."

Murray raised an eyebrow, laughed, and took both of the doctors aside.

They whispered together. I wandered over to regard Dr. Braceland's big orange goldfish, one eye bulging at me in a small glass jar over by a south-facing window. In a minute, Braceland hurried over to my side. "Now you understand," he said, "you're putting yourself in here? That means you can take yourself out any time you want."

I nodded. And then I settled in, persuading myself the Institute wasn't so bad. It was something like the Novitiate, with a time for this and a time for that, but better than the Novitiate. I had a little white frame cottage to live in, with a television room where I was able to see footage on the funeral of President Kennedy (something I had missed in Rome) and watch the college bowl games. I slept eight hours a night and took a long nap every afternoon. I strolled the icy grounds with some of the men and women in my group. I played some furious basketball. I learned a little about oil painting (and did a passable portrait of Mary, from a picture I had brought along with me). I had daily talks with Dr. McCawley, and took a lot of tests.

A psychologist administered one test that gave me some insight into my personality. It was a set of four cards that told a story. I was supposed to put them "in order." I studied them, rearranged the cards, then nodded to the doctor when I'd finished. "That right?" I said.

As he scribbled furiously on his chart, I looked back at the cards and realized that I could, by rearranging the cards, tell other stories, each as "correct" as the other. I felt foolish. Any sequence was an acceptable sequence. But if I was so concerned about having my first choice deemed "right," then I was as rigid as Ottaviani. Now *that* was depressing.

On January 4, I picked up the *New York Times* and found Gus Weigel's obituary on page 1. The story said he had died of a heart attack at the Jesuit's *America* House in New York. And that he was only fifty-seven. Apparently, he, too, had been suffering from battle fatigue, but, instead of taking a rest, he had continued with classroom work at Woodstock and a full schedule of outside talks as well. I should have been happy, that my stay at the Institute forced me to slow down. And that my tests had turned out well. Three weeks into my stay, Dr. McCawley said my condition was not serious. I was the kind of person who worked too hard. I was depressed about my marriage. And I was a little paranoid because I thought a Jesuit priest was having an affair with my wife.

"Well, yes," I said, "I kinda knew that. What other evidence do you have that I'm paranoid?"

He waffled on that one. "We can't isolate paranoia. It isn't like typhoid bacteria, that we give you pills for, and send you home." Paranoia, apparently, was more of a relational thing. It was my stance toward the world around me. Dr. McCawley couldn't see any evidence that I was paranoid in this setting. At any rate, he saw no reason for me to stick around any longer. I could go back to Rome if I'd agree to see Dr. Ayd on a regular basis.

Dr. McCawley said my wife seemed ready to have me back. He had phoned her (at my expense, $98 worth) and she told him that we had won first prize in a raffle at Santa Susanna, the Paulists' church in Rome, where many of the town's Americans went to Mass. It was a two-week cruise around the Mediterranean. She wanted me to get her some cruise wear in New York. Furthermore, I had gotten four or five letters from her that were full of loving encouragement, full of news about the Christmas toys that Santa had brought the children, and how their eyes had goggled at the Christmas tree. She had news about our friends in Rome, the Novaks and the Cogleys and the Sheas, and all of the permanent Jesuits in Rome. She mentioned the names of just about everyone except Malachy Martin.

25

My optimism about Mary got a pretty good pounding by the facts. She wasn't at the airport when I arrived. I found her standing in the *ingresso* of our apartment in her red cotton nightshirt when I opened the door at midnight, studying me, staring at me. "You should have stayed in Connecticut," she said, "where you could get help."

I shrugged. "Dr. McCawley decided I could do just as well here, under the guidance of Dr. Ayd. I thought he discussed that with you."

"Yes," she cried. "And he also wrote me and said I should see Dr. Ayd. He said I should become involved in the therapy, too. 'Therapy? Therapy?' I don't need any therapy,"

I swallowed hard and dug into my bag. "I've got the things you asked for, for the Mediterranean cruise."

Now she didn't want to go on the cruise that we had won at the Santa Susanna raffle. She laid down some new rules: no questions, no recriminations, no intercourse. She wanted to live her own life. In fact, she had removed her wedding ring and said she was in the mood for a divorce. I was too domineering, I could not accept her "as a person."

I gulped and walked into the kitchen for a glass of water. I couldn't help notice some of Malachy's things in the house: a pair of his undershorts in our laundry room, a bag of his pipe tobacco tucked in a bookshelf, his fingernail brush in my bathroom.

But I said nothing about Martin. I spoke to Mary about the new "insights" I had into myself. The stresses of the past year had only "brought out the latent weaknesses I've managed to live with for some time." I was going to work on "my ambivalent feelings toward women."

"Yes, yes," she said, "you've been saying that in your letters." She headed for the bedroom. Over her shoulder, she said, "You'd better go see Dr. Ayd."

"At one in the morning?"

"Tomorrow. First thing tomorrow."

I tried to pray, but I had only angry words for God. Next morning, I put off phoning Dr. Ayd, and fired off a bunch of letters to some priests and bishops I knew, telling them I was suffering from a bit of battle fatigue, and asking them for their prayers. Some wrote me back. Michael J. Buckley, a Jesuit classmate from Los Gatos, wrote me from Austria, where he was taking his fifteenth year of formation. His letter helped me far more than its author ever knew:

> Great heavens, Bob, take care of yourself. Your news about yourself came as a shock. I have some sort of unconscious image of you as the iron man, the one who doesn't wear out or run down, probably stamped into my psyche during those embryonic days of Novitiate in which you ruled mightily as scullery boss. And to hear that you were running low came as a sickening surprise.

⋙

I REESTABLISHED MYSELF at the office and tried to find more time for the family I'd been ignoring. I even started coming home for lunch. Almost invariably, Mary would just be hanging up the phone when I appeared and then, after lunch, she'd take off in her Fiat 500 — "to go shopping," while I played horsey with the kids, or took them for a walk in the nearby Villa Sciarra.

Mary and I went to a few dinner parties together, where she assumed an unusual, know-it-all attitude with everyone. We remained miles apart. Mary made one concession: she agreed to say one Hail Mary with me every night before we went to sleep.

I tried to keep calm, bit my tongue when I wanted to rave. But I had to talk to someone — not to a cleric or a shrink employed by the Jesuits or anyone with an institutional stake in all this. Mike Novak? Yes, why didn't I think of him sooner? We were together all fall, and I never said anything to him about my personal troubles. Now, I was beginning to wish I had.

On my way home to lunch, I stopped off at the Pensione Baldoni, where he and his Karen had settled in, she to paint, he to barrel through his book on the second session, *The Open Church*. He was dictating the thing on a recorder, just as if he were Erle Stanley Gardner writing his seventieth mystery story, but Mike was writing something much more difficult, a reflective essay on the new kind of Church that had been aborning at Vatican II.

I marveled at the thick stack of paper on Mike's desk, the typewritten record of his dictation. "What do you do with this?" I asked, curious about his writing routine.

"I read it over and then send it off to Macmillan."

"I could never do that. I have to write and rewrite and then look at the whole thing and rewrite some more." That wasn't exactly what I had done the last year, when I wrote my book in six weeks. But then, I didn't just sit down and dictate it either.

Mike shrugged. "I couldn't do what you did. I couldn't cram my book with all your facts and all your color. Your book was you. My book is — me." With an air of triumph, he said, "And I'm making my deadline, too!"

I thought the pressure had taken its toll on him: now he looked like he was the one who needed a rest, and I said so with a laugh.

To Mike, that sounded like an invitation to ask about me. He searched my eyes and said, "How are you?"

I walked away from him and looked out the window, afraid that maybe he'd find some evidence of madness in my eyes. He saw a sign of madness anyway, a departure from reality at least, in my very walking away. I turned back to him and, with a forced calm, told him what I'd found when I got home, Mary's hostility and all the indications that Malachy Martin may have been spending a good deal of time at Via Quirico Filopanti 2. I narrowed my eyes down to two slits and said, "I don't see how they could do much, with the kids and the two maids around all the time."

I paused, because Mike was shaking his head, then rushed into a recital, to demonstrate that I was not paranoid: "I don't think Malachy and Mary are actually going to bed together. But they might as well be. Mary seems to be spending a lot of time with — somebody else, maybe him. And none with me."

Mike frowned. "Better not to kid yourself, Bob."

"What?" I said.

"I think they *are* having an affair." My head spun. "Karen and I have seen them around town together, at Necci's, at Romolo in Trastevere, laughing, having a good time."

I removed a pile of papers from an antique chair and sat down on it so heavily that it creaked. Mike was a gentle soul with a high, almost girlish voice. Now he roared, pounding his fist on the desk, "Goddamn it! I wish I'd paid more attention. I should have gone over there. I bet I would have found them together. I wouldn't have let Malachy do this to you. I wouldn't have. But I was writing this book." He waved at the pile of notes and papers all around him.

Now Mike had given voice to a fantasy I had had back at the Institute of Living. I'd fly back to Rome prematurely, and find the two of them together and zap them both with — what? I'd buy a gun in New York and then I wouldn't call ahead, I'd stake out the apartment and wait and — then I'd break into my fantasy and tell myself that this...was... sick.

Now I *was* going mad. Trembling just a little, I drove to Dr. Ayd's, and he prescribed some tranquilizers for me. He told me to try to relax and to come back and see him every other day. I hurried home — it was about three in the afternoon — and found that the kids were there with the maids, and Mary was out. "Where?" I asked.

"Uscita," said Annamaria. Oh, just out. I went into our bedroom and rifled the closets and the bureau. I didn't know what I was looking for, but I found it. Under some of Mary's lingerie, I found a cellophane strip, both ends torn, with seven little yellow pills lined up inside. I had to take the strip over to the window to read the tiny inscription on the pill: "Searle. 5 mg." What the hell was this?

Ever the workaholic, I went back to the office and when I returned home at 8:00 P.M., I couldn't talk to Mary, couldn't even look at her. And I couldn't go talk to Martin. I would have killed him. I had to do something, so I went to Martin's superior, Roderick A. F. MacKenzie, rector of the Biblicum. He was tall and angular, a kindly, soft-spoken man who seemed truly disturbed when I told him that I suspected that my wife and Father Martin had been keeping company during the Christmas holidays.

"What, uh, proof do you have?" I handed him the sorry little bag of Malachy's leavings, and he pulled out a pair of shorts and a fingernail brush. He shook his head and said, "This is proof?"

"I had some paintings, too. They were nude studies, half-finished. I found them in our guest room when I got home from the U.S. in August."

"You have the paintings?"

I stammered. "They've, uh, disappeared."

"Did they have Father Martin's signature on them?"

"No," I said. "But Mary certainly didn't paint them. She doesn't paint."

He shook his head and frowned. "How do you know Father Martin painted them?"

"I, I, I'm sure he did," I said. "He brought his paints and an easel to Lavinio last summer."

"That's no proof."

"Yeah. But." I hesitated, then blurted, "She's taking birth control pills." There. I told him. I hadn't wanted to use that information. But I had to. Father MacKenzie shook his head and closed his eyes. "She's not taking them for me," I said in a rush. "She hasn't let me get close to her for months. For eight months."

He drummed his fingers on his desktop, then peered over his spectacles at me. "Where did you say you'd spent your time last month?"

"I was in a nut house," I said matter-of-factly. "In Connecticut."

He spread his palms. "Well," he said. He handed back the paper bag.

"You don't believe me, do you?"

"A man's innocent until he's proven guilty. You know that."

"I will prove it," I said. "I guarantee that. In the meantime, what am I supposed to do?"

"I think you'd better get some professional help."

I grabbed my coat and stuffed the evidence back in my briefcase and started for the door. Sure, I said to myself, I need professional help. I need a professional killer.

I phoned Jack Shea and asked him to have lunch with me. He worked in the political section of the U.S. Embassy in Rome, but I knew he knew some agents for the U.S. Central Intelligence Agency. Maybe he'd have some ideas. We had a long lunch in the cellar-restaurant called Tinello, and we talked about everything except Mary and Malachy. Finally, when we had finished our coffee and dessert, when I could put off my truth-telling no longer, I blurted my whole story.

He put his hand on my shoulder and heard me out and, when I had finished, he said quietly, "Maybe Rod MacKenzie doesn't believe you. But I believe you. I don't doubt it for a minute. I've seen the two of them together. I wondered about him last summer."

"Last summer?"

"Remember? You had come over to our place at the beach, with Malachy? We had a house guest, a young woman from Paris, and we were having drinks at home and then going down to the pier for dinner?"

I nodded. "I remember." I was still choked up and it was better for me not to speak, but I thought how curious: Mike Novak and Jack Shea, two laymen, believe me instantly, while John Courtney Murray, a priest, thinks I'm paranoid and takes me to a nuthouse, and R. A. F. MacKenzie, also a priest, thinks I'm paranoid because I've been to a nuthouse.

Shea said, "Well, maybe you remember he spent the whole cocktail hour talking to our friend in French?"

"Uh huh."

"You don't understand French?"

"I can read it. I couldn't understand a thing they were saying."

"Well, there was no mistaking Martin's intentions. He was putting the make on her. He spent most of his time telling Nicole dirty jokes. I was talking to you, but I couldn't help overhearing him."

"Why didn't you say something to me?"

"Would that have helped?"

"Well," I said, "I always thought the man was a homosexual."

Shea hummed at that. "I think he's tri-sexual."

"Tri-sexual?"

"I think he'll try anything sexual. He's a real rake."

"I have to have some proof for MacKenzie."

"You want to get Martin transferred out of Rome?"

"I don't know."

"I know. I think he's gotta go." He said he knew a few private eyes.

So I hired two private investigators, for ten thousand lire a day, $16 plus expenses. That's about all they were worth. I visited their office on the Piazza Ungaria, more like a little closet, with cheap linoleum on the floor. The man who did the talking was six and a half feet tall, wore a well-tailored gray flannel suit and two days growth of beard. His partner was only a little more than half his height, with a ski jump nose, like Richard Nixon's, and Nixon's five o'clock shadow. I gave them our home address, along with snapshots of Mary and Malachy Martin, and I instructed them to tail Mary for several days, and then we'd figure out what to do next.

On the first afternoon, they reported, Mary drove to an open area near the Forum and met Martin. He got in the car with her and then the detectives lost her Fiat 500 in the traffic. There were about a million of these cars in Rome, most of them white, like Mary's.

The second afternoon, they tailed her to a hotel, the Columbus, where she met Martin, with another man, not a cleric, whom they described as *"un Polacco."* She was there with them somewhere in the hotel, the detectives couldn't say where, from 5:20 to 7:00 P.M. They told me what the *Polacco* looked like. I said the man's name was probably Zachariah

Schuster. I said he usually stayed at the Mediterraneo. They did some checking there, found that Schuster was registered and tipped a bellman to point him out. Yes, Schuster was the same man who'd been with Malachy and Mary.

The third day, they tailed Mary to the Hotel Massimo d'Azeglio. She entered at 2:55 P.M. and emerged at 6:15. They made some inquiries to see if she, or Martin, was registered there. Negative.

But the people in the hotel undoubtedly tipped off Martin because, on the fourth day, Mary emerged from our home at 10:50 A.M., got in her Fiat, made a series of "vicious turns," and took such a circuitous route to the Lion Book Store that it was obvious she knew she was being tailed. She met no one, and was home by noon.

The fifth day, she drove straight to a rendezvous point near the Forum, parked along the curb and sat there in the car. My detectives sat in their car, watching her. Then a third car screeched up behind them. Two men climbed out, private detectives from another agency, tailing my detectives tailing Mary. They accosted my two clowns, demanding to know why they were following the American woman, their client. My detectives professed ignorance. They said they worked for the Vatican, and pulled identification cards out of their pockets stamped with bold block letters: *VATICANO*.

"Her detectives raised their eyebrows at that," reported my private eye, the tall one. "They concluded we were working for the Vatican. And we let them think so." He added, as an afterthought, "And the other one, how do you call him, Father Martin? He was standing on the corner with a smirk on his face."

I called these fools off the job, sure now that I had blown the only chance I had to prove that Mary and Malachy were spending their afternoons together at some hotel, doubly sure that I had only made her little game infinitely more exciting for her by providing some delicious intrigue. I also felt foolish. I suspected Malachy wasn't putting up his money for private eyes, but getting it from Mary, who was getting it from me. So I was financing both sides of this production. This was like a cheap French farce.

I was too disturbed to sleep more than a couple hours a night. Morning after morning, I would awaken about three and lie there in the dark, thinking, thinking, thinking, if only, if only, if only. Mary wasn't resting too well, either. She started talking in her sleep. One night, as I lay there staring at the ceiling, Mary cried Malachy's name in a dream.

Next morning at breakfast, impassively, I played back to Mary all the words in her dream. She turned white, stared at me, rose without a word, went to the phone, rang for Dr. Ayd and asked for an appointment.

So now we were both talking to Dr. Ayd. Mary wasn't in therapy. I was sure she was talking about our relationship. But Dr. Ayd wouldn't tell me what Mary was telling him. He said to me, "Try to be as kind and considerate and loving as you can be, under the circumstances. I can see some changes in her. When she received the mink coat on her birthday, she was more pleased than she could admit to you."

I saw no signs of progress. At the end of our nightly Hail Mary together, Mary had started to add the invocation, "St. Jude."

To which I gave the automatic response: "Pray for us." I was still a Jesuit, still believing in the power of prayer and in the efficacy of a saint's intervention. Yes. Jude was the right saint to call upon. St. Jude is the patron saint of hopeless causes.

26

I needed to feel good about myself, and, providentially, my editors at *Time* came up with a special assignment that would help me do just that. They wanted me to begin reporting on news tips that I'd wanted to pursue for months now, that the Church might be rescinding its ban on birth control. The Church's teaching dated back to a 1931 condemnation of contraception by Pope Pius XI. If the Church was going to reverse that position, the knottiest moral issue for Catholic couples everywhere, the news would hit like a hurricane.

I knew of no reporter who even suspected there was a story here. It would be my scoop, and I had to be at my creative best to break it loose. Most of the theologians who were rethinking the Church's position on birth control weren't ready to make their thoughts public. Theologians didn't normally seek a forum in the "secular press." They talked among themselves, or wrote nuanced articles in learned journals that were circulated to a few hundred of their peers. And if their arguments with the official Roman position appeared in *Time,* who could assure them the Holy Office would not come thundering down on them?

Religion Editor John Elson told me to tell my sources that *Time* would handle their quotes with discretion. That is, we'd quote their reasoned arguments, but we wouldn't reveal their identities. In Washington, newsmen often used this kind of quote, "not for attribution," to protect their sources. On a delicate story like this one, Elson said, I could protect my sources in the same way. In this case, their identity was not the most important thing. Their information was.

I got the information. In France, Belgium, and the Netherlands, I interviewed a couple dozen Catholic bishops and theologians — behind closed doors — and found that many of them were reformulating a whole new theology of marriage and sexuality, coming to new understandings of "the natural law" and ending up with a position decidedly different from the official Roman view. There was little doubt that many of them were turning away from the old moral textbooks, urging their Catholics to grow up, and start consulting their own consciences. For more than a week on the road, I found liberal theologians telling me, "There is something good and wonderful about making love. The Church has forgotten to teach it."

At the Collegium Albertinum in Nijmegen, I had an evening visit with two Dominican priests, Edward Schillebeeckx and Willem Van der Marck. Schillebeeckx was then considered one of the Church's top ten theologians. After they served coffee and passed around cigars, these men both said they thought the Church would have less difficulty reformulating its teaching on birth control than it would have in trying to explain how it was that the Church could change its teaching.

Father Schillebeeckx said, "There's a job ahead, to explain all this in a way that shows that the Church isn't simply changing, but, rather, deepening its teaching on the meaning of sex in marriage."

I said I thought it was more important for the Church to serve the people of God with some new insights, less important for the Church to save face. People changed their minds every day. Why couldn't the Church change its teaching on this important issue? "Would the world lose its faith in God if the pope said, 'We've changed our mind'?"

The two Dominicans puffed on their cigars, looked at each other, then smiled at me. "That's a good question," said Schillebeeckx.

"Very refreshing view," said Van der Marck.

I resolved to bring that view to the pages of *Time*. I had no personal axe to grind. Mary and I had never used any form of contraception, but that demanded no special heroism from us. Up until recently, we had wanted a dozen kids, and I was on a career track where we could probably afford them. Still, I believed there was some important muckraking to be done here, and I thought my reporting might help overturn the tyranny of an authority with a very limited view of marriage, one that I believed was having a damaging effect on millions of Catholic marriages.

In Rome, I was told, Catholics couldn't buy contraceptives, because they were outlawed. Romans had their own form of birth control. They called it abortion. During their childbearing years, one doctor told me, some Catholic women had ten, twelve abortions. Or more. They did it themselves, with wire coathangers. And sometimes they even baptized the mess that came out.

☙

I FINISHED UP my reporting on a swing back to France and phoned Mary from Paris. "Are you coming to Paris for the weekend?" I asked.

"Of course," she said, and her tone was happy enough to make me believe that maybe, just maybe, we could close the gap between us in Paris, as we couldn't seem to do in Rome.

I sat right down in the offices of Time-Life in Paris to write my file, knowing that the editors in New York would believe my news only if I gave them everything I had. I wrote furiously. The average *Time* file in those days was a few thousand words. When I was done with my reporting on this story, the man in *Time*'s teletype room told me I'd written twenty-five thousand words.*

I'd finished with my file when Mary arrived at Orly on Friday afternoon. She had her own agenda. She didn't come straight to the hotel, she stopped off (I later discovered) to see Zachariah Schuster and two other friends of Malachy Martin's in the Paris offices of the American Jewish Committee. That night, we had a quick dinner and saw a thriller called *Charade,* with Cary Grant, Audrey Hepburn, and Walter Matthau. We were clutched by the movie, and held each other at the climax, when Matthau, Hepburn's "friend at the Embassy," turned out to be the psychotic killer.

I hoped that this sharing (even though it was only a movie), would somehow bring us closer. I even hoped that Mary might see that if this droll character played by Matthau could be a villain, maybe Mary could admit the possibility that her droll friend Martin could be a villain, too, as I was now convinced he was. We went back to our hotel, and had a drink at the bar. Neither the movie nor the drink had any warming effect on Mary. When Mary smiled, she smiled a twisted, almost cynical smile, and then she spent an hour in the bathroom when we retired to our suite at the Crillon. Only two words passed between us: "Good night."

On Saturday, I decided to turn my reportage into a text piece for *Life.* I cabled New York, sought and got an assignment from Hugh Moffett to do an article for him on the Church and birth control. This meant that I'd

*I expanded my reportage to do an entire book on the Church's battle over birth control, *The Politics of Sex and Religion.* It was published by Sheed and Ward in Kansas City in 1985. Sheed and Ward produced it in London under the title *The Encyclical That Never Was* in 1989.

only lined up more work for myself. I spent all day Saturday writing for *Life* instead of strolling Paris with Mary. My text was full of theologians theologizing, and popes pontificating, and when I had it cabled to New York, I knew it was awful. It didn't make the magazine. I was sorry I'd even tried.

That night, we had cocktails at the apartment of a friend of Mary's (who turned out to be a friend of Martin's), then we booked a table at the Folies Bergère. It was a dismal attempt to be young and gay and alive in Paris. Bare-breasted beauties were all around us, dancing, singing, and waving their ostrich feather fans. Through the whole dinner show, I tried a few conversational ploys. Mary hardly uttered a word. "We seem to be on different wave lengths," I said.

She said, "This isn't the place to discuss things." She paused. "We ought to have a serious talk, soon." She smiled with her mouth, but not with her eyes, pursed her lips, then made a little popping sound with her mouth, and lit a cigarette. I reached across the table and broke the cigarette in two. A little flustered, Mary lit another. I also broke that one in half, and popped my lips. We left the show early and retired early and, in the morning, we were on our way back to Rome.

ঞ৹

WE ARRIVED HOME at noon. Just before I left for the office, I placed a Minifon wire recorder under the large reclining chair in our guest room, where Mary was accustomed to talk on the telephone, and punched the RECORD button. When I returned home that evening, I slipped into the guest room, grabbed the recorder and took it out to the car. I sat in the front seat and rewound the spool, then punched the play button.

Only a few minutes into the spool came the sounds of someone dialing the phone, and then Mary's voice saying, *"Padre Martin, per favore."* After some long seconds, she announced in breathlessly loving tones, "I'm back, I'm back, I'm back. Uh. Uh. He went to the office. He won't be back until about uh, seven." I couldn't hear what Martin was saying, but Mary's side of the conversation was full of fondness. She congratulated him for finishing his commentary, and trilled, "We have to celebrate!" They talked about meeting later that afternoon, then Mary had to break off the conversation because Betsy had gotten into something.

I sat there on the front seat of my Volkswagen, staring at the machine, pondering what I had learned: not very much that I hadn't already figured out for myself, except for the revelation that he was writing a book on . . . something.

I also breathed a sigh of something like relief. This recording gave me some proof that Malachy and Mary were having an affair. But it was very slim proof — nothing more than Mary's tone of voice. This was not the kind of proof that would stand up in a court of law, or even impress R. A. F. MacKenzie, but it was something that I wanted the general of the Jesuits to hear. I wasn't exactly sure what action I expected the general to take. I was sure there was power there, power over Martin that I could turn on, if I wanted to.

Soon, I would want to. The next afternoon, I came back to my office after a lunch with Ed Jackson and found Mary pawing through the things on my desk. I cleared my throat. She stood up, face flushed, and said, "We're finished. I simply don't love you anymore."

Mary was a real spectacle. She'd been shopping, and had gotten herself up in a new outfit, a full-length, black serge coat, buttoned all the way down the front, and a black felt hat with a stiff wide brim. It was a feminine treatment of the standard Roman clerical uniform. I tried not to laugh as I thought of an old Thomistic principle, *Omne agens agit sibi simile.* "Every maker makes an image of himself." Of course, I said to myself, if Martin is making Mary, why shouldn't she end up looking like him, too, right down to the very costume he wore, his usual Roman cassock?

I didn't feel calm inside, but said, without heat, "Okay, what next?"

She said she didn't know. Her voice sounded very far away. She seemed to be looking around my office as she spoke. "A separation," she said. "But I don't want to return to the United States. Maybe I'll go to Paris. Or London. Or maybe stay here in Rome." Finally, she said what was really on her mind. She wanted to know where my wire recorder was.

"What wire recorder?" I said.

"The wire recorder that you planted in our guest room yesterday," she said. She explained that Annamaria, our maid, had seen it under the big chair and assumed that Mary had put it there, to catch Annamaria in some forbidden conversation or other. "But no. You put it there, didn't you?"

Nemo se accuset, I said. It was the scholastic formula that Thomas Jefferson had used for the theoretical underpinning of the Fifth Amendment of the U.S. Constitution's Bill of Rights: "No one need incriminate himself." I was right. Mary's demanding an answer here was unconstitutional. The thought never crossed my mind that my action, bugging Mary's phone, was unconstitutional, too.

Mary studied me for a long minute, thinking hard. Then she shook her head, sadly, and popped her lips. She didn't have to say, again, that she didn't love me. As was now so often the case, when Mary spoke, Malachy Martin came out of her mouth. Now, in the popping of her lips, I knew that she didn't love me anymore. And, a weird corollary: I suspected that Malachy Martin was showing his perverse love for me in a new way, by making Mary into a some kind of devilish copy of himself. I shuddered at the thought.

⚜

I HAD LUNCH the next day with Jack Shea, and let him hear some of the recording. He said I should go over to the Jesuit Curia with it. And he couldn't help wondering what piece of Malachy's writing called for a celebration.

"Whatever it is," I said, "it'll be a lie."

Shea laughed. "Malachy's a menace, and he'll end up giving the Order a lot of grief. You've got a duty to tell them what you know."

Right after lunch, I took a cab to the other side of the Tiber and tried to tell James Naughton, one of the Americans on the general's staff, that I thought Mary and Martin were having an affair. He nodded impassively, expressing neither belief nor disbelief. He listened grimly to the wire recording. From the look on his face, I am sure my recording proved nothing in itself to him, because he didn't really understand the context of what Mary was talking about, and he couldn't hear Martin's side of the conversation. Still, he had to pay close attention to my angry presence. I was *Time*'s man at the Council. If Malachy Martin was fooling around with my wife, I could make trouble for the Jesuits. Anticipating a bit, I told Naughton that I didn't want Martin sent out of town. I said, "Sending him away would only give him added glamor in Mary's eyes."

But Martin's rector at the Biblicum, Rod MacKenzie, was soon giving Martin his marching orders. He sent Malachy to Jerusalem, for an indefinite stay, as soon as he could get a plane ticket and a visa. And, of course, MacKenzie's order did make Malachy a martyr, in Mary's eyes, which blazed when she gave me the news about Martin's transfer. I was sick, she screamed, to accuse an innocent man, and get him sent away to boot.

All I could do was make a little popping sound with my lips, for emphasis.

· 233 ·

A day or two later, I got a note from Malachy telling me he was leaving for Jerusalem. He signed it with a salutation: "Happy Valentine's Day."

✐

NOW MALACHY MARTIN had even more sympathy, not only from Mary, but also from a good many of our mutual friends in Rome. Frank McCool told me, "Everyone thinks you've done a terrible thing." I wasn't so sure that Malachy's exile was my doing. I checked with Father Naughton and he swore he'd said nothing to Father MacKenzie. I was inclined to believe him. He had nothing to gain by lying. But someone must have told MacKenzie about Malachy and Mary. Someone who knew. As a friend of mine in the New York financial world put it recently, "Adulterers think they are so damned clever, sneaking around, thinking that nobody sees what's going on. All the while, they're leaving a trail of breadcrumbs that even Ray Charles could see."

All the clerics in my scenario, however, seemed as blind as the jazz singer. When news of Malachy's ouster dribbled into England and the U.S., our friends there, too, thought I had flipped my lid. T. D. Roberts, John Courtney Murray, George Higgins, Gregory Baum, they all seemed to know I had done Martin in.

✐

ON SATURDAY NIGHT, February 22, Mary and I sat through a movie, *The Victors*, a classic with a poignant, ironic scene in it that I would never forget. In a dramatic long shot, the tiny figure of a deserter marches across the snow to his execution before a firing squad, while Frank Sinatra's voice comes across with a modern Christmas carol, "Have Yourself A Merry Little Christmas." When Mary and I stopped for a bite on the Via Veneto, Mary said she thought I ought to ask for a transfer back to the U.S., "where the climate will be better *for us.*"

Eagerly, I gobbled up this news. Go back to the U.S? Together? Sure! We talked about what this meant for the whole family. I could get *Time* to send me to California. There, I said, Mary would have a better chance to develop her own things, go on for a master's degree in psychology, whatever she wanted. Next day, a Sunday, I wrote Clurman in New York. "The time has come," I said, "to move on." I said that I had pioneered on the Council coverage, that others could pick up where I left off, that I wanted to be involved in the presidential campaign of 1964. I said I hoped all of this didn't discombobulate him and/or Ed Jackson.

· 234 ·

It probably did. I got a terse cable back on February 27. "OKAY I'LL OBLIGE. CLURMAN." Dick asked me not to become "a lame duck" in Rome, because he needed me as an active correspondent in Rome until he could find a replacement. He said he was sorry I wanted to leave. He assured me this would have no bad effects on my career.

Of course, it would, but I told myself, "Career, hell. All I want now is my family." I knew that staying in Rome wouldn't help me keep my family one little bit. And a new start back in the U.S. might help change everything. That's what I was thinking. Mary had something else in mind. She started acting secretively again. More surreptitious phone calls. More afternoon jaunts into the city. I felt sure that Martin had slipped back into Rome. I phoned our stringer in Israel to have him check to see if Martin was still there. He was, and this news only made me crazier. I put the oafs from the detective agency on Mary's trail again, and they reported that she was spending her afternoons at the Hotel Massimo d'Azeglio. I started to do some serious drinking.

One night, after trying to talk sense to Mary and finding no success, I hurled an expensive crystal tumbler (and the martini inside it) into our marble foyer, scattering shards of glass all over the hall. The next night, at bedtime, when Mary said she wouldn't say a Hail Mary with me, I put my hands around her neck and squeezed, gently. I didn't intend to hurt her, I just had a point to make, forcefully. But she didn't know what my intentions were; she'd read, or seen, *Othello* and she was frightened. She screamed, and when I released her, she jumped out of bed and said she was leaving.

"Well, then, go," I shouted. I gripped her arm firmly and escorted her to the door, shoved her out into the hall, and slammed the door. She was wearing her red cotton nightshirt, the one that matched mine. I went back to bed, then, a half hour later, answered the ringing doorbell. Two policemen were standing there with Mary. They wanted to put me under arrest.

Speaking the most idiomatic Italian of my life, I told them they were making a big mistake. They listened respectfully, noting, at the same time, Mary's insistence that I be carted away in handcuffs. When they got out the cuffs, the maid, Annamaria, who'd been standing in the kitchen doorway, called to one of the cops and spoke quietly to him, while I pleaded with his partner not to cuff me. I did not convince him. He was snapping the cuffs on my wrists when the other officer approached and took him aside. They spoke for a moment or two and then they turned to me and

Mary. They made a plea for us to compose our differences, said a quick good night, and then they were off.

"Oh, you shit," Mary said. "You were so charming. I've never seen you so charming."

I shrugged. I'd heard about the rat-infested Roman jails. "You're lucky," I said with menace in my voice. "Lucky they didn't take me off. Believe me, you're lucky." I popped my lips, for emphasis.

The next day, Mary came to the office and said she had to get away. She wanted to go back to the U.S., see her folks, spend some time with them, think things over. "Great," I said. I had the office get tickets for her and the kids, and, in three days, I was putting the three of them on TWA Flight 801 for New York, where *Time*'s airport broker met them, got them right through customs and whisked them on to a waiting flight for Milwaukee. I wept all the way back into Rome, but I was sure that things would get better now. They couldn't get any worse.

27

I was in a daze when I returned home. I waved a silent greeting to the maids in the kitchen, and wandered back to our bedroom. I was shocked to find that Mary had taken, or gotten rid of, all her things. She'd left nothing personal behind, nothing to be shipped along with our household goods to California. Empty closets. Empty bureau drawers. In the master bathroom, a dripping faucet, wastebasket overflowing with jars of cosmetics and old lipsticks and an empty box that said Modess. I wandered back into the bedroom, and spied the heel of a shoe peeking out from under the bed, got down on my knees and found a possibly forgotten pair of pumps, and next to them, a blue cardboard carton labeled Enovid. It contained what was left of a year's supply, nine bright purple folders, each containing twenty pills in plastic strips, stamped with the legend, "Searle 5 mg."

Still wearing my trench coat, I slumped into a chair and closed my eyes. Soon, Annamaria and Emma were standing over me and clearing their throats. "Yes," I said, "what is it?"

They looked at each other, hesitant, then back at me. Annamaria said, "We knew that *la signora* and Father Martin were having an affair. On December 6, the very day you flew off to America, Father Martin was waiting for *la signora.*"

Emma confirmed that. "He was right here when *la signora* returned from the airport with Archbishop Roberts. And then, when the archbishop went back to England two days later, he was around every day. Almost every afternoon, *la signora* would give us money to go off to the cinema with the children. And when we returned, they, *la signora* and *il padre,* would be alone together here."

I wanted to shout, "NOW YOU TELL ME!" I told them to wait a moment. They followed me into the kitchen and watched as I quaffed a big glass of water. I moved to the dining room and asked them to take a seat with me. "Okay. Okay. Go on. Go on."

"About a week before Christmas," Annamaria recalled, "*la signora* explained that she would be going off to Paris to meet her parents for Christmas. She couldn't take the children. Emma was to care for little T. D. at her home in Rome. Annamaria would take Betsy up north, to her own family home in Valdagno. She would give them each a hundred thousand lire. *Il padre* seemed to take a great deal of interest in the arrangements. It was he who went down and purchased her train tickets for Valdagno."

"But *la signora* didn't go to Paris for Christmas," said Emma. "I phoned here on Christmas Day. *La signora* answered the phone. I hung up, because I didn't want her to know that I knew she was only telling us a story about going out of town. Later, the vegetable man told me *la signora* was here all through Christmastime. He made daily deliveries. He saw *la signora* and" — she made a face — "*il padre*. Every day."

"The vegetable man?" I cried. "The vegetable man!" I slammed my forehead with the heel of my right hand. Apparently, everyone in town knew about this adultery but me. I interrupted the maids a good many times. It took them at least an hour to get through their stories.

Annamaria's tale began way back in August, when we first hired her as a *bambinaia* at the beach in Lavinio. She wasn't there long, she said, before Father Martin had made passes at her, told her he loved her, and wanted to go to bed with her. She soon realized that it was *la signora* he wanted, not her.

She was "not too suspicious" when *la signora* and *il padre* moved back to Rome from the beach in late August, because *la signora* was "so pregnant." But in December, she knew for sure they were up to something. *Il padre* was promoting her trip to Valdagno, persuading her to take little Betsy into the Italian Alps in the dead of winter, even though the tot was suffering from a bronchial condition. "I didn't want to have these ugly suspicions," she said, "because I had such respect for *la signora*.

"But I had many doubts about *il padre*. He said he was going to the Holy Land for Christmas. That was a lie. When I returned here on January 3, I rang the bell and I had to wait a long time. Finally, *il padre* answered the door in his barefeet. He said he was surprised to see us. We weren't supposed to be back until January 5. *La signora* was in bed, he said, because she wasn't feeling well. And when she came out of the bedroom, I could believe she wasn't well, because she looked pale and afraid. I realized then she hadn't gone to Paris, and that he hadn't gone to the Holy Land. Her dirty laundry and his dirty laundry were very much in evidence."

"It was clear," said Emma, "that he'd been wearing your red nightshirt. I found it in *la signora*'s bedroom, dirty, although it was clean when you left for the United States." It was becoming clearer to me now. This was not only a tale of lust, but of envy as well. Malachy's envy was compelling him not only to take what I had, but become what I was.

Emma said, "Obviously, *il padre* had moved in. He had been writing something on your typewriter."

"Writing something?" I said. "What? Letters? Correspondence?"

"No," she said. "Something much bigger. A thick manuscript."

When the maids had finished the rest of the story — and they had had much more to tell about Mary's duplicity through January, February, and March — I took a drive, stopped at the little park on the top of the Janiculum, and looked out over the city. I couldn't help thinking of the children. The notion that Mary would send them off, and at Christmas, too! The lump in my throat began to grow. To think that Mary had actually written me at the Institute to describe the Christmas she had had with the kids. This was not the Mary I knew. Under Malachy's direction, she had become a deceitful wretch. Now I wondered what other deceptions she and Martin had devised.

◈

IN THE DAYS that followed, I lived mainly on gin, spent most of my nights staring at the ceiling in my bedroom, trying to process everything. At the office, did a pretty good imitation of a foreign correspondent at work. I spent extra time updating my huge file on birth control — which my editors were treating with caution. They decided they would hold up the story until they could get a detailed piece on the Pill into the Medicine section. Even then, they didn't rush into print with my reports about the new Church thinking on birth control. My twenty-five-thousand-word file, reduced to three columns of type in *Time*, would not run until the issue dated April 10.

Alone now in Rome, I spent much of my time trying to prove I wasn't a nut. I took my two maids to our Time Inc. lawyer's office in Rome and had them swear affidavits about the goings-on in the Kaiser household at Christmastime, then had copies of those statements stamped and notarized on two parchments and delivered them to Father MacKenzie at the Biblicum. He sent me back a note. "Not being acquainted with the persons who made them," he wrote, "I am unable to form a judgment on their trustworthiness. But, even if accepted at face value, they would not prove your suspicions true."

I phoned him. "What'll it take to convince you? Technicolor movies of the two of them — fucking?"

There was a long pause. The poor man was caught in a terrible dilemma, damned if he believed me, damned if he didn't. He said, "I hope your impending move to the States will help you resolve your troubles."

At lunch a few days later, I told my friend from the U.S. Embassy, Jack Shea, about my harsh words to MacKenzie. He dipped into his briefcase and pulled out some unbound galleys for a book called *The Pilgrim*. Shea said it would be published in the summer. "You might show this to MacKenzie."

"What is it?"

"The pen name is Michael Serafian," Shea said, "but the style is pure Pushkin."

"Malachy's book!" I grabbed it and turned quickly to a passage concerning the *schema* on the Jews. I skimmed it, then told Shea, "It's Malachy all right, and it looks like a fabrication."

Shea was way ahead of me. "Uh huh. I've read the whole thing. It's also an attack on Pope Paul VI."

I flipped back to the front of the book. "But he dedicates the book to the pope."

"Believe me, he attacks him, too."

I grimaced. All through December, Malachy hadn't only been sleeping in my bed with my wife, he'd been concocting tall tales, on my Olivetti and in my apartment, about the second session of the Council. And trashing the pope, too. "This guy is incredible," I said.

"A real asshole. But you have to give the devil his due. He succeeded in selling this garbage to Farrar Straus." Roger Straus was one of the most distinguished guys in the New York publishing world. And his partner, Bob Giroux, had discovered Thomas Merton's *Seven Storey Mountain*.

⚜

I MARVELED at the devil's handiwork, too, but my fascination compelled me to keep putting together the pieces of a story that fascinated me as much as anything I'd ever worked on for *Time*. I went back to Ayd, not a patient now, but a sleuth who had a notion that Ayd must have known more than he was telling me when I'd first appeared on his doorstep in November.

I had several visits with him before he started opening up with me. It was I who had been his patient, not my wife, nor any of my friends, yet he seemed to cling to the fiction that he had had a confidential relationship with them. Finally, he had to admit, "I'm afraid there was a conspiracy here."

"Martin was involved in it, wasn't he?"

"He was the first one who told me you needed psychiatric help. I believed him. We discussed the problem of getting you to come over and see me. The idea had to be your own. That's where Father Beuzer came in. He was in one of my classes at the Greg. He knew you. Why not have him plant the seed? If you were having problems, then you'd certainly want to see me."

"And I did come to see you."

"But why?"

I looked at Ayd and laughed an embarrassed laugh. "Because, if I was paranoid, I wanted to deal with it."

"Fair enough," said Ayd. "But, you know, that was my first clue that you weren't paranoid. People who are paranoid don't put themselves into the hands of a doctor like me quite so easily as you did."

"What was your second clue?"

"When I saw Malachy and Mary together. I saw her admiration for him, but he wouldn't look at her. Maybe he could see I was watching him. There was something wrong here, but I couldn't name it."

"And when was that?"

"Toward the end of November, Martin brought a delegation to tell me about their concern for you."

"*Martin* brought a delegation?" I said.

Dr. Ayd sighed. "He came with Mary. And John Courtney Murray. And Archbishop Roberts."

"God damn!"

"Yes, I know. It must be pretty depressing to think that your best friends were in on this."

"But how," I said, "do you know that Martin brought them? Maybe the others brought him?"

Ayd gave me a long look. "Just an informed hunch. He made the appointment. And all the time they were here, Martin didn't say a word.

If the others brought him, they did so because he had some information to offer. He had none. And when the others were finished, they seemed to defer to him. And then, when he said he had nothing to add, they all left."

"And the upshot of the meeting?" I said. "What did you all decide?"

"Murray suggested that you had to put yourself in a clinic. I say this in my own defense. I didn't go along with him. I didn't think you needed anything more than a well-deserved rest."

"You didn't recommend the Institute of Living?"

"No. I didn't even know you were headed there. I don't know how you got there."

"As far as I know, it was Murray's idea. Or maybe Martin's. But it was Murray who persuaded me to go, he took me there. He signed me in."

Ayd clucked. "That's not the way it's supposed to be done. Institutions like this are supposed to take in patients referred by doctors, not by laymen."

I laughed. "Well, the great John Courtney Murray isn't a layman, is he?"

Dr. Ayd shook his head. "I'm afraid that Murray's name and reputation meant more than it should have at the Institute."

"Dr. Ayd, why didn't you tell me about Martin and his goddamn delegation? If I'd only known Martin was conspiring to get me out of Rome, I could have done something before he was able to have his way with Mary."

"They were having an affair long before that."

"You know that?"

"I suspect that."

"When?"

"Huh?"

"When did they start having their affair?"

Ayd said he believed it was back in August, when Mary was still pregnant with T. D.

"Hell," I said, "no wonder the little guy didn't want to come out. They had to do a Cesarean section, you know." I bowed my head.

He put a hand on my shoulder. "If I'd said anything to you, I'd only have been trying to play God."

I straightened up and looked him in the eye. "It was easier for you to do nothing?"

"I guess so."

I squinted at him. "In doing nothing, you *were* playing God, weren't you?"

"What do you mean?"

"Through this whole thing, God hasn't been doing anything. And neither were you."

Ayd coughed in embarrassment and shook his head. "It's an old mystery. The mystery of evil. If there is a God, why does He let these terrible things happen? We don't know. We just don't know. But some of us still believe."

I was thinking that one over as I rose and put on my jacket. Finally, I said, "I believe in God all right. It's just that I think He's something of a shit."

∽

I COULD HARDLY WAIT to tell my colleague Ed Jackson about Martin's machinations. He wasn't surprised. "Hell, in November, Martin came into the office here with Mary and Roberts and Murray."

"Here?" I said. "They all came here? What for?"

"They wanted me to have you transferred out of Rome. They said they could see that the pressure on you was beginning to tell. They said you were losing your judgment."

"What did you tell them?"

"I told 'em I knew you'd been working hard, but I couldn't see that your work was suffering. For awhile there, maybe, you went beyond the bounds."

"What do you mean?"

"If you'd asked me, I would have advised you not to sign that critique of the *schema* on the mass media with Cogley and Novak. You were making the news instead of reporting it. But your criticisms were right on the mark. You weren't losing your judgment. In fact, in light of what's happened, I think you had pretty good judgment. Especially about that weasel."

I demanded to know why Ed hadn't told me about that little visit from the weasel and "my closest friends."

He shrugged. "They asked me to keep it confidential."

I shook my head. That was the trouble with secrecy. People always found a way of misusing it. "Well," I said, "maybe it's over now. I think Martin's out of the picture. Mary's back home in Milwaukee. Maybe I can win her back."

· 243 ·

Jackson frowned. "Why would you *want* her back?"

"She's my wife. I married her for better or for worse."

Jackson gave me a wide-eyed, incredulous smile. "Now, you *are* losing your judgment."

Clurman stopped at Fiumicino to see me on his umpteenth trip to Vietnam. He told me I wasn't losing anything except a little weight. (I *had* lost twenty pounds in the week that Mary left with the kids.) "Your reporting's still good," he said. "The magazine should have run that piece you did last week on Nixon's stopover in Rome. On the twenty-fifth floor, they are still talking about your massive file on the birth control thing." He told me, there and then, "If you want to stay in Rome, you can. If not, I'll send you anywhere you want. Name the place."

I told him I wanted Los Angeles. "I think Mary and I can do better in our own culture. Rome has been bad for us."

"It's been great for you," he said. "It hasn't been good for Mary."

"I'd still like L.A. I can get Mary and the kids back if I go there."

He echoed Ed Jackson. He didn't understand why I'd want Mary now. Still, he wasn't going to renege on his promise. "Okay," he said. "You can report to Marshall Berges in L.A. on May 1. I'm going to bring Israel Shenker in here from Moscow." Clurman knew Shenker's experience reporting on the Kremlin would help him at the Vatican. The bureaucracies in both places had much in common. Brilliant move.

☙

MARY STAYED IN MILWAUKEE two weeks, and then she was off to visit her brother in Phoenix. She paid a call on my mother there, told her our marriage was "all washed up," that I'd rejected my new son, that I'd tried to choke her to death in Rome.

I phoned Mary in Phoenix. She seemed vague about her plans. I asked her to wait there for me, that I would be leaving Rome in a week or so. Just before I left Rome in mid-April, I phoned Mary again. She wasn't there, but her sister-in-law spoke with me.

"When will Mary be back?" I asked.

"We don't know."

"Where is she now?"

She paused. "We don't know that either."

"Uh huh." It was obvious to me that Mary's family was protecting her — against me. "Look," I said, figuring I had nothing to lose by coming right out with the truth. "I don't know what Mary's told you. She's been having an affair with a Jesuit priest in Rome. His superiors had to send him off to Jerusalem."

"Oh," she said, with a touch of excitement in her voice. "Mary got two airmail letters today. From Jerusalem."

"Peggy," I said. "Do us all a favor. Don't send those letters on to Mary, wherever she is. And don't open them. Just put them in an envelope and send them to the superior of the Biblicum in Rome. The letters could provide the proof the Jesuits need to fix this guy's wagon."

She said she would. I gave her Father MacKenzie's name and address on the Piazza Pilotta. Peggy didn't send the letters. When I left Rome, I felt MacKenzie was still under the impression that I was a nut, a nut who had tried to smear one of his good men and true.

ớᴘ

WHEN I CHECKED IN with Clurman's office in New York on April 14, there was a letter waiting for me from Mary's brother-in-law in Milwaukee. "Mary is currently living near Las Vegas to establish residence for a divorce," he wrote. "I spoke with her attorney yesterday and I gave him your New York address...."

A divorce! I shouldn't have been surprised. I was. Now I was certain that Mary was still under the influence of Martin. I thought back to my last conversation with Dr. Ayd. Like many psychiatrists, he thought he could solve any problem if only he could give it a name. He had said that Martin was a sociopath, and recommended I read Cleckley's classic work on sociopathy, *Mask of Sanity.* Ayd said that the sociopath is a completely amoral individual who can think of nothing but his own pleasure. His guess was that Martin had done this before.

"Done what?"

"Played around with other women. Married women. Anyone and everyone."

"Now that," I said, "is an interesting thought. I just wonder—"

"What?"

"How do I go about proving your theory?"

Ayd said, "I haven't a clue. I'm a psychiatrist, not a detective."

Hmmm, I said to myself. I could be a detective. If Mary could just get a glimpse behind the mask....

ớᴘ

AS SOON AS I arrived in New York, I phoned William Van Etten Casey, the Jesuit from Holy Cross who had stayed with us in Rome for three weeks last May. I told him that I was being transferred to L.A. "Uh huh," he said. "So the Curia got you, too."

"Too?"

He said he'd heard that Martin had been sent to Jerusalem. There was a rumor that his enemies in the Curia had put the heat on his superiors in Rome and gotten him run out of town.

I sighed and told Casey, "Malachy Martin probably planted those rumors himself. The truth is more shocking." I gave it to him in about two teary sentences.

He heard me out, then told me he'd fly down from Boston. He wanted to see me. He was in New York the next morning. We strolled all over midtown, up to Lincoln Center, then back across Central Park. It took all that time for me to tell him the whole sad story, and its even sadder denouement: that, up to now, I hadn't found one single Jesuit who believed me. Casey believed me.

I could have expected that from this most unclerical of clerics. He was a good Jesuit who had always called them as he saw them, even the little hypocrisies of the Society itself. He rather liked being "agin' the government" of his own Order. He was a celibate who knew how to love, an unpretentious but serious scholar, a fine editor, and he was devoted to Sacred Scripture, the Broadway stage, the *New York Times,* and good dry sack.

"Hell," he said, "if you'd relayed any of your early suspicions to me, I could have confirmed them. When I was staying with you, way back in May, Martin would phone your house two or three times a day. He and Mary would chatter on for an hour at a time. I was a dunce. I thought, 'How nice, that Bob and Mary have such great friends in Rome.'"

※

I STOPPED in Phoenix on my way West, hoping to find out where Mary had gone. If only her brother and sister-in-law would give me a break. I paid them a call. Neither of them would tell me where Mary was, because they'd promised Mary they wouldn't.

I nodded. "That makes sense. You have to be on her side."

Her brother said, "We're on her side, but we're on your side, too. In fact, now we know that Mary's been telling some wild lies about you. We know she's been involved with this character, Martin, and is still involved."

They wouldn't say how they knew. My guess was that Peggy and Jim had opened Malachy's letters. Peggy seemed amused that Mary had taken everyone in so completely. "Mary talks about Msgr. Mark Hurley and Msgr. Higgins, and John Courtney Murray as if they were all in this together, approving everything."

"Well," I said, "why don't you tell them the truth?"

"I've tried to talk to Murray," Peggy said. "He's in Phoenix, staying with the Luces. In fact, Mary talked to him a couple of times while she was here. She said he was very sympathetic. He believes her, believes she's fleeing from you because you want to kill her."

Jim said, "We know now that Mary's making a big mistake."

Peggy grimaced. "I got nowhere with Murray. Why don't *you* go over and talk to him? I have a feeling that he's got some power in Rome, that he can do something about Martin."

I zipped over to see Murray at the Luce's winter home in the Biltmore Estates. Murray told me that he'd been suffering from some vertigo. But, even allowing for that, he seemed distant. He said he was sorry for me, "But getting well is something you have to do yourself."

"Getting well?" I said. "You don't understand." I told him about the testimony of the maids, and Dr. Ayd's revelations about the delegation that had come to see him, a delegation that included Martin and the great John Courtney Murray, a delegation that looked, now, like a conspiracy. I tried to keep cool through this recital, but I am sure my voice was filled with reproach.

Murray shook his head, with obvious pity for me. This was a view of things he couldn't abide, because it made him look like a fool. He stood and walked me back to my car.

When we reached the car, I turned to him. "You don't believe me," I said.

He said, "I, I think it's a, a construction."

I drove off, wondering what it would take to melt the perpetual lump in my throat.

28

With advice like Murray's, maybe someone else could have said, "Forget it," then dropped the whole thing. I couldn't. My Novice master had always said, "Pray as if everything depended on God and work as if everything depended on yourself." I prayed. And then I went to work.

In my first week on the job in California, I made it a point to make a dinner date with Mark Hurley. He was now an auxiliary bishop in San Francisco. If he was among those who were helping get Malachy established in the United States (and unwittingly helping bring Mary and Malachy together again), he needed a little more information than he was getting from Martin, Higgins, and Murray. Hurley used to show up at our Sunday nights, but I didn't know him very well. As far as I was concerned, he was just one of the American *periti* staying at the Villa Nova, a pensione that Msgr. George Higgins and company had made into a kind of Roman clubhouse. He was, therefore, one of the good guys. To me, he looked like an Irish detective lieutenant, or a National League umpire: fair. As far as I knew, he'd taken no active role in getting me out of Rome, or promoting the cause of Malachy Martin.

We had dinner at Doro's, a restaurant with red velvet wallpaper that was filled with fine art, right next door to the law offices of the famous, flamboyant Melvin Belli. I felt more comfortable in this ambience than I would have felt in Hurley's favorite Irish pub. Doro's was the kind of place I'd become accustomed to on my Time Inc. expense account. I ordered a bottle of Romanée, and while we sipped the rare French burgundy and munched on escargots, Hurley listened to my story about Mary and Malachy.

He said he had a hard time believing it, for two reasons: (1) John Courtney Murray assured him that I was sick, and (2) he knew that I was a hard worker. I said that Murray was going outside his competence to make any definitive statement about my mental health. And I said that I didn't understand how my being a hard worker made it impossible for me to see what was happening before my very eyes.

He shook his head. He said Malachy had been writing him almost every day, keeping him abreast of everything. "We feel sorry for him."

" 'We?' "

"George Higgins, John Courtney Murray, Ray Bosler, John Quinn."

"Bosler and Quinn, too?" Two more highly placed American clerics. I marveled to see how the circle was widening. I said, "Why don't you just call a meeting of the American hierarchy and get up a purse for Malachy?"

"We have been sending him money," admitted Hurley. "We can get him established over here as a diocesan priest. We think we've got him a job teaching in a small Catholic college in the Midwest." As a schemer who was taking Malachy's side against me, Hurley got an F for telling me what was going on. But then, he wasn't trying to be a schemer. He was just a simple pastor who cared about helping people.

"You don't believe he has any designs on my wife?" I said.

"Absolutely not. According to Malachy, you've made everything up."

"Why would I want to do that?"

He smiled. "Because you're psycho?"

He wouldn't have made a joke like that if he really thought I was psycho. So I plunged ahead. "Look," I said. "Mary's somewhere in Nevada right now, getting a divorce. But I understand Malachy writes her almost every day. Do you honestly think he's been trying to stop her? Or that he's urging her on?"

"I don't know that he's writing her every day," Hurley said.

"You don't have to believe me," I said. "Would you believe Mary's brother? Or her sister-in-law? I think they know what's happening."

Hurley said, "If they know something I don't know, I want to talk to them. I want one of them to phone me as soon as possible. By tomorrow night."

"I'll have Jim phone you," I said. "But how will you know it's Mary's brother phoning you? I could hire someone to do it."

Hurley laughed. "Let me worry about that. You just get him to call."

ঔঢ়

I LET a week pass, then I dialed Hurley and asked him what was happening.

"I talked to your brother-in-law," said Hurley in a low, sad voice. "He gave me all the proof I needed. He had two letters from Malachy to Mary. He read parts of them to me. There wasn't a doubt in my mind that it was Malachy who had written them."

"No doubt?"

"I've gotten a lot of letters from him. He has a certain style. These letters were from him, all right."

My heart leaped. But I was cautious. "Well, were they just friendly notes? Or what?"

He said, "They're incriminating. I phoned George Higgins today and told him the sad truth: 'We've been the victims of an incredible hoax.'"

I was glad. But I didn't gloat. It had taken me a long time, too, to see through Malachy.

I never saw the letters Jim had read to Hurley over the phone, and neither did the Jesuits in Rome. Jim simply refused to send them along. As far as I knew, Malachy was still "in good standing" with the Soc. And he was waiting for Higgins and company to bring him to the U.S. Now, it looked like he would have a longer wait than he had counted on. At least, he wouldn't be getting any more help from Higgins. Wasn't it odd, though, that he would solicit their help, but not call on the help of the Jesuits he knew in the U.S.? My guess: that the Jesuits already had his number.

❧

IN THE MEANTIME, I had surprised Mary by not storming into Nevada to contest the divorce. *Time*'s law firm in L.A. had referred me to a good attorney named Grant Cooper, who advised me I had nothing to gain by making an appearance in Nevada. "If you go there," he said, "she'll still get the divorce and custody of the kids, too. She'll also get half of everything you own, to boot."

"And if I stay out?"

"Then the courts can only dissolve the marriage. But the State of Nevada will have no jurisdiction over your property."

"What about arranging to see my kids? Isn't that a normal part of any divorce agreement?"

Cooper grimaced. "This is a hopeless case. The best thing you can do about those kids is forget you ever had 'em. When they grow up, they may come looking for you. But it's useless, now, to fight for 'em."

I wept, wept with the tears of a Rachel, mourning for her children "because they were not." Later I told myself that Cooper had no crystal ball. I'd get my kids.

Mary had already emptied our substantial U.S. checking account, and had been planning, apparently, on some kind of continuing financial support from me. Now that she couldn't get a court to order up that support (because I'd failed to appear in Nevada), she was upset. "It is, of course, your right," she wrote in a note mailed to my office in Beverly Hills. "Nevertheless, I do think that some agreement on division of property would be more sensible and just...." She said she was taking civil service exams in Nevada and would be looking for a job there. "I'm not returning to Europe," she said. "I plan to stay in Nevada."

Mary asked me not to tell her parents that she had filed for divorce, because "they have taken this all very hard. I do think, Bob, that only you and I should settle these matters, and not involve legions of family and friends. I well understand the worry and concern of others. But we are discussing your life and my life, something that no one else can do for us."

I wrote back, care of her attorney in Las Vegas, "You're right. 'Only you and I should settle these matters.' If only you had followed this plan from the time you first began to feel alienated. If only you were following it now.'" I knew that Mary was still under Malachy's influence, that he was not only telling her what to do, but giving her advice on how to do me, too. Only a few days before, I learned that Mary had written Clurman in New York, asking Time Inc. to make sure I be put under psychiatric care in L.A., because I could be "homicidally dangerous." I was sure that idea didn't come from Mary, but from Malachy.

Clurman paid no attention to Mary's note. He told me to just keep turning out the kind of files I had done on the Goldwater-Johnson campaign in California. I thanked God that Clurman had the wisdom and the integrity that some of my clerical friends had so sorely lacked, and I mentioned the incident, in passing, to Andy Kopkind, one of my new friends in the L.A. bureau of *Time*. Andy nodded. "Yeah, that was good of Clurman. But it wouldn't hurt you to go see a shrink. I think you could become obsessed by all of this."

He was right. There was a danger that I'd turn most of my energies into the Malachy project. I told myself I had to be careful not to do that. But if, to Mary, Malachy was still a knight in shining white armor, then I had good reasons to unhorse him. I felt compelled to do some more detective work. If Malachy had a past, as I thought he might, and if I could prove it to Mary, maybe I could prevent her from following this guy — to her own sorrow.

In this, I may have been kidding myself. Maybe I just wanted the satisfaction of nailing this guy. Maybe I felt I could handle this better if I knew Malachy was simply using her, if I could learn that their "love" was really just a rat fuck.

But how could I reveal the rat? Would I have to uncover his entire history? This could take months, years. I felt like the reporter in the Orson Welles movie who had to travel the world looking for the meaning of Charles Foster Kane's last word on earth: Rosebud. Neal Gabler has pointed out that the world itself has come to be molded in the image of the movies. He writes in *Life the Movie: How Entertainment Conquered Reality* that "entertainment has gradually infested our own personal lives, converting them into 'movies,' too."

I didn't have months, or years to pursue my movie mystery. Mary would win her Nevada divorce in less than six weeks. That meant that I had only a few weeks to follow Malachy's spoor. So I couldn't track him systematically; I'd have to start looking now in the most likely places. But where were the likeliest places? Last spring, Malachy had told me he'd gone to the Rome airport to see an American woman he'd known in Jerusalem. She was leaving her husband and heading for Kentucky with her children. I wondered: was it possible that Malachy had had anything to do with *that* family's breakup? It was a lead, but a slim one. I didn't even know the woman's name.

On a hunch, I phoned Mary's brother in Phoenix. "Just a shot in the dark, Jim," I said. "Has Mary ever mentioned a family Malachy knew in Jerusalem?"

It just so happened that Mary had. She told Jim that when Malachy was in Jerusalem he had made the acquaintance of an American diplomat, and his wife. Name was Blake, he thought. Somehow (somehow!) the wife had fallen in love with Malachy. When he didn't reciprocate, she became hysterical. She had tried to commit suicide, then flew to Rome with her three children to see Malachy. He went out to the airport, calmed her down, and put her back on the plane for the U.S. She was somewhere in Kentucky, Jim thought. Malachy had warned Mary about her. "That Blake woman," Malachy had told Mary, "would do anything to get even with me."

That was Mary's version of the story, one given her by Malachy. I knew there had to be another version. Or versions. What were they? How could I find out? I checked on Bill Blake with the U.S. State Department, with the U.S. Army, the Air Force. And drew a blank. I started phoning the information operator in every large city in Kentucky, to see if there was a listing for a Mrs. William Blake. I didn't know *her* first name. I made ten or twelve unsuccessful phone calls to Blake residences, on the order of: "Look, I may have the wrong number here. But did you ever live in Jerusalem?"

This was like looking for a pearl on the mudflats of Milpitas. I had better luck developing more details on Malachy's other deceptions. From Jesuits who had studied with him, I learned that on several occasions he had gotten permission to attend learned meetings in far-off places, then returned and written up accounts of meetings that had never existed. The truth is that the meetings were figments of Malachy's imagination, concocted to cover up his journeys to — who knows where? Another time, he received permission to visit the U.S. to see his dying sister. When he came back to Rome, he had all the priests at the Biblicum saying Masses for the repose of her departed soul. The truth was that his sister was alive and well and living in Schenectady, and that he hadn't heard from her in fifteen years.

♫

DURING ALL THIS TIME, of course, I had work to do, and did it. I was covering the presidential primary campaign, and I started following Senator Barry Goldwater around the West. Toward the end of June, I came back home to Phoenix with the senator and a large press contingent. Barry's daughter was getting married. While we newsmen were waiting around for the wedding day, and attending daily non-news conferences given by the senator's press secretary, I phoned Mary's brother, to see what he'd heard from Mary.

Surprise! Mary was there, with the kids. She wanted to talk to me. She wanted me to come over and see Betsy and little T. D., if I could get away. A chance to see my kids? Of course. I said I'd come over as soon as I could. And that I wanted to take her to dinner that evening. She agreed.

That afternoon, I got Charles Mohr of the *New York Times*, a former *Time* correspondent, to cover for me, and I took a trip over to the McArdles. It was ninety-eight in the shade and my three-year-old was playing in the front yard of the only home on the street with a dried-up lawn. She gave me a puzzled look when I drove up. "Betsy?" I said.

"Daddy!" she cried, and ran toward me. She talked my arm off and introduced me to her little brother, now almost a year old, who even then had the devilish grin he has today. The babysitter told me the grownups were out shopping, and so, for a half-hour or more, I played with my kids, bouncing them on my knees, chasing them around the yard, and sprinkling them with the garden hose, until I collapsed from the heat. I think that if they had asked me to help them make mudpies, I would have done so — and eaten them, too. We went into the house. Betsy took my arm and dragged me into the guest room to show me one of her dolls. "You're crying, Daddy?"

I said, "I think I have something in my eye. A cinder." I wanted to change the subject. "Are these your mother's things?" I said, pointing to the closet. Betsy nodded.

I didn't know what I was looking for, but I found it immediately: an envelope jutting out of the pocket of a cotton housecoat, and found two letters addressed to Mary. They were from Malachy. I caught my breath. Were these the Technicolor movies I'd been looking for?

I grabbed them and stuck them in my pocket. I wanted to leave right away, but I gave the kids the horsy back rides I'd promised them, down the hall, out to the backyard, and back through the kitchen. When the sitter said it was nap time, the kids protested, but I was grateful. "Tell Mrs. Kaiser that I was here," I said to the babysitter on my way out the door. "I'll be back later."

※

"COPIES," I SAID to myself. "Where can I make some copies?" I raced to a real estate office on Camelback Road and sauntered in, trying to look nonchalant, but my breath was short and my heart was pounding. "You have a Thermofax machine?" I asked.

"We do photostats here," said a man behind a desk. "Fifty cents a page."

"Mind doing these?" I said, handing over the letters.

He eyed them, shrugged, and made me five copies of each page. I threw down a $10 bill and started out the door, but then returned and said, "I'd better take the negatives, too." I retrieved them from a wastebasket, almost tripped going out the door, made it to the car, and zipped off down the road. Several blocks down the street, I pulled over and started reading.

The letters were typed, one signed "Malachy" and the other "Your black rat." The signatures were in Pushkin's hand, and the paragraphs ran on in pure Pushkin style. He blathered on about the coming marriage of Malachy Martin and Mary McArdle:

> I can tell you this: you will never want for excitement and wonder and love, and I will give you the life and loving you were made for but never had until God discovered me to you and you to me. I believe that being bonded to you in holy matrimony will be very very different from any notion I can now conceive, but I feel that the intimacy and the love and the compenetration of each other's being is something we have already. . . . I hope you will have purchased our rings, yours and mine, my dear, before I come to you, the rings that the Italians call *anello*, the matrimonial ring. It will be a symbol of our togetherness, of your womanliness and my manliness, and of the complete control that we each have one over the other.
>
> You have won my head and my heart and you have become the darlingest, daringest, dearest thing on this planet, in this galaxy, in this universe, all because of a blessed concatenation of circumstances that could never be repeated in a hundred million shakes of the divine dice. . . . If you'll recall, my moment did not come right away. (The most beautiful words ever spoken to me: oh, yes, dear, fear not, I am yours. No one ever spoke words so sweet as those to me.) Even now, I can summon up the memory of your glistening limbs on that first eve, your raven locks shining in the moonlight, your moist, half-open eyes, your moist, half-open lips, my love, my dove, my panting doe. . . .

I wanted to throw up, but I turned to Malachy's second letter. It was filled with more, much more of the same treacle, and it ended with a request that Mary kiss the children for him, "because they are the responsibility of both of us now." He said he was sailing to Naples and would arrive in Rome on May 31. She should write him there at the Pensione Alto Adige, not the Biblical Institute.

I hurried to my hotel in Scottsdale, and addressed four envelopes — to Father Rod MacKenzie at the Biblicum, to Father James Naughton at the Jesuit Curia in Rome, to Dr. Francis Braceland at the Institute of Living, and to Father John Courtney Murray at the Jesuit House of Studies in Woodstock, Maryland. I folded the photostat copies, put them in the envelopes, took them to the post office, and mailed them on June 24, special delivery.

I could look myself in the mirror again, and not see a fool. I knew that I had not been imagining things, that I was not paranoid, or afflicted with some fancy disorder concocted by a psychiatric committee. The story was really an old one, as old as King David, at least: someone else had coveted my wife, and conspired to get me out of the way. But, unlike the cuckold Uriah, I wouldn't lose my life over it. I was smarter than Uriah, or luckier, at least. My intuitions saved me, but I couldn't congratulate myself too warmly about that, because it had taken me too long to figure things out. My common sense had been dulled by my ideology.

That's what made me angry now — that I should have known better, all along. Since my earliest days as a Catholic, I knew about the *elementum humanum in ecclesia Dei,* the human element in the Church of God. One Saturday morning, with my fellow eighth graders at St. Francis Xavier Parish in Phoenix, I was playing basketball on the outdoor courts we had built for ourselves. During a break, a few of us wandered over to watch a couple of workmen pumping out the cesspool next to the sisters' convent. As we watched the waters from the cesspool spreading over the adjacent pasture, we were startled to see hundreds of white balloons floating along. They were coming up out of the cesspool.

"Those aren't balloons," said one of my classmates. "They're rubbers. We've seen 'em down at the mill." He was referring to the sewage plant that had been built for the city of Phoenix. We were still out in the country, in cesspool country, where condoms could tell tales.

"Haw haw," shouted Leo Samsky, a diamond in the rough who had spent some time on a sheep ranch. "I always *thought* the fathers fucked the sisters. Now I *know* it."

I was afraid he was right, and so were my mates, Dicky Hubbs, Albert Mangino and Jim Hudson. The cesspool served only the convent, there were no neighbors, then, and there were some virile young Jesuits around, some of them probably sent to Phoenix because they were having problems in California. The rest of the scenario was all too probable.

"What do you think?" I asked Eddie Shiya, one of the more mature guys in my class.

"Don't talk about it," he said. "Don't even think about it." I took his advice. Don't talk about sex and celibacy and sex and priests and sex and nuns and sex and the Church. And then it won't be a problem, right? Of course, he was right. It wasn't a problem, unless I chose to think about it. And I didn't. Until now.

29

It was a cautious meeting of two adversaries at Navarre's, one of the finest restaurants in Phoenix, but, free now of doubts about myself, I was more relaxed than I had been in a very long time. We ordered drinks. I waited for Mary to speak. She smiled and sipped her Scotch. I broke the silence and said, "I want you back." It sounded right. This is what I was supposed to say, wasn't it? Part of the pledge, "til death do us part?" But it didn't feel right.

At the end of the evening, in front of her brother's home, she told me what she was supposed to say, that maybe she had made a big mistake. We were both lying.

I took my lie one step further, embraced her, kissed her on the neck and told her, "I understand, Mary, I understand. You need time. Take as much time as you want."

I followed her into the house, took Jim McArdle aside and slipped him the letters I had lifted. "Put these back in Mary's housecoat," I whispered. "And don't tell her."

Jim did tell Mary. He had settled on a policy of telling us both the truth, insofar as he knew it. As a result, Mary came to my hotel the next day. (I had left at 6:00 A.M. with Senator Goldwater for a one-day jaunt into Mexico on his Aero Commander.) She identified herself to the front desk as Mrs. Kaiser, got the key to my room and turned it upside down looking for my copies of those letters. When she couldn't find them (they were in the trunk of my rented car), she phoned Malachy at the Biblicum, to warn him that the charade was over, at least as far as the Jesuits were concerned. As I surmised from a glance at the telephone charges on my hotel bill, she also had a long talk with her lawyer in Las Vegas.

In Rome, properly warned, Malachy was on the lookout for any missives from me to his superior, Rod MacKenzie. Several days later, on June 27, he intercepted my letter to MacKenzie containing the incriminating photostats and put it in his pocket. But he had to assume other copies were headed elsewhere. He packed his bags and left a message for MacKenzie. "Since persons unknown — maybe the Arab Christians who wanted to scuttle the *schema* on the Jews — are making an attempt on my life, I will have to leave the Biblicum immediately."

∂₽

NOW, AT LEAST, Malachy was not going to get further support, moral or financial, from the Society. I doubted that I had succeeded in scotching whatever plans he and Mary had been making. But I still felt that someone — perhaps not me, but someone — could convince Mary that she was on a trail leading nowhere. That might not be easy. Malachy appeared to be the kind of person who enjoyed intrigue. And he had won Mary over to the same life. Conspiracy was an aphrodisiac.

I phoned my own coconspirator, Father William Van Etten Casey, my balding Jesuit leprechaun with the Boston accent, and asked him to help. I knew he was planning a trip West anyway, and so, from Holy Cross College in Massachusetts, he phoned Mary, who was still in Phoenix. He spoke on the phone with her at some length, and arranged to meet her in Phoenix the very next day, and did so, for three hours. He got nowhere with her, and he reported his failure (I was back in Los Angeles) in a few angry words.

Casey told me, "Mary affected a lofty attitude. She was worldly-wise, knowing, self-assured. She was no longer mother's little girl, or Bob's child bride, but a sophisticated woman of the world."

He said that Mary made a case against my ten years in the Society: they rendered me unfit for marriage. She had made a mistake in marrying a man with such a background. I laughed at the irony. Malachy had the same background as I.

Finally, Casey said to Mary, "I can see that it's all over between you and Bob. But what about these rumors I've been hearing about you and Father Martin?"

Mary launched into another attack on me — for the damage I had done to "Father Martin" by my accusations.

Casey heard her out, then asked again, "Is there any truth in these reports?"

She told him, "Well, frankly, the story is true. Malachy and I are in love. We plan to get married in the near future."

At that point, the mailman arrived with several letters for Mary. Two of them were from Martin. One of them was in code and Mary was so pleased with its cleverness that she showed Casey the letter and explained the code. The other envelope contained the letter I had sent to Rod MacKenzie, along with the photostats of the Martin letters I had found. Malachy wrote that my actions "proved conclusively" how mentally ill I had become, that she should forget me, and that he was speeding up his plans to leave the Jesuits and join her.

Mary was "aglow with excitement." Casey took his leave. Now he knew all the facts, and he could make his firm conclusion: "Bob Kaiser was the innocent victim of a cruel liaison between a devil and a fool."

Casey lashed out at Mary before he left her, telling her that he'd report all of this to me, and advise me to "grab the kids as soon as you can." Mary skedaddled back to Nevada, and told her brother she never intended staying in Nevada. She planned a European rendezvous with Malachy in Paris, where she thought she would be given a job by the American Jewish Committee.

The news hit Mary's parents hard. Her mother went on heavy medication. Her father, fighting off cancer with daily cobalt treatments, refused to open a birthday gift Mary had sent him from Nevada. They told their son Jim to tell Mary, "When you leave Nevada, don't come to Milwaukee. We have no daughter anymore. We do not know how one person could hurt so many."

※

NOT MORE THAN three days passed before I got a phone call from Frank McCool in Chicago, where he was teaching a summer course. He said he was "sorry about everything that has happened." But he couldn't seem to expand on that.

I was as unable to express my feelings as he was. I said, "I'm sorry, too, Frank. Goodbye."

I got a warm note from Rod MacKenzie. He said Malachy had intercepted my letter to him. But he had seen another copy of the photostats. He said, "This is, in effect, the color movie you spoke of. This is evidence. And I accept it as decisive. . . . I am sorry if you think my unbending attitude made things worse. I did what I felt I had to, treating a man as innocent until he was proved guilty. I deny that I ever thought you were crazy, or hinted such a thing to others. I did think you were ultrasuspicious. Now I must admit your suspicions were right."

He had a postscript. "No apology called for, for harsh words. I never held those against you, especially in view of the strain you were and are under."

I wouldn't have wanted anything more from MacKenzie. But John Courtney Murray turned out to be something of a blockhead. His stiff note gave with one hand and took away with the other. "I was badly wrong in my judgment with regard to the relations between Malachy and your wife, and with regard to both of them personally. I offer you my apologies, with all necessary fullness." But such an admission wounded his great pride. (I sometimes thought he took his initials, J. C., too seriously.) And his pride pushed him to retaliate. He said he had a written report from the Institute for Living, one that not even I had seen, and he wanted me to know the psychiatric diagnosis was not good. "You are suffering from a chronic undifferentiated schizophrenic reaction which is not quiescent but causing progressive deterioration." And, therefore, that I was "in need of intensive psychotherapy." Zap.

Murray ended with an unctuous disclaimer. He only told me of this diagnosis "out of concern" for me. "It is bad enough — in fact, tragic — that your marriage has broken up. I don't want *you* to break up."

I thank God I was able to see — again — that Murray was acting outside his competence. He was a theologian (and a specialist inside that discipline, at that), not a psychiatrist, and he was handing on a mere conclusion without any knowledge about the psychological protocols that backed it up. I was hardly on the verge of "breaking up" — as Murray would have it. If I was going to break up, I would have shattered long ago, thanks to him and his clerical gang, who persuaded me to leave Rome at precisely the time when my wife and kids needed me most, with a wolf at the door. (I apologize to my environmentalist friends who have such great esteem for the wolf, and my apologies, also, to the noble wolf.)

I took great pleasure in putting down Murray's note, able, finally, to turn my back on Murray's own self-asserted, but bogus, authority. I signaled the moment by shouting, "Fuck you, J. C." An obscene stepping stone in the drama of my growing up.

Growing up: a common expression, but an uncommon experience. Many of us fear growing up. And those of us who can summon up our courage to do so find opposition from those who think they are trying to protect us. Those who are identified by social philosophers as "emerging" will understand what I am trying to say: Blacks, Chicanos, Arabs, Chinese, women of all races. . . . I think we all share the same feeling: the thrill of taking charge of ourselves.

There was a religious component in the process of my maturation. I had to renounce a whole series of little gods: my parents, and my surrogate parents and the authority figures who would make things easy for me, if I only let them. Not many years ago, I loved one of the richest women in the world. We talked about marriage, but, as it turned out, we wanted different things. I often wonder what might have happened if we had married. Regrets? Some. She was a delight to be with, and she could have also made things very easy for me. But then, if I let her make things easy for me, I wouldn't have been my own man. I would have been hers.

I say this is a religious insight, because I fit it under the First Commandment that God gave to Moses. "Thou shalt have no other gods before me" is really an order from God to all of us: to take charge of ourselves, think our own thoughts, and feel our own feelings. In other words, to grow up.

For a long time, I didn't understand this. I entered the Society of Jesus because, Peter Pan-like, I did not want to grow up. I left the Jesuits in order to grow up, and thought I was doing so as I plunged into the workaday world of newspapering, then marriage and a family and the whirl of Time Inc.

But something inside me that still liked structure and order and discipline was still alive. I had taken off my black robe, but I hadn't really seized responsibility for my own thoughts and feelings and actions. To be sure, I chronicled the Church's "growing up." But I was unable to grow up myself. I still had a childish dependence on others, particularly on the Jesuits.

We are all victims of our early training. I can still hear my own father's negative admonitions, repeated as far back as I can remember, and on into the fourth decade of my life: "You can't do that." In every worthwhile thing that I ever wanted to do, I felt that I had to push the image of my father aside before I could make the attempt.

For me, the Jesuit Order was only a substitute for my father, whose own negativism had forced my mother to pick up her boys and flee. And then, when I turned away from the Order, my father-substitute, I found that I had so absorbed the Jesuit way of looking at life that I was still making decisions as if I were a Jesuit. Which is to say not making my own decisions at all. Up until very recently, I found I was still dreaming occasionally of my life in the Order, or using characters from that old scenario in my current dreams, and that sometimes these characters, no matter how benevolent, were trying to tell me what to do.

The Jesuits became the authority symbols that were preventing me from becoming my own person. I can imagine that other emerging peoples (and I put most women in that same category, *emerging*) have their own inhibiting authority symbols — parents, teachers, preachers, whoever. With the best of intentions, these authority figures have tried to block off the dawn of new possibilities for those they have "loved." As a result, I can imagine that today there is a black physicist somewhere telling himself, "You can't teach at Harvard." I can imagine a woman with her MBA saying to herself, "You can't run General Motors." I can imagine a Chicano congressman saying to himself, "You can't be governor of California." All because someone, some authority figure, made them believe, "You're a black. You can't do that. You're a woman. You're a Chicano."

I would rather think that all of us will grow up insofar as we are able to turn off those inhibiting voices of authority within us that keep telling us what we can or cannot do. Those voices are nothing more than idols, projections of own childish attitudes that stop us from being free — that is, grown up — men and women.

We can't grow up as long as we worship idols. This was a lesson that God tried to tell the ancient Jews, and that He keeps trying to tell the rest of us today. The ancient Jews, of course, did not always listen. And we do not always listen — to our own sorrow.

For years, I was guilty of this idol worship. I didn't call it that. At first, during my teenage years, I called it hero worship. There were a whole series of heroes, ending with the Jesuits. (Maybe those of you who aren't Catholic can understand if you substitute the phrase "U.S. Marine" for "Jesuit." A good many ex-Marines still worship the Corps.) In my life, I idolized the Jesuits, and I was always ready to exalt any Jesuit who stuck his head up above the crowd. All unwitting, John Courtney Murray helped me smash one of the idols that prevented me from growing up. I had to learn that, though Murray was a famous Jesuit, Murray was just a man.

Once I realized that, I started wondering about the clericalism that prompted Murray to rush, automatically, to Malachy's aid, even to the point of blinding himself to the reality — that the man he was defending (simply because he was a member of the same boys' club) was no different from your average lawyer or stockbroker or computer salesman who is always ready for a little extra nooky on the side.

Murray was caught up in a special kind of clerical error, to think that a priest was, ipso facto, set apart from the rest of mankind. And I was no less innocent than Murray. We were all afflicted with a kind of institutional ideology, a super-Catholicism, something like the super-Americanism that says, "My country right or wrong, but right or wrong my country." Neither I nor any of my clerical friends would have dared say that priests cannot be tempted, or succumb to temptation. In particular cases, however, we were inclined not to see the obvious — because we didn't *want* to see it. We had this blindness, an unconscious inability to challenge the assumption that the priesthood itself makes a man immune to the kind of feelings that men of all kinds have felt from the beginning of time.

Enforced celibacy also implied something else — that sexual intimacy was something that priests (and religious women) could forego without doing violence to their very identities as men (and women). In a way, we in the Church were trained to think that sex was not important. (There was a kind of corollary to this doctrine: that women weren't important either.) Now the whole Mary-and-Malachy thing told me that I should not be surprised if some souls said, "Nonsense!" and proceeded to rebel against such a system. That's what Mary and Malachy were doing, rebelling against the system, and devil take the hindmost.

Of course, the devil did. Every rebellion has its consequences, sometimes mayhem and murder. Here, as in most tales of adultery, the woman was the one who ended up being hurt the most. At this point, Mary had been shunned by her family and ostracized by her friends and was waiting for Malachy Martin to join her in the U.S., even while he was being abetted by his friends in the clergy who were getting together a purse for him so he could "save his priesthood."

જી

BUT I AM getting ahead of myself, and the story of my own obsession. The day after I received the note from Murray, I phoned Dr. Braceland in Connecticut and asked him what the doctors meant by a "chronic undifferentiated schizophrenic reaction." Now, in the summer of '64, he wanted to eat those words. "We wrote them down on our report," he said, "for the insurance."

"Huh?"

"The insurance companies will accept 'schizophrenic reaction' as a reimbursable illness. They wouldn't have paid us if we had reported that the only real evidence we had of any sickness was your tendency to project, which resulted in some paranoid attitudes regarding your wife."

I laughed. "And so the truth was that my so-called paranoia was only an indication that I was beginning to get the picture."

He laughed too. "Yes, that's true." I could almost hear him squirm.

Now I thought I had him. I said, "So, doctor, Father Murray thinks I need psychiatric help. Do you think I need psychiatric help?"

"Yes."

"But why?"

He paused — too long. I could hardly expect the great Dr. Braceland to confess that he was afflicted with his own kind of clericalism. Or that he had to protect the great Father Murray. After some umms and aaahs, Braceland said, "Because the circumstances now seem sufficient in themselves to put anyone into a disturbed condition."

"I see," I said, bidding the doctor good-bye, and cradling the telephone as gently as I could. I wanted to slam it down and swear. Yeah, I was disturbed. In fact, I was outraged at Malachy's masterful efforts to have me take myself out of Rome, thousands of miles away from my family, and clear the way for his final seduction of my wife and the possible alienation of my children. I was so depressed by the sorry state of affairs that I could not attend Mass that Sunday without weeping. That was the sick reward I got for my obsession. Did I enjoy being unhappy?

I did not. Early on a Tuesday morning, I am presenting myself in the office of an elderly Los Angeles psychiatrist. He is not a Catholic. I have made sure of that. And so I can trust him in ways I cannot trust Dr. Braceland. I tell him my story. When I am finished, he says, in a slightly Viennese accent, "And why do you think you need a doctor's care?"

I say, "I am depressed."

"No," he says, "This is not depression. This is life. Depression is pathological. These feelings you have. They are natural. You have been hurt. You are sad. You should be sad. But the cure for that is — living. Stop worrying about your wife. Start living. Make some new friends. That's the best thing you can do. Live. Enjoy."

❧

AND NOW I AM in the prow of the *Impromptu*, a sturdy, double-masted ketch, wind blowing in my hair, sailing to Catalina with a fellow reporter from the *Time* bureau and four other bachelors. I spend an extended weekend in the sun, enjoying the sailor's life at the Isthmus: good food, good drink, good company, water skiing, snorkeling, reading a novel by William Goldman called *Boys and Girls Together*. At the Isthmus bar on Saturday night, a slim, blonde Nordic goddess who looks like she has just stepped off the cover of *Vogue*, approaches me. Tanned legs, tight white shorts, blue tube top, warm white smile. "Pardon me," she says, "but do you have the correct — match?"

I giggle. It is a real turn-on, knowing this woman is coming on to me. She smiles and tells me her name, Karen McCaffery.

She is about to begin her senior year at San Diego State. I tell her I work for *Time*.

She wonders if I can straighten out her misfired subscription.

I tell her, "I do not sell the magazine. I write for it."

She says, "Are you kidding me?"

I say, "Can I buy you a drink?"

She says she'll have a gimlet.

"Gin?"

"No, vodka."

We are among the last to leave the bar, and together we catch the last water taxi back out to the boats. Her father's boat and my boat are anchored on adjacent moorings. The sea is all phosphorescent. Her face is aglow. "Go for a swim?" she asks.

"Now? It's almost two."

"Get your suit on, and I'll see you right — there." She is pointing to a spot off her starboard bow.

In a few moments, in the waters of Cherry Cove, alive with summer plankton, we make playful patterns of light underwater. She performs an underwater ballet. We hardly touch.

At dawn with my buddies, I set off waterskiing, hard. At 9:00 A.M., I am calling on Karen at Dr. McCaffery's sloop. Mrs. McCaffery says Karen is still asleep. "No, I'm not," she says, looking over her mom's shoulder. Throaty voice. Tousled locks. Long cotton T-shirt. Nothing more.

"We're sailing to Avalon at one," I tell her. "Wanta go along?"

She says, "Yes, yes, I'd like that, yes."

⸜⸝

THE NEXT WEEK, miraculously enough, courtesy of *Time*'s bureau in Jerusalem and Ma Bell, I finally located Mr. Blake. Unable to find Mrs. Blake by calling telephone operators in Kentucky, I had written to our stringer in the Middle East, and asked him to see if Bill Blake was still stationed there. In less than a week, I had Blake's address and telephone number at the U.S. Embassy. At three o'clock one morning, lying in bed and staring at the ceiling of my apartment in Hermosa Beach, I decided to phone Jerusalem. I told Blake who I was and I said I had a hunch that Malachy may have had a hand in the breakup of his marriage, as he had in mine.

Blake seemed frightened by my call. He said he couldn't tell me anything, and that he wouldn't give me the name and address of his wife. If I wanted to communicate with him further, I could do so, through his lawyers in — Frankfort, Kentucky.

Ah, Frankfort! That was one city I hadn't checked. I phoned Frankfort information. Yes, they had a Mrs. William Blake. I got her phone number and lay there, weighing discreet ways of approaching this woman. I wasn't sure there was one.

Next day at three, I took a direct approach. It was exactly the right one. "Mrs. Blake?" I said.

"Yes."

I told her my name and said I worked for *Time*. "I knew Malachy Martin in Rome," I said.

"Really?" She seemed excited.

"I am going to be in Kentucky this weekend. Can I see you?"

I needed to say no more. "Please, please," she said. "Stop by. And, oh, by the way, my name is Jill."

At week's end, I was winging my way to Frankfort, Kentucky, where I rented a car and drove out to find an address on Cherry Hill Lane, a simple frame house on a leafy road without sidewalks. A zaftig blonde wearing a cotton housedress that was not quite buttoned up all the way came to the screen door. "I'm looking for Jill Blake," I said.

"I've been expecting you. You're Kaiser, right?" I nodded. "Come in." She gave me a glass of iced tea, and wondered immediately if I was an emissary sent by Malachy Martin.

"An emissary? Hardly." I decided I had to tell her the simple truth. I said, "My wife and Malachy Martin are having an affair. He's telling her they're going to get married. I don't believe he will ever marry her. I have to persuade her that he is one of the biggest bullshitters of all time."

Jill Blake frowned. "Yes," she said. "I can see that we have to talk." She arranged for a sitter to come stay with her two young children, and then I took her off to dinner at a nearby restaurant, where she did most of the talking, and then, after we returned home, she tucked her children in bed, and talked to me through most of a balmy July night on her front porch. She wasn't a woman who, as Malachy intimated, "would do anything to get even" with Malachy. In fact, she was getting a divorce so she could be with Malachy. She'd never known anyone like him, so kind and so handsome and so much able to make her feel like a woman. Jill said, "He told me one night, 'The two greatest thrills a man can have is to hear a woman cry out in the ecstasy of love and to cry out in the pain of childbirth.'"

Well, I thought, this man has some great lines. He should have written for Warner Brothers. And now my hatred for him soared. It appeared he had manipulated this young woman, encouraged her to split from her husband, just as he had manipulated Mary, with the same results.

Jill confirmed my surmise with some facts. Malachy had been in Jerusalem in the summer of 1962 when she'd needed him. She'd just had a baby and she was crestfallen at the sight of her own stretch marks. Malachy said he loved her stretch marks and he covered them with his kisses during the days and nights when Blake was away on his nation's business. Needless to say, Jill had fallen for him then, and had kept hoping he would come back to her. She had corresponded with him when he went back to Rome, but when he stopped writing in December 1962, she attempted suicide. In May 1963, her husband took up with another woman, and so she flew into Rome with her children and saw Malachy at the Rome airport. There, he told her, "a providential concatenation of events" precluded him from following her to the U.S. He said he still loved her.

And she still loved him.

I had to give Malachy grudging credit. When he seduced a woman, she tended to stay seduced. I left Frankfort the next day, but not before I made a simple pitch to Jill Blake. I said, "Won't you do me, and my children, a favor? Write a note I can give to Mary. Tell her how you and Malachy were left alone together, how he tried to console you, to bring out your womanliness, to possess you, and how he made you believe he would marry you. If Mary were to know that she hasn't been the first — and I have proof she really thinks she has been Malachy's first — then maybe she'd have a different view of all this."

Jill Blake said she would think it over. She soon wrote me in Los Angeles. "I would help you with Mary," she said. "But, knowing what you told me of the situation, I believe she will wait a long time for Malachy.

My letting her know about Mal and me might only make her want him more."

Jill kept the best for last. "Watch out for prowling tigresses," she warned. "Especially the kind who would cheerfully gobble up a man who loves children. So goes it." She said she'd gladly trade places with Mary. She wanted me.

This movie-plot was sagging. Now it had all the aspects of a bad soap opera. I wrote Jill and suggested that maybe it wasn't too late for her and her husband to get back together. She responded to that by flying to California. She phoned me from Anaheim, where she was visiting friends. Could I see her that evening?

I picked her up at a spacious hillside villa, and took her out to a posh restaurant not far from Disneyland. I have a good recall for events and even conversations of long long ago, but I cannot remember what we talked about. I can only recall that when I returned her to the villa, she told me to make myself comfortable in a cozy room dominated by books and some fine art. It was probably the closest thing to a tigress's lair that she could find on quick notice in Southern California. She disappeared for a moment or two, then reappeared wearing nothing but a tan. She had lovely breasts. I was too curious to run and needy enough to stay.

On the next night, Jill appeared on the doorstep of my beach home in Hermosa, smiling and unbuttoning her blouse. She had a plane to catch for Kentucky early in the morning. "I'd like to stay till then," she said.

I was easy. For much of the night, we made love, and, at dawn, when I tried to leave my bedroom so that I could die in peace and alone on my couch, Jill woke, ran to me and threw her arms around my neck. "Fuck me," she said.

This was a woman of more than average feeling. I said to myself, if Malachy Martin had been Jill's master in the art of love, what passions had he perhaps ignited in Mary? I was fascinated by the thought. And, in my Pollyannaish way, I told myself that maybe, when Mary and I got together again, Mary would be as passionate as Jill. I thought of the old Spanish proverb. Was God going to write straight with crooked lines, again?

30

I never saw Jill Blake again. She wrote me and thanked me for providing her with an ear, a heart, and a few other things besides, just after she had cried out to God in her loneliness, "Please, if You're there, send me somebody to be a friend now. I just can't go on like this much longer."

I wrote her, too, but the main item on my agenda was Mary. Couldn't Jill write that letter, telling Mary the truth about Malachy? Jill temporized, and then, one day in late August, I got a wire from a friend in London, telling me that Mary and the kids had left Nevada and arrived in England. Mary had persuaded her father, our banker, to send her all of our joint savings. She had also borrowed money on my insurance policy, which was written in her name. Now she set up an apartment in Chelsea, and soon, according to my spies in London, Malachy Martin moved in.

I screamed inside over that news. But it wasn't the picture of Mary's being with Malachy that flashed through my mind. It was the thought that he might start in on some devilment with the kids. An old picture had played in my memory, of Malachy tickling Betsy on her bare tummy with his chin, what looked like an innocent and playful thing at the time, but now was something else for me to think about. . . .

After checking with Clurman, who had some misgivings about my vacation plans for Rome, I took time off and jetted from L.A. to Rome on October 18. The Council's third session was under way. I needed to be there for some of that: this was an extension of Pope John's Council, but in a much different sense, this was my Council, too.

On my first afternoon in Rome, I slipped unnoticed into an empty seat at the American Bishops' Press Panel and was pleased to find that Israel Shenker, my replacement at *Time,* was asking good, mischievous questions. Charles Davis, the English theologian, who was sitting on a chair to my left, whispered to a ruddy Protestant clergyman on his left, "That's the man who took Kaiser's place at *Time*."

"Oh, I know all about Kaiser," said the ruddy fellow. Is there such a thing as a leering tone, as well as a leering look? He had it. I leaned over and peered at him and my doing so gave Father Davis a start, because he hadn't known I was back in Rome, and, in fact, sitting right next to him in the crowded basement room of the U.S.O. I leaned over to the ruddy Protestant and said, "Hello. I'm Robert Kaiser." Now he looked even ruddier.

I asked no questions of the panel. Afterward, many of my journalistic colleagues came over and shook my hand. Some of the clerics, such as Msgr. George Higgins and Father John Long seemed a bit embarrassed in their greetings. Many of the others hugged me and said they were praying for me, and for Mary and the kids. That was about all they could say, and I think that Father Jorge Mejía, now Cardinal Mejía, had already spoken for many in a note he had sent me from Rome in September:

> ... there is not much to be said: I suppose we, your friends, have all to take our part of the guilt and pain and atone for one another. While we were all enjoying your company and your hospitality, something horrible began creeping among us which was to take a part of your life. Can I feel just and innocent, and look the other way, and put the blame on somebody else? I have the minimum of Christianity not to be able to do so.
>
> So I want you to know that I come to you oppressed by the impression that as you were opening to us the gates of your happiness, we were plundering it away from you.
>
> It's a mean thing to say that Rome will never be the same without you. It is your life which will never be the same. But it is the clear duty of your friends to try to give some hope to your soul: I don't know how and when, but I am sure that in the middle of darkness you will sometime see a light. I wish I could help you to see it soon.
>
> You are our brother in hunger, thirst, sickness, nakedness, in prison. God will ask us what we did for you, after tearing your happiness to pieces. And I want to have something to answer.

I had dinner that night with Jack and Mary Shea and a long lunch the next day with Father Bill Moran, who told me that the Biblicum was pretty upset over Malachy in July. They'd seen his fanciful commentary on the second session, *The Pilgrim,* that had savaged Pope Paul VI (though the book was dedicated to the pope!). That didn't upset them as much as the news about what he had done to me and my family. Moran told me that letters addressed to the Rev. Malachy Martin, S.J., were being returned to the senders by the people at the Biblicum with "the Rev." and "S.J." scratched out and scrawled over with the words: "departed, address unknown."

It took some doing for me to locate T. D. Roberts. When I finally found him living in a large, chilly hotel room in an inconvenient part of Rome, he looked cold and hungry — and sheepish. I wanted to ask him why he had joined the conspiracy against me last fall, but I didn't have the heart. Anyway, I knew why: because, at the time, he didn't realize that it was a conspiracy, or, at any rate, anything other than a conspiracy of goodness. The real question was, how could he be so stupid? I didn't ask that one, either. I am sure there was something about me, my lack of warmth toward him, perhaps, that made even those words unnecessary.

Despite my manner, it was obvious that T. D. was trying to make some amends. He said he'd been keeping in touch with Mary. Before he left London for the third session, he'd introduced her to two English women who might be able to help her, if and when she needed help. "Up to now," he said, "she hasn't seemed to want any."

He showed me letters he'd received in Rome from each of the women. They had the same basic story to tell: Mary was still under the poisonous influence of Malachy, and didn't seem to know it. In early October, according to them, Malachy had convinced Mary that I was on my way to England, to kill her, which prompted Mary to ask one of the women for refuge. She and the children spent the night at this woman's apartment, then, unaccountably and without fear, she returned the next day to her own flat in Chelsea.

One of the women wrote T.D, "M.M. is fanning the flames all the time to widen the chasm between Mary and Bob." She said he told Mary she should see me only in the presence of an attorney. And now — a bizarre turn, I thought — she reported that Mary and Malachy were threatening Archbishop Eugene D'Souza of Nagpur, India, "with exposure." The woman was puzzled. The archbishop had come to London as a friend, took Mary out to dinner, even gave her $100. And for that, Mary wanted to expose him? For doing what?

T. D.'s informant wrote, "Venom pours out of Mary, and she can only think of vengeance. But vengeance for what? I am blowed if I know."

It was obvious to me where the injections of venom were coming from. Malachy was the vengeful one, and he was programming Mary.

T. D. confirmed this. He handed me a third letter, a nasty missive addressed to him and signed by Mary, but in a style that was pure Pushkin. There were words in the note that Mary didn't know how to spell, words and phrases that weren't in her vocabulary — like "initiative" and "recrudescence" and "unadulterated bunk," "at the end of my tether," and "the States." The letter could have only one intent: to drive T. D. away from any further contact with Mary.

After I finished reading that one, I shrugged and stared at T. D. with a look, I am sure, that was close to despair. Reading all of this took something out of me. I wondered then whether I had any more sympathy for Mary. I could understand passion. I didn't have much tolerance for stupidity.

"You can keep these," said T. D. Roberts. "Use them with discretion." He pushed the letters back to me.

I stood and asked him if he needed anything.

"Yes," he said. "See if you can get me some chocolate bars. I'm not getting enough to eat. I can't seem to get warm."

∂∫

T. D. HAD GIVEN ME Mary's address in Chelsea, and I wrote Mary a note, and enclosed some cash. I told her I was in Rome, that I wanted to see her and the children. I wrote:

> Mary, I don't know if there is a future for you and me. Sometimes, I find myself saying there isn't. Most of the time, I keep hoping there is. I love you. I miss the children. I think I've grown up a lot in the last year, and I think I understand more than I did. If the situation were reversed, I know I would appreciate some understanding on your part. Please write immediately and let me know how you feel. Is there still a chance for us?

Two weeks later, I got a minimal, dead-pan note from Mary. "When you arrive in London," she wrote, "please phone me. I will then make suitable arrangements. You ought to see the children."

That night, I took George Hagmeier, the American Paulist priest-psychologist, out to dinner at Cesarina, a fine Bolognese restaurant on the Via Piemonte, and grilled him about the potential psychological effect of my seizing the children and taking them back to the U.S. with me. He said such a move might have a traumatic effect on little T. D., now only fourteen months old, but that it would probably not harm Betsy, just turning three. I pondered that, got a referral to a detective agency on Chancery Lane in London, and asked the agency to put a watch on the apartment in Chelsea, so I could get a reading on Mary's typical movements over a three-day period.

I consulted Jack and Mary Shea as well. Jack frowned when I told him what I was up to. "Look," I said, "I just want to get the kids away from her now, while the other guy is still in the picture. He'll be gone soon, I have no doubt about that. When that happens, then Mary will have to come back to the U.S., if she wants the kids. She can have them, under the regulation of a California court, but I will have them close to me, too."

Jack and Mary said they could go along with my plan. "Well," I said, "I don't even have a plan. Just a wish, right now." I said I was going to consult with an English lawyer about the legalities involved, and talk with the detectives, to see if Mary left the house at a certain time every day, or what. "If she leaves the kids with a sitter, it shouldn't be too difficult. I'll just show up and whisk the kids off and get 'em on a plane."

"And if Mary doesn't let the kids out of her sight?" asked Jack. "What then?" I said I didn't know. I'd just have to think of something. Jack said, "Look, you may not have to use these, but if you do...." He dug into a satchel and came up with several small pills. He said, "One of these could put Mary to sleep."

I smiled. "Just drop one into her tea, huh?"

Jack shrugged. "They're harmless. It's up to you." I thanked him and put the knockout drops into my briefcase.

"Where will you take the kids?" asked Mary.

"To my family in Phoenix," I said.

"For a warm, safe, happy Christmas, huh?"

I laughed at that. The kids had spent last Christmas with strangers. Surely Mary couldn't object to another little trip for them this year — with someone who loved them, me.

JP

I H A D an altogether unpleasant lunch with Msgr. George Higgins. He said he was keeping in close touch with Malachy, so he could "save the man's priesthood."

"I piss on his priesthood," I said. I was appalled at Higgins' priorities. Malachy was a priest only if you went along with the old theology, which held that he was endowed with certain magical powers forever — no matter that he no longer had a Christian community looking to him for service. "This so-called priest," I said, "goes on with his seduction, and you continue to help him. What about my family? Matrimony's a sacrament, too, you know."

"That's your problem," said Higgins.

It was, of course, more than my problem. It was the Church's problem, as long as churchmen clung to the ancient celibacy bargain. Trouble was, priests like Higgins were part of an old-boy network of super-priests who continued to maintain that the future of the Church lay in maintaining the old, celibate priesthood — the notion that men are important and women are not, and that they can turn their backs on their own sexuality with impunity. Most churchmen know, at least subconsciously, that their power comes in some kind of trade-off: they assume celibacy and they are rewarded, in turn, with power. In order to make that bargain stick, these churchmen must deny their manhood, and turn their own blind eye to other priests who cannot or will not go through with the bargain. "It must not happen," they say, "and therefore, it doesn't happen." In order to maintain that blindness, they must also ignore or demonize women in order to stay in power, with disastrous results to their own authenticity.

Their denial doesn't cut off their sexuality; it just drives it underground. According to the most well-informed sources I can find in the American church, I can report that many American priests, even some bishops, are fooling around sexually — either with a woman, or women, or with other men, and no one cries, "Havoc!" I heard recently about a young priest in Phoenix, troubled by his sexual stirrings, who went to an older priest to tell him he had to leave the priesthood. "You don't have to leave," advised the older priest. "You can have any woman in town."

By what rationale? "Well," say these priest-seducers, "celibacy means we can't get married. It doesn't say we can't have sex." And so they go on their merry way, sleeping with their secretaries, or unhappy housewives up the street, or joining homosexual networks. I thought then (and think now) that the situation may be providential: when Catholics-at-large realize what is going on, they will demand an honest reevaluation of the whole celibacy issue and a declericalization of what we call ministry.

Higgins had said it was my problem. Well, insofar as it was, I intended to do something about it. Knowing now that I couldn't sever Malachy from his clerical connections, I decided to use those connections to some advantage. I'd lull Mary and Malachy into a sense of false security, by getting a message to them, through Higgins. "I'm going to London to see my kids a week from today," I told Higgins, betting that he would pass the news on to Malachy.

Then I paid the *conto* and hurried to Fiumicino in a taxi. I made the 3:00 P.M. flight to London, and was able to keep a late-afternoon appointment with my London solicitor. He said that, since there was no custody agreement, I was quite within my rights to take my own kids, if I could get them. "Under English law," he said, "you have as much right to them as your wife does. But you don't want to petition an English court. Then your children would be under the English court's jurisdiction for a long time to come. Better just take them."

Easier decided than done. My detectives said Mary had gotten on to them, knew she was being watched and wasn't letting the children out of her sight. I half gave up on my plan and phoned Mary to ask her when I could see Betsy and T. D. She said I couldn't take them anywhere; she would bring them by my hotel at eleven the next day.

⁂

MARY WAS WARY, feral, like a cat with her kittens, when she appeared with the kids, all bundled up on a cold, windy, rainy day. Just in case I might seize an opportunity to swoop them up, I had paid my bill and had my bag packed and in the porter's lodge with three airline tickets in my pocket. We stayed in the lobby and ordered tea. Betsy asked immediately if I was going to take pictures of her and her little brother. "Where's your camera, Daddy?" she asked.

I told her I lost it. In my haste to get out of Rome, I'd left the damn thing in the taxi.

Undaunted, Betsy chattered on, She wanted to play "Let's Pretend." Like, "Let's pretend, Daddy, that I'm the circus master and you're the people. Sit right over there. Now here I come, just ahead of the elephants." T. D. was tugging at my pants leg. He wanted to play hide-and-seek and come chase me. I tried to divide my time between them and caught a case of the giggles. Mary watched my every move, ready to pounce if I tried to run out with the children. We had tea served in the hotel lobby, but I didn't even think of giving a Mickey Finn to Mary. That seemed too bizarre. How would the kids feel if their mom lost consciousness and I ran off with them in a taxi? When our appointed hour was up, Mary rose, frozen faced, bundled up the children and whisked them off without a word about my seeing them again, tomorrow, next week, ever.

I rebooked my room at the desk, stumbled up the stairs, and threw myself face down on the bed, absolutely desolate. It was the lowest moment of my life. But I couldn't just do nothing. Next day, I phoned Mary to ask if I could come by the apartment in Chelsea to see the kids again.

"You saw them yesterday," she cried.

"I know," I said. "But I'm going back to California on Monday —"

"Well, go," she shouted.

On Monday morning, I decided on one bold try — for Betsy alone. I hired a limousine for the day, bought some travel clothes and Peter Pan slippers for Betsy, some toys and some clothes for T. D., and had the driver take me to Chelsea. I left Betsy's things in the car, and knocked on the door. Mary was prepared for me. She wouldn't even open the door, and said she was going to call the police. While she did, the kids and I made faces at one another through the barred windows of the lower-level apartment they were living in. When the bobbies came, I identified myself and told them I wanted to see my children. They took me to the door and made a plea on my behalf: a father ought to be able to see his own little nippers, huh?

Mary let us in. I handed over the toys and the clothes for T. D. He started opening the packages.

Mary said, "Don't you have anything for Betsy?"

"Yes," I said. "I have something in the car." I had no expertise in the dirty tricks department, and my intentions were all too clear as soon as I picked up Betsy and started for the door. Mary tried to hold me back, shrieking so loudly that the lieutenant in charge had to intervene.

I told the lieutenant that I was quite within my rights, and gave him the name and phone number of my solicitor. The lieutenant put two of his men at the door and phoned my lawyer right then and there. The officer nodded and said to my solicitor, "Yes, I understand."

I smiled. If the lieutenant was beginning to understand, maybe I was going to pull this off. Mary darted in to blunt this understanding. She whacked the telephone, effectively terminating the call, and started screaming that she wouldn't stand for my taking either or both of the children.

The officer took me aside and said, "You may be right. If you are, a judge will be able to confirm that. You lose nothing by waiting a day or two for that. In the meantime, I have to preserve the peace. That's my first job. And right now, you're disturbing it. You'll have to go."

I nodded. He was making good sense. And he had the authority and the power to make me go. I went. But I didn't want to lock myself (and my kids) in the jurisdiction of an English court. I looked at my watch, saw that I still had time to make a 1:00 P.M. flight to the U.S. I strode to my limo, retrieved another bag from the backseat, took it back to the apartment and gave it to one of the policemen. "This is for Betsy," I said.

<p>

I WAS BACK at work at the *Time* bureau in Beverly Hills on November 18, feeling like I had had no vacation at all. On November 28, I covered the Notre Dame-Southern California game, watched Ara Parseghian's undefeated Irish blow a commanding lead at half-time, to lose the game 20–17, and the national championship as well. In the Notre Dame locker room afterwards, I noted that Parseghian had written the half-time score on the blackboard: 17–0, along with the words, "Only 30 more minutes." It was obvious that he'd instructed the Irish to hold on. Instead of playing to win, they were playing not to lose. The risk-taking Trojans demonstrated the folly of that course.

I only wished that my own risk-taking had been as productive. It wasn't. I did not get my kids back, and my health started to crumble as well. After I filed my football story, I dashed to an 8:00 P.M. lecture on the Council which I'd agreed to give that night on the UCLA campus, and went to sleep in the middle of a rap session afterward at the home of a friend.

I was not only tired. I was sick. At midweek, I dragged myself to a doctor's office, aching and weary and jaundiced. He took one look at me and said, "Young man, you have to get to a hospital right away. You've got hepatitis."

31

For a month, I lay flat on my back at a hospital in Redondo Beach. My hepatitis was so infectious that, for a while, I couldn't receive visitors. And then, when I could, friends were advised by the nurses to put on gowns and masks before they entered the room. At Christmas, I flew home to Phoenix, for another month of enforced rest.

A cousin of Mary's in London wrote me. "You ought to begin to organize your life without Mary. I haven't any idea how one goes about doing this, but I repeat that I see no signs of her breaking." Not a month later, I would get another note, this one from Father Art Yzermans, who gave me an opposite opinion. He said he knew Malachy Martin was in New York City, and that he had broken completely with Mary. "Forget about Malachy," he said, "and work on your own mental outlook for the future. And keep in contact with Mary." I wrote back, scolding him:

> I think about practically nothing else except getting back together with Mary and the children. Under the circumstances, however, my psychiatrist, my priest friends, and a couple of other friends all tell me I am only destroying myself by even considering that any longer. Mary has left me, doesn't want me, doesn't write to me, has flown thousands of miles away to get away from me (or join her fucking Jesuit priest bastard liar fink).
>
> It is bad for me to "keep in contact with Mary." Every time I make contact, I am rebuffed. Just making the first move is emasculating enough. The added rebuff is almost unbearable. But you don't know anything about these matters. You're just a simple country priest, as you've told me repeatedly.

On February 1, I reported back to *Time*, bought a Pontiac convertible and leased an apartment in Beverly Hills. I was ready to make a new life for myself. I had gotten letters in the hospital from Karen McCaffery and Sally Tooley and Patti Gallagher. (For some preternatural reason, I liked Irish women.) And I spent a lot of nickels talking to each of them on the phone. Now I started dating them, and a good many others, too. The Daisy Discotheque, then the ranking disco in town with the movie set, became my neighborhood pub. I started working on my tennis game and I found a group that liked to play touch football on Saturday mornings.

Out of the blue, I got a letter from Jill Blake, with a note enclosed for me to send on to Mary. It was laughable because it was such a loving remembrance of Malachy Martin that it could only swell the man's stature in Mary's eyes, not lessen it. I kept it, along with some other memorabilia of my soap opera period, which I thought was now ended. I didn't know how I could ever remarry in the Church, but I told myself I'd have to figure out a way: maybe the Jesuits could help me get "a Catholic divorce" — that is, an annulment based on psychological immaturity, Mary's *and* mine. In fact, Father Casey undertook to write up a brief and he submitted it to ecclesiastical lawyers for their critique.

Karen McCaffery and I had seen each other a few times during her senior year. There was still high voltage between us, but we kept the sparks contained. Each time I saw her, Karen looked like she'd stepped out of a fashion layout. She was tanned, talkative, lively, and, after a martini or two, terribly earnest. On the day she graduated from San Diego State, we went sailing to Catalina with three other couples, slept side by side in separate sleeping bags on the afterdeck, water-skied, and swam together. On the sail back to the mainland, we exchanged kisses for the first time and when we landed at Marina del Rey, she told me she had decided to move to L.A. for a summer modeling job, which would give her enough extra money for a trip to Europe with her best girlfriend in the fall.

I told her she could move in with me.

"Are you kidding me?" she said. I was not. The next week she brought her things to my apartment in Beverly Hills. She said, "Separate bedrooms, no strings attached. Okay?"

I took her literally. I guess I was waiting for her to make the first move. Before she (or I) could make any moves, Father Casey dropped in on me. He was on his way to another stay in Fresno, and he was there in my living room when Karen came home from a modeling stint. Her eyes widened at the sight of him, and when I took *him* out to a Hollywood premiere, she split — lock, stock, and hair curlers. All her things were gone when I returned at midnight. She left a note saying she could not understand why I did not let go of the Jesuits, as she, raised a Seventh Day Adventist, had let go of the repressive Sevens.

A few weeks later, however, Karen came to a large, crowded party I was giving on a Saturday night at my Beverly Hills apartment. Every time I turned around, Karen was there, with open arms and open mouth, and when the last guest had departed about 2:00 A.M., she made that first move, the move that I was waiting for. I made the rest of them.

ঙ৷৷

KAREN AND GANEA, her college friend, departed for Europe in early September of 1965. I bought a new IBM Selectric and started to write a memoir about my misadventures with the Jesuits, and all the errors of all my clerical friends, then and now. Karen wrote me letters almost every day, from London (where she paid a call on Mary and the kids to deliver several outfits and toys for Betsy and T. D.), from Scotland, and from Paris, where she and Ganea enrolled in the *Alliance Française*. They were the only passionate love letters I have ever received and each of them urged me to hurry and finish my book so I could come over and join her in Paris. Sure, just like that, write a book in six weeks?   .

True, I had done that before. I couldn't do it now, for a number of reasons, mainly because the story I had to tell wasn't over yet. And I had no distance on it.

I noodled around. Karen continued to write. I grew increasingly restive over her being free in Paris and passionate, and my being locked down in Beverly Hills and lonely. And the Council! The Council was drawing to a close. I wanted to be in on it.

I wrote Karen a note and told her I'd be at Orly in a week. Meet me. I had three months' vacation coming: I'd write my book in Paris and Rome, and then in December and January at St. Anton, where I would write in the mornings, and then spend the rest of each day playing with her. It was a fine fantasy: we'd ski from ten to two, drink Austrian beer and eat pastries *mit schlag* after skiing, listen to zither music in the evenings and make love all night under down comforters.

ঙ৷৷

IT WAS EVENING in Paris when I got off my flight from L.A., lugging my heavy IBM Selectric typewriter, but only midday on my biological clock. I spied Karen in the waiting crowd on the other side of the customs barrier. Her face was flushed with an excitement which even I, a sexual infant, could understand. We embraced — there in the airport, and then all the way into Paris in a cab and then in our hotel, almost until dawn. For three days, we wandered all over the Left Bank, over to the Louvre, and up and down the Champs Élysées. We explored exotic restaurants and each other. I thought of my three days in Paris with Mary: the worst trip ever. And now another Paris, with Karen: the best.

I told Karen my ski plans. Mary had suddenly become more amenable, and I was able to negotiate a visit with my kids in London. I would go see them for three days, then return to see Karen in Paris, then continue on to Rome. I asked her if she could join me there in December when her classes were over at the *Alliance Française*. "Yes," she said. "Yes."

ৡ৶

I SPENT THREE DAYS in London, playing with the children, while Mary went to her job each day. If the kids were a delight last November, they were a double delight after another year's growth. Little T. D. was talking now, wondering if I could fix things. Betsy had developed her role as a circus ringmaster, and she involved both me and T. D. in her fantasies. We wandered around to parks and took the tube everywhere and visited the British Museum. This time, I had a new camera and lots of film to take the expected pictures. Evenings, Mary talked about quitting her job and going back to the U.S. What about Malachy? Mary had no details to give me about him, except to tell me that he was gone, out of her life, and for good.

The first night, she took me across the street to a neighbor's guesthouse, and when she unlocked the door, she told me, "It's cold in here." I agreed. She said, "You can turn on the gas fire."

"Uh huh."

"Or I could keep you warm."

I laughed. "I'll try the gas fire." Mary made no further passes, and then, after two short winter days in London, it was time for me to go. Mary and the kids drove me to Heathrow for my flight to Rome.

I climbed out of the car and told Mary she and the children needn't come into the terminal. I leaned over and kissed her on the cheek. "I want to do the right thing by you and by the kids and by myself," I said, wondering how I could do all these things simultaneously.

"I know you do," Mary said. "I know you do."

⚜

KAREN WAS WAITING for me, again, this time at the airport called Le Bourget, smiling ruefully, not flushed this time, but terribly intense. "I didn't think you'd show up," she confessed. "I thought I'd never see you again."

We stayed up all night together. Karen knew now that I wanted her. I didn't have any doubts about her. And she didn't have any doubts about me.

⚜

AT THE INVITATION of Father John Felice, I stayed at Chicago's Loyola University campus in Rome, wrote my book in the mornings, mingled with my old friends and newspaper colleagues in the afternoons and evenings. Rome was the same. I wasn't. Oh, I was delighted to see my friends again, and I found they had added a new wrinkle: they had a journalists' Mass every evening at the Salvatorians' church off the Via della Conciliazione. Afterward, we would go out for noisy dinners together, all the old crowd and some new people, too, Catholic intellectuals and writers from many lands who were here in Rome, as I was, for the historic denouement of the Council, to be in on the birth of the new Church, one in which we Catholics were beginning to understand the worldly dimensions of our belief.

The old Church was the hierarchy — bishops and priests (but probably not the nuns, who, I was coming to see, were as out of sympathy with hierarchy (and patriarchy) as I). The new Church was everybody, the entire "people of God." The old Church played ecclesiastical power games. The new Church would be involved in the ongoing process that some theologians called "the redemption of the earth." The old Church did a lot of talking, issued encyclicals and bulls and interdicts and excommunications. The new Church, according to some of its most charismatic leaders here, notably Archbishop Dom Helder Pessoa Camara of Recife, Brazil, and Cardinal Giacomo Lercaro of Bologna, Italy, was a Church that had to listen, because it was poor. In one famous speech of this fourth session, Lercaro tried to explain: "Poverty implies for the Church an awareness of

· 283 ·

her own inadequacies, joined with boldness in making the adaptations demanded by a true sense of history and a spirit of humility."

But if the Church was poor and humble, I was even poorer and more humble. My Jesuit friends in Rome were encouraging me to take Mary back. I'd married her for better or worse, hadn't I? And rehabilitating Mary would be a grand project, wouldn't it? I couldn't find it in me to do that, to simply will a reconciliation because it was the right thing to do. I needed time to do that, wasn't even sure if I could, or wanted to. I wrote and told Mary that I wasn't coming to London for Christmas, that I was in love with Karen, that I planned a trip with her to St. Anton in December and January, where I would write and ski.

Mary wrote back immediately, astonished, full of reproach. She urged me to think of the children, of her, of myself, and she hit me in my soft underbelly: "The children and I assumed you would be with us for Christmas. You must have conveyed that impression to Betsy, because she continually speaks of Santa and Daddy coming to see her at Christmas. Betsy and T. D. are just at that age where the holidays, with all the decorations and excitement, mean so very much."

In a hurried note, I said that maybe she was right. I made no promises about our future together. I said that I was scrapping my Austrian plans and coming to England for Christmas with the kids. I didn't know what I'd do with Karen, or she with me.

Mary replied with a softer, conciliatory letter, filling two airmail folders with her scrawl. She told me that she had been foolish, idiotic, immature, rash, and naive. She said she was sorry for hurting me, and that she had learned from her mistakes. She said we probably both needed a session where we could each bring out our own feelings about the events of the past three years. She had put together all the pieces of the Malachy puzzle, and now she could say she felt nothing for him. The man she thought she had known didn't exist.

From others, I had already heard how Malachy Martin had kissed Mary good-bye in March, promising to send for her and the kids — "our charges" — as soon as he got settled in New York. His letters slowed to a trickle. Then, when they stopped coming in July, she paid a call on Malachy Martin's brother, a monsignor in Dublin. She told him that Malachy and she had planned to marry. Did he know where Malachy was?

"Dear girl," he said to her sadly. "I don't know. I must tell you, you are the fourth woman who has come here asking me the same question about Malachy. All of them have essentially the same story to tell. That they were in love with Malachy and thought Malachy was in love with them."

"Four women?" Mary demanded. "The same story?"

He nodded, and said, "And one rather attractive young man." He raised his palms heavenward and said, "I'm sorry." He pursed his lips, then let go with a little explosion of air that made them go pop — meaning, Mary knew, "That's just the way it is."

32

In Rome, I was getting no place with my book. I was still too close to the whole thing. I decided to do a bit of reporting — on the hottest Church issue of the day, on the changing of Church thinking regarding birth control. Doing that reporting in Rome, now, was a snap. Many of the theologians on the pope's commission were here, most of them eager to talk to me, and I was assembling quite a file when Karen wrote me from Paris: people there had turned ugly, and so had the weather. She was on her way to Rome, a couple of weeks ahead of schedule.

When she arrived, glowing, Rome was wet, windy, and rainy. We escaped to Naples on the Rapido, and then caught an old tub for Capri, which pitched and shook so violently on the passage over that we both thought we were going to die of the heaves. Wet and bedraggled, we walked halfway around the island so that we could get a hotel that would provide us with a glorious view the next day. We restored ourselves with a hot bath together and a nap and a romantic late supper. In the morning, we marveled at the sunup over a promontory that kissed the coral sea around the island and illumined it with ten thousand glorious radiances. Karen and I bought some bread and cheese and wine and explored the island and talked. She told me she was sick of Europe, and homesick: she wanted to go back to California and to her family for Christmas.

"That's fine," I said. "Then I can spend Christmas in London with my kids. And I've got this piece I'm doing for the *Ladies Home Journal* on birth control. I need to do some more research on it, in the Netherlands and Belgium. Then I'll be back in California by New Year's."

Karen nodded. Yes, that would work just fine. We'd see each other at New Year's, and ski some other time.

When we returned to Rome, we took up residence in the Hotel Columbus on the Via della Conciliazione, only a few hundred yards from the Vatican. Karen met my reporter colleagues in Rome, went with me to the journalists' Mass every evening, shared some favorite restaurants, helped me discover some new ones. We were at supper one night with several veterans of the Council, and a new friend, the Jesuit Peter Hebblethwaite, editor of the *Month*, a journal of religion and culture produced by the Jesuits in Great Britain. At one point, Peter asked me where my daughter went to school. "Peter," I said, "Karen is not my daughter. She's my girlfriend."

On December 2, I dashed off in the late afternoon for an interview on my birth control story with Father Bernard Häring, a member of the pope's birth control commission, and one of the pope's own personal theologians. In the parlor of the Redemptorist College on Rome's Via Merulana, Häring hugged me, then took me up to his room on the third floor. He seemed more than eager to talk to me. Though the pope had already appointed a special commission (including Häring) to advise him on the birth control question, Häring had a plan to get the whole thing presented to the Council itself. He didn't see why the Fathers of the Council could not produce a statement which, in principle, at least, would help the Church solve its own dilemma. When the interview was over, it was quite dark outside. He escorted me to the stairs and there, in the light of a dim bulb, asked me about Mary.

I said I understood that the other man in the case had left her in London and for good. "She seems eager for a reconciliation and wants me to come to London for Christmas."

Häring's blue eyes lit up. "Go back to her," he said. "Go to her. Take her back. You won't regret it."

I didn't know how to deal with that. My new self (the one that was trying to be honest with my own feelings) said that I couldn't take Mary back. My old self (the one that always listened respectfully to authority) said that I ought to do so. In my cab back to the Columbus, I heard an old plaintive refrain from my Novitiate days, "Never, forever, never, forever." They were the words of my Novice Master, words, he said, chanted over and over by the damned in Hell, whose greatest torment was that they had no more hope: "Never, forever, never, forever. . . . "

In the hotel lobby, the concierge said a lady was waiting to see me — in the bar on the second floor. I expected to see Karen. It was Mary, just flown in from London. "I went to the *Time* office," she said breathlessly, and with a slight British accent. "They told me you were at the Columbus."

Oh, God! Karen is upstairs in the room. Mary is down here in the bar. I had to get Mary out. I took her by the elbow, left some lire for her waiter, led her outside. We turned left into St. Peter's Square, deserted and chilly. I fumbled to button up my trenchcoat. Mary pulled her mink more snugly around her neck. We strolled on the cobblestones, about twenty turns around the square. Mary did most of the talking. She'd realized that her letters weren't doing any good, so she had come to make her case in person. She wanted me back. Now. She kept talking about the children, showed me some recent pictures of the kids by the light of the fountain in the middle of the square.

I thought of St. Ignatius and his preamble to the Spiritual Exercises — designed to order one's life so that one would "never come to a decision because of any inordinate attachments." My heart was pounding, and my head was filled with images of the children, Betsy playing circus master, and T. D. tugging at my pants leg. "Okay," I said finally. Let's try it. Let's get together again."

She sighed and said my name, and threw her arms around my neck and kissed me, warmly, lingeringly. "Bob! You're so good."

"There's just one problem," I said, pulling back from her. "Karen's with me. She's waiting for me now." I looked at my watch. "I'm overdue. I've got to go break this news to her. And it isn't going to be easy."

Mary said, "You've got her right there in the Columbus? What will people say?"

"I don't give a damn what my enemies say. I have the impression that my friends understand, and approve."

Mary frowned, started to reply, then stopped when two burly fellows came up, tapped us politely and said they were putting both of us under arrest.

Perchè? I demanded. "What for?"

"For kissing in public," one of them said. He turned and pointed theatrically to the pope's lighted window above. His voice deepened, as if to underscore the seriousness of this charge. "And underneath the window of the Holy Father himself!"

Mary said to me, "Oh, Bob. Tell him — "

"No," I said. "Let's see what happens. I'm curious about this."

We went along meekly to the office of the magistrate right there on the edge of the last gigantic Bernini colonnade. The courtroom was little more than a tiny shed, like a comedy kiosk on the border of Liechtenstein. The magistrate, a round fellow who was trying to look serious, read us something in Italian, which I took for a lecture. It was probably just the relevant Roman (or Vatican City) statute, which included a fixed penalty of so many lire. Then he asked us where we were from. I said I was an American. Mary said she was an American, too. He asked us for our passports.

We handed them over. The magistrate looked at each of them, and then he did a double take. He turned in exasperation to one of the detectives. *Ma sono sposati!* "But they're married!"

The detectives looked at us in surprise, then at each other. One made a flapping motion with his right hand, which probably meant, "What kind of married people go around kissing anywhere, in public or private?"

I pazzi Americani, said the other. "Crazy Americans." As if being crazy and being American explained everything.

The magistrate said, "Case dismissed."

❧

I PUT MARY in a cab for the Hotel Flora, bought a bottle of Johnny Walker, and hurried over to the Columbus to tell Karen. "That must have been some interview," she said.

"Yes," I said. "How about a drink?"

"No," she said. "I don't much feel like a drink." She lay down on the large, king-sized bed in our room and patted a place for me to come and lie down beside her. "Somebody's been phoning. A woman. Wouldn't leave her name."

I hesitated, then blurted the news. "The woman who was calling. It was Mary. She flew in tonight from London. She was waiting for me downstairs. We talked. I'm going to take her back."

"Now I'll have a drink," Karen said, blinking back tears.

We both had a drink, and then another. We both cried. And we talked through much of the night. We did not go out for dinner. We finished the bottle of Scotch. And when we finished talking, we lay there stiffly, holding hands, hardly sleeping.

I took Karen down to the Stazione Termini early the next morning, so she could catch a train for Florence. She had a girlfriend there, a college classmate from California who had married a man from Florence who was in the glove business. We walked down the platform together until we found her first-class coach. The train whistle gave a mournful blast. I

set Karen's bag down and took her by the shoulders and said, "Karen" — "
"I never want to see you again," she said, bursting into tears.

<p>

I WENT BACK to the Columbus, checked out, and moved into the
Flora with Mary. She said she was going to have lunch with Father Bill
Moran over near the Biblicum, but wanted to have a quiet little dinner
with me that night at the Columbus. She said she would meet me at
the U.S. Bishops' Press Panel. We met there, chatted with some of our
friends for a good long time, then walked over to the dining room of
the Columbus. This time, Mary didn't forget that December 3 was my
birthday. She had a small surprise for me: one sympathetic, happy guest
to share this moment with us: Archbishop Denis Hurley of Durban, South
Africa, a man who had only had kind words for both of us during all the
trauma of the past two years.

And she had a gift for me as well. "I looked and looked all over town
for something symbolic," she said as I was unwrapping it. It was an
exquisitely crafted, full-rigged, triple-masted schooner. I told her it was
beautiful, but I was puzzled by it. I was no collector. "It's symbolic," she
explained. "Of a long trip. Ended now."

After dinner, we went to a gathering of Americans in Rome, mostly
reporters, some theologians, a bishop or two. Sen. Eugene McCarthy and
his wife, Abigail, were there, and Abigail came up to me and whispered,
"Why don't you warn people?"

"You mean about Mary and me, together again?" I said. She nodded.
I shrugged. "I didn't have much advance warning myself."

Mary ended up at one end of the room, I at the other. I bumped into
Father Rod MacKenzie. He asked me if I had any news from England.
I smiled and said, "Mary's with me. In fact, she's right over there." He
glanced across the room and saw her talking with Frank McCool. He
stiffened and frowned. He said he was glad we were together, but he
couldn't care less about talking to Mary.

That Sunday night, we called a final reunion of our old Council crowd.
We held the party in a hall on the Loyola campus, and it was almost like
old times. T. D. Roberts was there, looking tired (too tired to even wrinkle
his nose) and decrepit, Archbishop Hurley, Archbishop Eugene D'Souza,
Bishop John Wright, Fathers Häring, Murphy, Mejía, Stransky, Heston,
and all the Jesuits who had been more or less privy to our melodrama:

Tucci, Long, Moran, McCool, Calegari, and some of my journalist friends: Gary MacEoin, Jan Grootaers, Jean Vogel.

They all came to give us their blessings, and to tell us how happy they were that their prayers for us were answered. In effect, Mary and I — together now — were confirming their faith that God was in his heaven and all was right with the world. Some of them knew that all was not right. After the party, MacEoin told me he didn't give us more than a couple of weeks. "Mary has changed," he said. "She was a brazen hussy tonight. Did you see her prancing around in her micro-mini-skirt and flirting with all the clerics?"

I had seen, but I didn't want to think about it. I fantasized, instead, about all of our friends who had been cheering for us, and all of the angels and saints in heaven, smiling too, overjoyed that Bob and Mary were back together again.

Mary left next day to return to London and the kids. A few days later, the Council was adjourning on a high note of pageantry. With my press pass, I was able to wander into St. Peter's, where I found a couple thousand prelates, surrounded by aides who were helping them don their ceremonial robes. I found Jesuit Father Stefan Schmidt with Cardinal Bea; Schmidt was the cardinal's secretary; he had been a friend to Malachy and a source for me. I stopped and told him, "Mary and I are back together."

"Of course," he said with a huge, happy smile, as if it that was the most expected piece of news he'd ever heard. "It is one of the fruits of the Council."

I wondered about his metaphor. To me, right now, the fruit was an unripe olive and I wanted to spit it out. When the ceremonies (which were held out in St. Peter's Square) had ended, when the last prelate had long departed and no one was there except me and the pigeons and the workmen who were cleaning up the litter, I sat forlorn on the steps of the basilica and looked past the bleachers and the scaffolding they had rigged for the press photographers off Via della Conciliazione, the street of reconciliation. I wasn't reconciled at all.

I had to ask myself: What did I really feel about Mary? What did I feel about Karen? For most of the day, I walked all over the city, across the Tiber, around the Pantheon, over to the Forum, back to the Fontana Trevi, up the Via Veneto, into the Borghese Gardens, back to the Tiber, across the Ponte Cavour, past the Castel Sant'Angelo, back to St. Peter's Square. I saw no one, spoke to no one.

I sat down again on the steps of St. Peter's and tried to sum up my thoughts and feelings about me and the kids and Mary and Karen. I wanted the kids, I didn't want Mary. The pope's own theologian said, "Take her back." But it was clear now to me that our marriage had crashed. All the pope's horses and all the pope's men couldn't put it together again. Mary and I were getting together for the wrong reasons, to confirm for our clerical friends the power of their own prayers. But why should I be responsible for their faith? It would survive without my help. They could get along without me. The question was, could I get along without me?

I wanted to take possession of myself. No more using the Church as a crutch, or churchmen as a conscience. I loved Karen, and I wasn't conscience-stricken about that love at all, no matter what the rulebook said. Now, for the first time in my life, I wanted to make my own decision, right or wrong or maybe. I wasn't against the rules; I just wanted rules that worked for me, not against me.

I phoned Mary in London and said I wouldn't be with her anymore. I would come to London for Christmas, or take her and the kids back to Milwaukee for Christmas. But I didn't feel right about us together anymore. That was about it. Our connection was bad. I hung up the phone.

❦

I FOUND KAREN in a glove shop in Florence. She looked at me reproachfully for a long moment, then took my hand. "I got your gold bracelet in the mail yesterday," she said, shooting the cuff of her navy-blue peacoat so I could see she was wearing it. "I must admit you have good taste." We walked along the banks of the Arno for an hour or more in the weak afternoon winter's light. She was hurt, hesitant. She said, "I'm not sure about you."

I said, "What the hell do you mean you aren't sure? I am here, aren't I? Here because I want you?"

"Uh huh," she said. "I guess you do." The hurt look in her eyes told me she needed more tender words from me, more tender touches. She got them, right there on the Arno, and then again and again as we strolled back into town. We kissed in front of every jeweler's shop on the Ponte Vecchio, in front of Donatello's Annunciation at the Santa Croce, at the bar of the Excelsior, at a later dinner that night at Giovacchino's, and then in our room at the Continental-Lungarno. I made it clear that I wanted her, and her alone, and she made it clear that she wanted me.

EPILOGUE

In theory, the Fathers of the Second Vatican Ecumenical Council opened up the Church. They made it more catholic and less Roman, less legal and more loving. In their new definition of the Church as the people of God, they seemed to renounce the Church's old medieval and Renaissance role as a lordly institution in society, and identify it with the poor and downtrodden of this world. Only in this fashion could the people of God go forward with Christ's "redemption of the earth" — as servants of all.

There is a theory of growth behind all this. God gave us the sun overhead and the earth beneath, pure water and green grass and all the natural wonders of his creation, all the creatures on the earth and in the sea. What we do with all the wonders of creation is up to us, men and women with free minds and free wills. We can be whatever we want to be, as long as we do not freeze ourselves in a posture of adoration before idols of all kinds, bowing down before men or money or power or beauty — or any symbols whatever.

"God made man," Elie Wiesel once said, "because He loves stories." His statement presupposes that God gave men and women free minds and free wills, that we wouldn't be predetermined to go marching through history like so many mechanical toys, but try to take possession of ourselves and make our way in our own ways. That's where the fun comes in. Our own lives are like good movies that keep us on the edge of our seats, wondering what's going to happen next — and keep surprising us with every new turn of the plot.

If you're attracted by this kind of a God who likes stories, you also have to think He doesn't know what's going to happen next any more than we do. That makes sense. If He knew the end of every story, that would ruin the story for Him, wouldn't it? I rather like Wiesel's God, the God who turns us loose and then sits back and looks and listens and, undoubtedly, laughs (and cries) at our stories. I'd like to think that God has gotten a good laugh and a good cry out of mine (and is still getting a chuckle and shedding a tear or two as I keep making my bold, or sometimes fearful, moves).

Whether God is like that or not, who really knows? God figured into the story as I have told it, at almost every turn. At times, He became a principal player. Sometimes He was a hero, sometimes a villain. Sometimes He was very much in charge, sometimes He acted as if He didn't really give a damn. The ongoing question in my story was an old one: was God good?

I realize that applying the human word "good" to God is an anthropomorphism. It is only our human expectations of God — that He be good as a father or a king or a president is good, for example — that create our human disappointments with Him. In every game, there are winners and losers. Does God, then, love the winners and hate the losers? Does God demonstrate His predilection for one army and smite the other, though both call upon His help?

There must have been a time when I thought so. At one point in my story, I felt that God was something of a shit. I was only being a reporter then, reporting my own feelings. I am not the first man in history to feel this way. Faced with adversity, with suffering and disease and death, men and women have always tended to cry out, "Oh, God, why me?" Job sits on a dunghill and weeps and utters the same wonder.

Why does God permit evil at all? This is one of those ultimate questions for which, I believe, there is no humanly satisfying answer. Poor human beings that we are, we can only use human concepts and human language to express our views of the divine. None of the words are really adequate, and I think that if we found one that was, we humans would make a thing out of it and worship *it*.

In fact, some Christians have done exactly that with the word Jesus, the Word Made Flesh. In *Franny and Zooey,* the J. D. Salinger novel, Franny keeps repeating the Jesus prayer, as if uttering the word Jesus itself will somehow make her free. The repetition does not make her free, just something of a freak, a Jesus freak.

One of the ancient peoples, the Jews, have known this for a long time. In the purest form of Judaism I know, among the Hasidic Jews, there is no attempt to use any human word for God, because these devout souls know that none of the human words, in any language, are adequate to express who or what God is. Is God always good? Does He always watch over us and keep us from harm? Does He make sure that every baby is born with a perfect pair of everything, and never a case of AIDS? Does He always reward the just and punish the wicked? Not so far as anyone has noticed.

So how are we to think of God? In 1980, I asked the question of Karl Rahner, one of the world's leading Catholic theologians. (Yes, I was still consulting Jesuits; they were not my idols anymore, but they were and are my species, after all.) Father Rahner said, "God is — and always will be — incomprehensible mystery."

I said, "But Father, what do you mean, *always will be?* What about the beatific vision, when we're in heaven, when we will see God face to face?"

"Then," said Rahner, his eyes getting wider with his own wonder and his own wisdom, "we will be face-to-face with — " he paused dramatically " — incomprehensible mystery."

There was something very satisfying about that formulation. I accepted it, not because it was Rahner, the Jesuit, who said it, but because the notion made such good sense, and because it made idolatry impossible, even and especially the worship of authority.

Then it was that I knew: I could use authority to help make me wise, but I didn't have to make authority an idol.

AUTHOR'S NOTE

Malachy Martin fled to New York City, a renegade Jesuit and a renegade liberal as well, and soon became the darling of the U.S. Church's lunatic fringe, which lionized him for a series of fantastical books about demonic possession and the skullduggery of traitorous prelates within the Vatican itself. He died of a stroke in 1999, maintaining as he had all along that he had a special dispensation from the pope to serve as a freelance priest in good standing, dispensed from his vows of poverty and obedience, but not from the vow of chastity. It was all a pack of lies. For thirty years, he lived as a kept man under the roof of a rich Manhattanite, the ex-wife of a Greek shipping tycoon.

Mary never heard from Malachy again. She became a psychologist in Massachusetts and, some years later, married a lawyer and became a mother again.

Many of my better sources at the Council passed on.

On February 21, 2001, two of my Sunday night regulars (and two of the kindest men I have ever known), Archbishop Jorge Mejía, head of the Vatican Library, and Jesuit Father Roberto Tucci, head of Vatican Radio, were made cardinals in the largest consistory ever.

I ended up marrying Karen, and we had a baby boy, who grew up to be a teacher.

As children, Betsy and T. D. lived their summers with me. Betsy became a social worker and a great mom, T. D. a newspaper reporter and an ambitious cyclist.